Praise for *The Khan*

'Mir offers us a fascinating glimpse into a world rarely portrayed in fiction.'

Guardian, best crime and thrillers

'With *The Khan,* Saima Mir delivers a once-in-a-generation crime thriller and in Jia Khan has created a female South-Asian protagonist who is fierce, passionate and absolutely compelling. This is not simply black-and-white on the page. It's blood. It's emotion. It's tears, anger, betrayal and revenge. An outstanding debut which deserves to be read widely.'

A.A. Dhand, author of *Streets of Darkness*

'This impressive debut reveals a world in which monsters exist "in the guise of friends and behind smiling faces". It is a considerable achievement.'

The Times, best crime fiction

'Compelling and gritty.'

Cosmopolitan

'A tremendous debut (Jia Khan is a fascinating, multi-layered protagonist). Timely, authentic, immersive and powerful. Hints of *The Godfather.* SUPERB.'

Will Dean, author of the Tuva Moodyson mysteries

'Bold, addictive and brilliant.'

Stylist, best fiction 2021

'The book operates on various levels: crime family saga, character study and an exploration of clan-run organised crime. A sterling debut.'

Vaseem Khan, author of
The Unexpected Inheritance of Inspector Chopra

VENGEANCE

SAIMA MIR

POINT
BLANK

A Point Blank book

First published in Great Britain, the Republic of Ireland and Australia
by Point Blank Books, an imprint of Oneworld Publications, 2024

Copyright © Saima Mir, 2024

The moral right of Saima Mir to be identified as the
Author of this work has been asserted by her in accordance
with the Copyright, Designs and Patents Act 1988

ISBN 978-0-86154-156-0
eISBN 978-0-86154-157-7

Typeset by Geethik Technologies
Printed and bound in Great Britain by Clays Ltd, Elcograf S.p.A.

Oneworld Publications
10 Bloomsbury Street
London WC1B 3SR
England

For all the women who have set themselves free.

'The tree is known by its fruit, not by its roots.'

Spanish proverb

PROLOGUE

The old man stared at the metal roller door of the industrial unit and hesitated. He slipped his hands into the pocket of his thick coat, pulling out the heavy bunch of keys that opened every door on this sprawling industrial estate. The bitter wind gnawed his fingertips as he went from key to key, looking for the right one. He knew each one by sight, but anxiety left his head foggy. Eventually, he found it.

He knelt before the steel tambour and took the padlock in his hand. The keys slid in easily, as if newly oiled.

The chill this morning was harsher than usual, and he was grateful to his wife for forcing his hat and thermals upon him. 'That's how local people survive this cold,' she'd said.

Thirty years had passed since they'd set up home in England. She was still as smart now as she had been then. So much so that he wished he'd listened to her about the thick army socks she'd gone to hand him as he'd left home, but he was a stubborn old fool and couldn't have her win all the battles.

The 6.00AM call from the police had caught him off-guard, and he wouldn't have had time to do much more than get dressed and leave if it wasn't for his wife. Their years together had taught her when to speak and when to wait, and so she hadn't pressed him on the issue of the West Yorkshire Constabulary. Instead, she had shored him up with the practicalities of love, ironing him a shirt, making sure he was warm, filling him with food. He'd wiped the sleep from his eyes and sipped his coffee.

His daughters were already dressed when the call came. They were in the kitchen, frying up scrambled eggs with tomatoes, fresh coriander and green chilli, and making piles of hot toast with melted butter.

'What's this? No Weetabix today?'

'Ami said you were heading out early, so we thought we'd surprise you,' said Abida as she kissed him on the cheek. She was his eldest child, the one who had changed everything. 'Besides, between tutorials and lab practicals, I don't have time for lunch,' she said.

He reached into his pocket and took a £20 note from his pocket, tucking it into her bag when her back was turned. The thought of her joy at finding it would sustain him all day.

The old man's chest puffed with pride at the sight of his daughters, each one's eyes as bright as their destiny. This was why he had come to this country, to build something different for the next generation. This was why they stayed.

His girls wouldn't be forced to cook and clean for their husbands like some of the daughters of his friends. Seeing the squandered potential of all these brilliant young women as they served undeserving men made his blood roil.

He wasn't going to let that happen to his daughters. They would have choices and know their worth.

'Sorry, I can't drop you at the train station today, beta,' he'd said. 'There is some urgent business I need to take care of.'

'It's OK, Abu. We'll walk. Seema needs the exercise,' Abida had teased, making fun of her middle sister, who pulled a face in return, and they'd laughed.

'Allah bless you, my darlings,' he'd said to his daughters, praying they would always be this happy. 'You are the keepers of my izzat, and I am the keeper of yours.'

He knew there wasn't anything he wouldn't do for them – which was why he was afraid of opening the industrial unit now.

There had been two squad cars waiting when he'd arrived in his beat-up Peugeot. He'd hesitated, reluctant to leave the warmth of the car. In there he was secure, surrounded by good memories, and who knew what was out there.

He'd thought about Abida as he'd pulled on the white hazmat suit the officers handed him 'as a precaution'.

'I understand you've been ill?' the detective constable said.

'Yes, I had vertigo. The GP came to my house.'

We won't need you to come in a few years' time, he'd said to the doctor. *Both my daughters are at medical school.* And then he'd added, *Are you married?* The GP had shaken his head and made polite small talk with the young medical students before leaving, asking about courses and placements. A ray of hope had warmed the old man's heart then. He wanted his daughters to have careers and live their lives, but he also wanted them to find love. An honourable kind of love that meant no one would speak ill of them.

And now, here he was in the industrial estate, assisting the police with their investigation.

He heaved the handle of the roller door. Behind it was the small unit of a multi-purpose space with an office at the rear. It screeched as it moved up and back into the ceiling of the unit. He looked down at the bright-blue shoe covers he'd pulled over the soles of his boots and stepped gingerly inside.

The smell of bleach hit hard, settling inside his nose, burning the inside of his nostrils and stinging his eyes. He reached out his hand, tugging at the light cord. The tube light hummed before turning on and filling the room.

The thing that struck him was the brilliant white of the walls. They had been marked and grimy last time he was here. Whoever had painted them hadn't done it well, though: flecks of emulsion were spread across the ground like white speckles on a grey egg. The detective constable followed him in, gazing around at the walls and floor, taking it all in.

'We're going to need that CCTV footage,' he said to him.

'Of course.'

As he headed towards the back office, the detective stopped to examine an orange velvet armchair that was decidedly out of place in the empty room. It looked as if it had been scrubbed within an inch of its life. He ordered the other police officers to seal off the unit and got out his radio to call in forensics.

The old man stepped on to the rug that lay between him and the office door. It made a squelching sound. He stepped off it and then on again, rocking back and forth like a child playing in a puddle. It was synthetic, a machine-made imitation Persian rug, perfect for hiding all manner of stains. He looked down at his feet: the plastic covers were now smeared with a congealing, brownish liquid.

A sickness rose as he realised what it was. He glanced at the detective, busy on the radio. He wanted to turn back, but he knew he had to keep his cool. He entered the office. It seemed pretty much the same as always, papers neatly placed on the desk, a kettle in the corner with two white cups and a box of Yorkshire Tea. He remembered why he was here.

He walked over to the CCTV recorder. The cameras were all off. He was sure he'd checked everything was on and working properly before leaving on Friday.

He cast his mind back. One of the tenants had needed to use the photocopier urgently at the weekend, and he'd been reluctant, uncomfortable at the thought of handing over the keys. But the man said it was for his daughter's school application, so he'd relented.

He clicked the keys on the computer and searched the database for security recordings. But there were none. Someone must have wiped them. He was scared now. What if the police didn't believe him? What if they said he was involved?

Something awful, something hideous, had happened inside this unit. The smell of the bleach, the whitewashed walls, the congealed liquid in the carpet confirmed it.

He felt faint, the room began to spin. He had daughters of marriageable age, and he could not get caught up in police business.

The old man stumbled out of the office, lurching towards the exit of the unit. Seeing he was in trouble, the detective stepped up to help him, catching him before he fell.

'Are you OK?'

'My blood sugar. There's chocolate in my glove compartment. Please.'

***

The area was swarming with forensics now. He watched from his corner of the car park, feeling sick to his stomach, wondering how much they knew. If only Abida hadn't got involved with that beghairat, if only she'd come to them earlier, it wouldn't have come to this. These boys were raised with no respect for women.

Abida had sobbed hard as she'd told him about the adulterated photos the boy had sent and how he threatened to use them. She needed her abu to help her.

And he would have done anything for her, paid any amount of blackmail money, if he thought it would end there. But he knew that wouldn't be enough. He had felt so helpless – until a trusted friend said they knew someone who could make the problem go away. Yes, he had done the right thing by making the call. His mind cleared. They couldn't prove anything. No money had changed hands. No names given or details shared. He didn't even know what they were going to do, only that his Abida would be free to get on with her life.

But the decision had cost him, and his wife had taken him to the GP. He'd felt so ill that he'd had to lie down across the hard plastic chairs in the waiting area.

For a moment he wondered where the boy was now. Then a police officer came back to check on him, and he realised he didn't really care.

It was going to work out. His daughter would be fine now that scumbag was taken care of.

She had been smiling this morning. Maybe she would like that nice young doctor.

Whatever happened, the old man would make sure she did as she pleased. It was the rest of the world that couldn't.

CHAPTER 1

Jia's jaw bore the shock of Maria's punch. Her sister had her in a wrist lock, one twist, one sidestep and a backhand to the nose was all that was needed.

The high ceilings of the once disused mill rang out with the thud of Jia's body hitting the mat. She stayed there for a moment, looking up at the beams, wondering what it would feel like to stay down.

Maria reached out her hand. 'Sorry, didn't mean to make actual contact.'

'You cheated,' said Jia, taking the help. 'Distracted me with talk of Baba's cabinet.'

'It's called the art of distraction for a reason,' said Maria. 'Best time to strike, when your opponent's mind is elsewhere.'

'Remind me not to go to war with you.' Jia took off her gloves and swigged some water.

Other women went to lunch; Jia Khan and her younger sister sparred. It was a weekly reconnect.

'You said there were some old things of dad's stuck at the back of the drawer?' said Maria, packing her gloves and pads away in her holdall.

'A few scribbled notes and an appointment diary from the year he and Bazigh Lala first arrived in London.'

'Anything interesting?'

'Some names I don't recognise – people he seems to have met with quite regularly for a time. A Mary. And a Henry Paxton. Idris is looking into it as he seems to think the guy might be a lord now. But you know Baba's handwriting, and of course Idris might be after the wrong Henry Paxton.'

'How would Baba become friends with an aristocrat? Strange, but then our father always was an enigma. I bet there are other things hidden around the house. You know how he was. Do you need an ice pack?'

Jia shook her head. There was a lot her father had hidden, most of it bad, some of it good, none of it known to Maria.

'That's good,' Maria said, 'because I must get to school early today. Ofsted are coming.'

She was a teacher at a local primary school. It was a profession far removed from Jia's, who'd been a barrister until her father's death, when she had taken over his criminal empire. There were few who knew he had been killed on her orders.

'That'll teach me not to spar with someone ten years younger,' murmured Jia as she watched her sister disappearing out of the door. She checked her face in the mirror. It had looked worse, but not for a long time.

Finding that diary had diverted her attention. Jia wanted to know more and had asked her cousin and consigliere, Idris, to find out who the people mentioned were, but it was proving difficult.

She picked up her bag. There was probably some arnica in the medicine cabinet that would help reduce the bluish tinge she could feel appearing along her cheekbone, although she knew her men would respect her more if she allowed the bruise to be as painful as possible.

The morning sun took her by surprise as she swung the metal door of the gym open. It had still been dark when she had parked her car earlier. It had rained all night and there were many pools of water. They'd mixed with engine oil and looked like stepping stones as they glinted in the sun. Jia understood she was looking at evidence of last night's car meet among the local lads. She'd have to ask her brother Benyamin about this.

She liked to train early, long before the world was up, before the demands upon her time descended, drawn to the silence and the beauty of solitude in public places. It made her mind feel clear and sharp, like the sound of a crystal bell.

Thinking of the sleeping city while she hit the punchbag always prepared Jia for whatever was about to come. She would follow up the session with a swim, then head outside for the newly minted tradition of buying a cup of tea from Mo at his karak chai van. The rituals of life were grounding and necessary when one ran an empire as large as hers. Routine allowed for clarity, something she needed now the company was expanding. Her family business had grown and with it had Jia's responsibilities.

She had once imagined she would get out fast, but now she found herself more and more complicit in the complexities of running a crime syndicate. And this made her crave structure and routine in preparation for the journey ahead.

She crossed the car park to Mo's van. He was an unassuming man in his twenties, but Jia could see he was entrepreneurial, steeped in his dreams and passionate about making good chai. A metaphor for the city, she thought, its eyes still wide despite frustrated ambitions.

Jia watched him pour the hot, milky tea from pot to cup and back again several times to make it froth and the perfect temperature to drink.

'How was the session, Jiji?' he said. That was how he referred to her, adding 'ji' to her name as a sign of respect and then shortening it the way youngsters do with familiarity.

Jia's cousin Idris was one of the few to also call her by that name, or one of the few she allowed to. It was unusual for people to banter with her as she was so formidable. While Mo understood her position in the city's landscape, the early hours and his tea-making skills made him brave, and she in turn permitted it.

'One day, Jiji, I am going have a fleet of mobile beverage vehicles. A van in every city in the country, and they'll be run by my daughter. Just like you run Akbar Khan's business.'

'Hmm,' she said, taking a sip. The tea was hot and unsweetened as she liked it. Mo had listened when she'd asked him to stop heaping sugar into the mix, adding that tea, like truth, should be delivered straight. 'It might just save your life if you ask your daughter what she wants,' added Jia.

Her father had sacrificed his youth so that she and her siblings could have a better life. For years she'd hated him for it, only understanding him after his death. There were so many things she would ask him now if she could. So many of his decisions were clearer to her but others were still opaque. But Jia's father was gone and there was no way to bring him back, and this was on her. The next time she'd see him would be on the Day of Judgement, when she would have to answer to Allah alone. Until then, she was the one delivering justice in this small corner of the world.

She had taken up martial arts when she moved south to London, learning under the same sifu for almost two decades and continuing to train with her online. When she returned home, Jia heard of a club hidden in the basement of a previously derelict mill that was now a shopping centre. The club opened long before the shops, and the car park was always empty when she arrived. She trained solo once a week and sparred with her younger sister Maria on another morning.

It was in the car park that she'd discovered Mo and his breakfast van, and he had become part of her training-morning ritual. On seeing her gloves, he had mentioned a martial arts class that originated with Muslims in Thailand.

'It's called silat, from the Sanskrit word *shila*, meaning "fight to support honesty",' he had said, and that had been enough of a sign for her, and she had joined.

These classes kept her head clear, and what she needed right now was clarity.

Her reasons for becoming the head of the Jirga had been complicated.

Mostly she had understood how many families would lose their livelihoods and the financial support her father had secretly been giving them for decades if the Jirga didn't continue strongly. And a power vacuum would be disastrous for the city.

Nowak, head of rival outfit the Brotherhood, had been vying for domination, and those who ordinarily would have replaced her father were too hot-headed to lead. They would have burned the city to the ground, leaving behind a pile of rubble.

She had killed Nowak to put an end to the turf war and have everyone accept her as leader. Jia's three cousins – Idris, Malik and Nadeem – had been with her that night, though she hadn't talked with them about what had happened since.

But a few nights ago, her cousin Nadeem had brought disturbing news of some of the families the Brotherhood had been supporting.

Some days life felt one step forward and three steps back. Now there was a problem.

Jia put her water bottle to her lips and thought of the families who had once worked for Nowak. She'd spent more on an empty bottle than they had to spend on food for a day.

She climbed into her car and turned on the ignition. As her seat warmed, she checked her phone for messages.

One was from her husband Elyas, a picture of their younger son, Lirian, sleeping.

'Reached out to the people you asked about,' said a message from Idris. 'Mary moved back to Cameroon. As for Henry, his people are being difficult. But might be because he's one of the wealthiest men in the UK.'

Deep in thought, Jia drove through the same streets her father had. He'd come to London in the 1970s and worked in a hotel for a while before moving north.

She passed thriving shops and businesses that had stood empty only the previous year. Jia could see that, because of her investment, advice and foresight, things were changing. Opportunity was all this run-down city in the north of England needed, she was convinced.

The buildings gave way to green swathes of land, and she turned into a private road lined with drystone walls. Before her stood the high gates of Pukhtun House.

A lone guard stood on duty, but Jia knew a state-of-the art security system was watching and recording at all times, because this was the home of the most powerful and feared family in the city.

This was Jia's home. It was the home of the Khan.

CHAPTER 2

1974

Akbar Khan stepped out of the Pembroke hotel and on to Park Lane, looking dapper. He pulled the maroon lapels of his velvet coat up high to protect him from a biting breeze. His brown hair shone in the sun like ambition, highlighted with threads of copper; both were gifts of ancestry.

He was buoyed by the prospect of new-found work, eager to harvest the mythical gold he'd heard London's streets were paved with, here to shape his fortune with hard work and a little luck. He'd just landed his first job.

It had been two months since he and his brother left Peshawar. They'd saved and borrowed to get to Britain. And once here, they'd walked the streets searching for work, laughed with old friends and made banter with new. He thought back to how much had happened in the last eight weeks.

The flight had landed at 9.00PM on a Monday evening in June, and he'd been surprised that it was still light outside, not even close to the time for Isha prayers.

His friend Mushtaq had been waiting at Heathrow, surprisingly dressed in a shalwar kameez. Akbar and Bazigh wore suits they'd had made in the market in Peshawar. Mushtaq's kameez was the colour of the bland Rich Tea biscuits he later offered them to go with their chai. Akbar Khan remembered the orange box of cake rusks he'd brought with him and took them out of his suitcase. They'd removed their shoes and were sitting on the floor of Mushtaq's room playing taj, just like they used to in their schooldays, the playing cards scattered on the rug in front of them.

The landlady had welcomed them with deep dishes of chicken karahi and roti. She had kind eyes, called them 'beta' and told them she was excited to have new people visit from her homeland. She was as eager to share information about her new home as to hear news of Pakistan. Her home was in the heart of Brixton.

'There are a lot of kalai here, from Jamaica, I think, but they are nice people.'

'Some are very aggressive.'

'Mushtaq, the gorai don't see the few shades that separate us. To them, we are all kalai.'

Embarrassed by the scolding, Mushtaq looked at the floor.

Akbar Khan wondered if his friend would have taken it so well if they had been back home in Pakistan, to be put in his place by a woman.

She was bold. If women could speak this freely in this country, then what could a man achieve?

Akbar placed a chapati on his plate.

'There is a shop in Tottenham Court Road,' she said, 'that sells kebab, and now we have a place where we can buy atta too.'

Bazigh Khan leaned forward to add some chicken to his plate, but Akbar put his hand on his shoulder.

'Forty-seven! Why are you stopping me? I'm hungry.'

Akbar Khan turned to the landlady. 'Bibiji, Mushtaq said he hadn't eaten meat since he arrived because it is not halal.'

'It's OK, baita. We don't mind so much, but for you, your uncle-ji found a farm nearby where we can go on weekends and buy fresh chickens. He slaughters them there and cleans them.' She picked up Bazigh Khan's plate and spooned some of the curry on to it. 'This chicken is halal.'

Akbar Khan relaxed. He placed a morsel of roti in his mouth. He hadn't realised how hungry he was. The responsibility of looking after his younger brother made him forget everything. 'Thank you, bibiji.'

'You know, this is London, and you will need to be less rigid here. It is either that, or the city will break you.'

Akbar Khan raised his eyes and met hers. His pupils widened like the aperture of a camera as the light declined. 'My Allah comes first.'

'Allah will understand,' she replied. 'As will you when you are my age. Allah always understands, beta. He is gracious and merciful.'

She hobbled out of the room, leaving the young men. She had come here as a bride at the age of sixteen, along with her husband. They had lived in one cramped room and saved every penny they could while she'd cooked and packed lunches for all the other desi men they knew. In time they had enough to buy a large house in a rundown area of London, with every room except their bedroom let to young men who reminded her of her brothers back in Karachi.

Akbar Khan reminded the landlady of her little brother, with the same fire in his belly and fight in his eyes. He was looking for halal chicken and offering his daily prayers, but he would be at the bookies and down the pub in no time.

She knew this because it was how it always was.

'Why do they call him forty-seven?' she'd asked her husband that night as they crawled under the quilt her mother had shipped to them from Lahore many years before. It had a deep maroon pattern on top and was plain underneath. It was so heavy, she swore it was filled with her mother, or her mother's huge love.

'He is Akbar Khan – AK – and he was born sometime between 1945 and 1947, around the time the Kalashnikov was designed. Like many of us, he doesn't know his birth date.' They'd laughed together and fallen asleep in each other's arms, glad their home now had indoor plumbing and they no longer had to brave the cold London nights for the outside privy.

Life was getting better. But the streets never felt like home.

CHAPTER 3

It was almost sunset when Jia went to meet Nadeem. Soon there would be fireworks in the sky.

The drive along stone-walled roads, with the fields on either side bathed in an orange glow, fed her soul. She had missed this living in London. The car climbed higher and higher, its engine taking the sharp incline with ease. The sky was cloudless. Jia knew it would be a perfect starry night, the kind where the radio seemed to play every track she'd loved when she was young and the moonlight hit every note.

The fields became a council housing estate, and she knew she'd arrived. She parked and looked over the valley. The view was as rich as the estate was impoverished. She pulled the collar of her coat up and heard the sound of the fireworks.

She checked her watch and was just wondering if Nadeem was running late when his car drew up. He took a navy peacoat from the passenger seat and pulled it on before walking over to his cousin, his hands in his pockets.

'When are you going to trade that thing in?' she said.

He turned back to his car. 'It keeps me humble,' he replied.

She raised her eyebrow and hugged him, knowing her car was conspicuous and not at all humble. They'd been raised together after Nadeem's mother had died, and so they were more like siblings; she respected his opinions. But Nadeem would be as aware as she was that being incognito didn't bring respect for a woman. The power that came with her being very obviously the Khan paved the way to the places she wanted to be.

The fireworks began, very bright.

'You know why those are called Catherine Wheels?' she asked as they crossed the street.

Nadeem shook his head.

'In the fourth century, Emperor Maxentius ordered a young woman, Saint Catherine, to be tied to a spiked wheel and tortured. He wanted her to renounce her faith. They say the wheel shattered when she touched it. She was beheaded.'

Nadeem looked at her, his face grim. 'I don't know why you women don't just rise up in your beds one night and kill us all while we sleep.'

'Which house is it?' Jia changed the subject.

They were standing in one of the city's roughest, grimmest estates. Although it was cold and dark, children in thin T-shirts were still playing outside. Jia found the lack of parental concern shocking.

The kids from these streets went to Maria's school and many of their fathers worked for Jia. She would ask her sister about it. It was time this behaviour stopped.

They walked through an underpass, the stench of urine so overpowering that Jia used her scarf to cover her mouth and nose. She stepped over countless, empty silver gas cannisters strewn across the pavement.

'Hippy crack,' said Nadeem with a sigh.

They came to a brown, peeling door of a flat.

Nadeem rapped hard. A shout, then whispers and footsteps followed. The door was answered by a short, round man with thinning hair and a warm smile. He stepped forward to hug Nadeem as if they were long-lost brothers. He saw Jia and stepped aside to allow them in.

There was no carpet or floorboards, just hard grey concrete. The wallpaper was peeling, and there were large brown patches on the wall which Jia knew meant damp. In a corner of the room a German shepherd was chewing on a large bone. Jia thought she saw a mouse run close to the wall. Worst of all was the stench. The house smelt like years of neglect and hardship.

Then a pile of library books caught Jia's eye, the spines neatly placed to make a perfect tower. They were a mix of science and literature, and among them she recognised a couple from the latest Booker Prize shortlist.

The sound of a baby crying startled Jia. She looked at the man, his expression tired and embarrassed. The thought of her own son Lirian living in conditions like these made Jia nauseous.

'I'm sorry,' said the man. 'My wife is trying to keep him quiet, but I'm not sure what is wrong.' His accent was thick, but his English clear.

'Costel came here a few years ago to study,' said Nadeem. 'Nowak paid their rent and a stipend in exchange for intelligence.'

'Nowak liked us,' Costel said. 'I don't know why, but he helped us. I have six brothers and sisters back home in Romania, and I wanted to send them money.'

'What did he ask you to do for him in exchange?'

'Nothing really big. We would eat together and talk about politics, religion, what was happening in the city, what I saw.'

'You were spying for him?'

'I'm not a stupid man. I know that at some point he would have asked me to do something…criminal, something bad, and I would have had to do it. But people like me have to take the chance so that our brothers and sisters don't have to.' Jia recognised herself in him. 'When Nowak died, we had nothing and we couldn't pay our rent. I finished my degree but then there were no jobs, and my wife was pregnant. And now we are here, in this place, a living hell.'

'Nadeem said you wanted to meet me.'

'I want to work for you. I need money. I cannot let my child grow up here.'

'I understand, but you worked for Nowak, so how can I trust you?'

'I knew him because we came from the same part of the world, not because I was like him or because I liked him. I know you value loyalty, and you can see what life is like for people such as me.'

Jia found Costel as impressive as Nadeem had promised.

'What was your university research into?' she asked.

'Blockchains.'

Now she was more interested than she had been. An idea was formulating in her head. 'As in cryptocurrency?' she said.

Costel nodded. 'In a way. I was looking at using blockchain technology to improve medical treatment.'

'I thought blockchain tech was about money.'

'It is. But it can be used for a number of things. It is just a virtual ledger that is cryptographically secure.'

Nadeem looked confused.

'Complex algorithms transform messages into a language that makes them hard to decipher and therefore difficult to steal,' explained Jia.

Costel added, 'Our medical history is split across multiple healthcare providers – the GP, the hospital, the dentist. The systems are incompatible and transferring records is slow. I was working on a way to create a permanent blockchain record, owned by a person, that holds all of their information in one place – ailments, allergies, lifestyle factors – to help doctors.'

'I hope that wasn't a waste of time,' said Nadeem a few minutes later as they crossed the road.

Jia remained silent, deep in thought.

Nadeem paused and then said, 'We did this to him when we took out Nowak. There are a lot of families like his, families that have fallen through the cracks.'

Jia knew this was true.

The decision to kill Nowak had been calculated, borne out of necessity. She had weighed up the pros and cons, and although she did not believe in the black and white of good and evil, she had felt the man who headed up the Brotherhood was on the side of the devil.

Now she wondered if she had possibly been blinded by her love for her people and her family, and the desire to survive.

She hadn't thought Nowak had a humane side, but perhaps he had, even if only slightly. And while killing Nowak had solved her personal problems, clearly it had created a void in the lives of those the Brotherhood had taken under its wing.

She needed time to think.

Looking over at Nadeem's face, the pain that filled it now, she could see he wasn't the man he had been. He was unravelling and had been since that day in Café de Khan when she'd put a bullet through Nowak's head.

'Sit with me for a moment,' she said to him, opening the car door. 'Let's talk.'

Nadeem climbed into the passenger side and felt the seat warm up beneath him. 'Maybe I was wrong about that old banger of mine,' he said. He was covering his emotion with humour, and Jia knew a little something about that. She knew too that he was kind, and he was brave. He had inherited the best aspects of their family, and his mind was having trouble processing what they had done and what they were becoming.

Jia wondered if she had asked too much of him. But she had only asked what she asked of herself.

He was still now, as if holding his breath.

Jia knew that if she ignored this, he would fragment. But there could be no turning back from what they had done, no way to undo killing a gangland boss, no way to erase it from memory. The feeling sat like a pebble in a glass jar, rattling at every tiny moment. She needed to fill the rest of the jar with sand, to dampen the sound.

'Nadeem, you need to find a way forward,' she said.

'I know.' A pause. 'I had some counselling in my early twenties,' he added, 'and I talked about losing my mother, about you guys, about my dad.'

Jia listened, letting him speak, knowing how hard it must have been for Nadeem to take that step, coming from a culture where men were expected to 'man up'.

The Khans loved one another, their loyalty was absolute, but expression of raw emotions to the point of vulnerability was as rare as it was painful.

Jia knew this better than anyone. Bitter experience had shown her vulnerability wasn't welcomed by her people, and it was often used against those who were open and honest about their truth. Nadeem knew this too.

'I can't really do that now, can I?' he laughed. 'Imagine telling a therapist about what happened. I don't know what to do. Is this who we are now? Is this it? I don't know if we're the good guys or the bad guys.'

'You're a good guy,' said Jia, her voice firm.

'Then why do I keep reliving that shot?' he said. 'It's like I'm trapped in that moment, and I don't want to be there but it's on a loop. It hits me at the strangest times, like when I'm driving past the restaurant. On Bonfire Night last year, I took Haala out to see the fireworks, and the smell of the fireworks took me back to that night, and I found I couldn't breathe.'

Jia knew about that night. Elyas had been with Nadeem that evening. Lirian had been unwell, so she'd stayed home. 'It's only a post-vacci-nation fever,' she'd told Elyas. 'You go, we'll be fine.' Elyas hadn't come back till late. He'd taken Nadeem home and stayed there until midnight.

'He had a panic attack,' Elyas told Jia when he got home. 'I've not seen him like that before. We talked a bit. He said he was worried about Haala's schooling, the eleven-plus, the usual parental stuff.

But I think that something else is going on. Maybe check on him tomorrow morning?'

Jia had been keeping an eye on Nadeem since then, but this was the first time she had directly spoken to him about it.

'You're the best guy,' she said. 'I should never have asked you to be part of that night.'

'It was my choice. I needed to be there. And now I need to fix this and get on. But I don't know how anymore.'

Jia didn't know either. But she knew that for him to feel safe, he had to believe she had everything under control. She took his hand in hers, the way she used to do when he was little and had grazed his knee.

'Let's get them out of that house for now,' she said. 'And we'll figure out what to do after that. We will make this right, OK?'

He didn't answer. So she took Nadeem's face in her hands and looked him dead in the eyes. 'I've got this, OK?' she said. She watched as the weight dropped from his shoulders and she saw a light flicker in his sunken eyes. And she understood what she had to do.

She would give him practical tasks, and then she would find a way to fix him, and in time she would move him out of the family business. There were enough of them to get their hands dirty. Nadeem didn't have to be one of them.

'How many families are there?'

He reached into his pocket and pulled out a piece of paper. He unfolded it before giving it to her. It was a list, itemised and printed.

'How did you know what I'd do?' she said, taking the paper and looking it over. It was much larger than she had expected.

'There's not much I know,' he replied. 'But I do know you.'

She looked down the list, names, addresses and ages. He had done his homework. She needed time to think as she couldn't promise too much.

'OK, let's figure something out,' she said. 'For now, let's extend that food delivery service that Imran Khan does from his cash and carry.'

The flicker in Nadeem's eyes had spread to his face, and it was beginning to glow.

'Go in there and tell them the good news.'

In his eagerness to extract Costel and his family from their damp-ridden existence, Nadeem practically fell out of the car. But something made him pause, and he turned back to her.

'Ahad talked to you?' he said.

She nodded.

'I tried to tell him you'd be cool, but he was worried. I'm glad he has you as a mother. It's not easy being different. Especially when you're a Pashtun.'

Jia felt something heavy inside the pit of her stomach. She was a terrible mother and she knew it. She had reacted badly to her elder son's honesty.

'I'm worried about him,' she said. 'What will happen to him? They will think the worst of him, treat him badly, assume the worst. Just like they do with me.'

'Who will?'

'People, the community.'

'Since when have you cared about "the community" – and what are we, *BBC Look North*? Would you turn up to a nice white village and say, "Take me to your community elders?"'

Jia laughed at his words, and she felt a little lighter, but she knew why she was afraid.

She thought of her father and wondered how he had felt when he landed in these colder climes, leaving behind his homeland. Maybe judgement was in their bloodline, a price they paid for the fight to survive.

She thought of Costel's child in that cold, dank house, and her head was filled with questions about actions and their consequences. She knew that she couldn't give too much time to these thoughts, because they were paralysing. Her life, her responsibilities, meant acting decisively and stepping forward, taking the punches and hitting back, until she won.

The world did not understand people like her. She couldn't hold that against it.

She herself had failed to understand her own father, and she had taken his life.

There were moments where she wished she had tried harder to cross the divide between them, a chasm that was cultural, generational and whose void was filled with self-righteousness, a void that she had drowned in, but they were fleeting moments. And Jia could not think about what was in the past right now.

The responsibilities upon her were growing, getting more complicated with each day, and she didn't have time to indulge herself.

She was the Khan, and she needed to decide her next move.

She started her car and called Idris on her way home. He picked up on the first ring.

'Could you find out where our suspected Henry Paxton likes to hold his meetings?' she said. 'Men like him are creatures of habit.'

They needed investment, and if Akbar Khan had connections with influential people, she should explore them.

CHAPTER 4

'You ever miss London?' asked Elyas.

'Not really. Once you've lived there for long enough, been invited to the "right" parties, achieved what you set out to, eaten at the best places, the shine comes off a little. It just wasn't fun anymore. Does that make sense?'

'I like being able to breathe fresh air,' he said.

'Besides, I'm there often enough, like this Friday,' Jia told him. 'Will you be able to hold the fort here?'

He nodded, putting on his headphones to catch up on the day's news. He was a journalist and so needed to keep abreast of what was happening.

Ahad was at university now, and with Jia working long hours, Elyas did most of the childcare when it came to Lirian, juggling it with his career.

Much as she loved her children, motherhood didn't come naturally to Jia, and she was happy to have her husband take the lead with bringing their boys up.

She was better at the kind of work that was respected by the world, the kind that came with pound signs. She knew this about herself, and that it was a trauma response to the lack of respect afforded to women for the burden their bodies and minds carried. Even in stories, godmothers were portrayed as gentle and magical beings who fulfilled wishes, while their male equivalents took lives and dispensed justice.

Jia saw herself in neither of these portrayals. Building a new world meant making sacrifices and finding a different way to live, and she chose to stand back from the day-to-day care demands parenthood brought.

'Isn't this the place we went to for dinner last week?' said Elyas, taking off his headphones and turning up the volume on his laptop so that Jia could hear.

'The body was found in the early hours by the dustbins at the back of this popular restaurant,' said a reporter's voice. 'In a statement released this afternoon, police say they are following leads but anyone with useful information should come forward.'

Jia was leaning back against the upholstered linen of her headboard, the duvet over her as she was reading. Elyas had his laptop propped up on a pile of grey cushions. 'That's the second body they've found after the guy that was killed at the industrial unit, the one who was left in the park, remember?'

Jia looked up from her book. 'How do you know they're connected?'

'I don't. Just a hunch.' Elyas picked up his phone and started tapping on it, before turning back to the computer.

Jia took a deep breath. She needed to wind down, and he had just gone into his news-journalist mode. If the murders turned out to be something she needed to concern herself with, that would become apparent soon enough. Idris would let her know, or the police chief would be in touch.

It had been a long and busy day. The kind that left her searching for sanctuary. She'd ached for the soft greys of her bedroom, the familiarity of the furniture, a mix of bespoke modern luxury and antiques that Akbar Khan had collected over the years.

The bedroom was a reflection of father and daughter. It helped that Akbar Khan had had good taste.

Bookshelves lined the alcoves on either side of the huge bed. Elyas had argued against its size, but she'd won him over by telling him she was used to sleeping alone. While he wasn't naive enough to assume that she had not had other relationships during their time apart when she was in London and they were estranged, he wasn't ready to know the details.

She lit candles and read books in bed. Elyas needed a constant flow of information from phones, iPads and Alexa.

Now, he turned his laptop towards her, the red of the BBC News website flashing up. The reporter was standing in front of the ornate stone entrance of what was once a Victorian chapel. Elyas hit play on the clip. Jia watched the camera pan over the building. It was bathed in yellow light. The video cut to the blue and white strips of a police cordon, signalling that something bad had happened there.

Jia turned back to her book. The daily reports of murders did not appeal to her in the way they did to her husband.

'Did you know about this?' Elyas asked, climbing out of bed.

'Where are you going?' she said.

'To get some water. Why didn't you tell me?'

'It slipped my mind. Idris mentioned it in passing but I didn't connect it with the other murder.'

He mumbled something under his breath.

'I can't hear you from there,' she said. She waited, listening to the sound of the toilet flushing. She heard the tap, water filling a cup, the low hum of an electric toothbrush and then more water. This was what he did when he was annoyed. It had been the same when they were young. He would leave the room, busy himself with something, and Jia would have to guess what was wrong. She was less patient now. She had no time for games and only headspace for precision.

Jia put her book down on the table beside her bed and slid open the drawer, taking out the tube of hand cream and smothering it on to the back of her hands. Since she'd removed the old diary from the back of the drawer, it slid smoothly into place. It had given her a glimpse into her father's life, a time that he had rarely spoken about, the toppled domino that had led her to this place.

The candle flickered gently, filling the room with the scent of lavender, jasmine and rosewood.

'It wasn't intentional,' she said to Elyas as he returned.

'You should have told me all the same.' He took his laptop and sat down by the window seat, looking out across the garden.

'It's of no relevance to us.'

'I just wish you'd told me,' he said, 'before you told Idris.'

'I didn't tell Idris. He mentioned it to me.'

Jia looked at the man she had fallen in love with in her twenties, the man who had carried a torch for her in her presence and during her long absence. She couldn't help but wonder if that was why they were here now. If she'd had to put up with this for two decades, she would have left him long ago. She waited in the silence, knowing that Elyas had something to say, but he kept his attention on his laptop, the keys bearing the brunt of his annoyance.

Jia sighed softly. There were days like this when she wondered what she was doing trying to keep this relationship afloat. She had been honest. She'd tried to tell him the truth about everything just after the fire, when Nowak was killed, but he hadn't wanted to hear it. Maybe she should have taken that as a sign to end the relationship, but she'd been pregnant. She hadn't wanted to raise a child alone, and as a single woman in her position, gaining the respect of her father's men would have been impossible if she were a single mother.

Decades had passed since her people left their homeland, but patriarchy was not held in by borders or contained by oceans. It lived in every corner of the world, basking in bright sunlight in some countries and lurking in crevices in others.

Elyas wasn't upset about the murder. It was everything else that was irking him, Jia knew. Living in her family home, being the default parent, Jia's strained relationship with Ahad, and of course the work she did, and that maybe she was closer to her cousin than to him.

'I just need Elyas to be honest, be angry,' she'd told her sister. 'But he's too busy being the good guy.'

As if on cue, their small son cried in the next room, and without argument or request, Elyas went to check on him.

The baby monitor crackled and Jia heard him soothing Lirian gently, the little boy wanting to be picked up. A faint whisper of singing, and Jia leaned towards the monitor, hearing some U2 lyrics.

The words were etched in her memory. They'd played the song on repeat lying on her bed together in their twenties, staring up at the ceiling, their fingers interlaced.

Life had seemed simpler, when good was what you were, not what you did. When 'All I Want Is You' had been enough, when the cradle had felt closer than the grave, when their story was untold and life had yet to become a tempest.

She reached over to put her glasses on the bedside table, her fingers accidentally denting the softening tallow of the candle burning beside her, making a ravine for the hot wax which stung and then cooled on fingertip.

Jia was still awake when Elyas came to bed an hour later, thinking about everything that had come to pass since the first time he'd kissed her. She wondered if he regretted it, if knowing what he knew now he would have walked away. She considered turning towards him and talking about everything, about the past, the here and now, and the things that were on his mind.

You are always the good guy, the one whom everyone likes. But for you to actually admit how you feel means telling me some truths. Are you strong enough to do that? is what she wanted to say to him. She wouldn't have liked his reply, but she'd have respected him for saying it.

In any other life, she would have taken his face in her hands and kissed it and asked her husband what was wrong.

He might even have told her, and they would have made love and fallen asleep in each other's arms. Their love affair had been about the two of them, but marriage was about community, and hers was particularly knotty.

When Jia had started out as a barrister, she had thought law was all clean lines and defined workings. Bad people went to prison, while good people were handed justice.

Experience had shown her this way of thinking was misguided, that, in fact, everyone was only one bad decision away from incarceration.

The family business was messy, and to some it felt outside the law of the land, but she justified her part in it. It was a peace she had to make daily with herself. But if she wasn't the Khan, children would go hungry, homes unheated, and lives would be lost.

Money was life and death; it was also self-respect, and those who had it could claim the moral high ground. Money brought with it choice.

Jia's dilemma was that she had enough money and status to remove the family from further criminal dealings and with no longer having to be part of the Jirga. But if she chose now to walk away, she would leave her people at the mercy of those who would exploit them. It was a heavy burden to bear.

She felt him move beside her, the bed covers pull slightly. He reached out and took her hand in his.

She blew out the candle and let the room fall into darkness.

They would talk, but not today.

CHAPTER 5

The day the body was dumped in the grounds of Pukhtun House began like every day had in the Khan household for decades.

It began with prayers.

Jia watched the warm water overflow from her cupped hands in to the basin before splashing it on to her face, over her ears and arms. She washed her feet three times, first the right and then the left, drying them on the bath mat, ready for prayer. She was bone tired and so grateful that the porcelain tiles under her feet were warm.

Now that she was running things, she saw her father's foresight in every aspect of life, how it ran like an artery through the business, the community and the family home. Even the comforting floor was evidence of that, a small mercy.

She looked at herself in the mirror. Her hair had more grey than she liked. She would rectify this. Having a child was hard; having a child in one's forties was even harder, but that didn't mean she should sacrifice her vanity.

She left the bathroom and picked up her soft cotton chador to cover her head before rolling out her father's old prayer mat. She slipped her feet on to the worn parts of it and said the Allahu Akbar. The Arabic words failed to hold her attention, and her mind kept wandering as she was so exhausted.

Lirian had kept her up most of the night with teething or trapped wind – who knew what it was. Elyas had handled everything alone with their eldest son, but he had been younger then. He had been so soundly asleep last night that Jia had gone to the nursery.

'You should hire a night nanny,' her mother had said.

But a woman who didn't trust herself couldn't trust a stranger to look after her child.

Jia was all too aware of her own failings as a parent, and maybe somewhere deep down she was trying to make up for having been a totally absent one to Ahad.

But there were other reasons for her tiredness today.

Nadeem had come to see her the night before with an update on Costel and the other families.

In the quiet of morning, Jia tried to focus on her prayer, sliding her hands down her thighs and on to her knees, and bowing. 'Glorious is my Lord, the magnificent.' The Arabic came easily by rote. But the spiritual connection was harder to make.

She knew life, with its twists and turns, and was intimately acquainted too with its darkness. She needed for there to be something bigger than her, but recently her faith had been dwindling.

Jia felt this acutely whenever her people came to her with concerns. As Nadeem had. He had aged in the last two years, and these days his eyes seemed sunken and shadowed. If it wasn't for his wrinkle-free skin, Jia would have wondered if he had turned to the illicit things her men sold, to alleviate his guilt.

'You have to forgive yourself,' she'd said the previous evening when they had spoken. 'We have to leave room for our own redemption.'

'It's only if we talk about what we have done that we find redemption,' he'd replied. His eyes locked on the polished oak-parquet flooring of her study that ran throughout every inch of Pukhtun House. As children their laughter had filled these rooms, and the attics and the cellars. But now the silence around them was swollen, filled with unspoken words about the men they had killed in cold blood, the damage they had inflicted, to bring the city back into the fold of the Jirga.

Turf wars claimed lives. Everyone involved knew that. But there had been unforeseen repercussions, things they had not considered back then – because how could they know how far the thread ran, and how tangled it would become?

Jia wondered if her father had always known what to do.

'We've all done something wrong,' she told Nadeem. 'No one is innocent in this world, especially those who think they are. This is life, not the afterlife, little brother. We did then what we had to do. We saved the city and who knows how many people. Nowak had no mercy, remember.'

Nadeem had cried. It was as if a dam had burst within him, and with his head in his hands, he had wept, and she had watched. She hadn't seen him cry since they were children, when it was natural to pick him up and wipe his tears – he was younger than her, and she'd seemed so much older.

Now, he was a man, towering above her, his beard peppered with white, and though she knew inside he was still that small child, she knew she shouldn't embrace him the way she used to.

But then, although cultural expectations and behavioural norms were hard to break, she put her arms around him as if he were a child again.

Emptied of sorrow, eventually he pulled back, still clutching her hand. 'Nowak would have killed us all,' she whispered. 'We had no choice. You have to trust that I won't put you in that position again, and we will make amends to those who are now collateral damage.'

Then Sanam Khan, Jia's mother, had taken Nadeem away to the kitchen, her arms around him tight, kissing his eyes and calling him 'bacha' as she asked if he was hungry. She had raised him as one of her own after his mother had been killed. In some ways she loved him more than those she had birthed. He was kinder to her, so grateful and gracious.

'Forgive me, oh Allah,' Jia prayed now, 'and raise me up, make good my shortcomings, and provide for me.' It would be morning soon, and the duties of life would be upon her.

She turned her head to the right and then the left, coming back to the world, ready to face its challenges. She needed to shore up the edifice of their lives, and that meant gaining more money and power. It was the only way she could do good.

She looked into the adjoining room, where Elyas was sleeping, curled around their son. She'd heard the toddler wake not long before prayers, followed by her husband's soothing voice as he slipped into the next room. 'It's OK,' he'd said to her. 'You get some rest. I'll sleep in the nursery.'

He was worried about her, she could tell.

He'd been watching her like a hawk, and when she'd confessed a few weeks earlier that her focus was suffering, he'd taken it as permission to step out of the shadows. She knew sleep deprivation wasn't good, but she wished he trusted her a little more.

She reflected on finding herself a new mother in her forties. With her first child, she hadn't experienced any complications during pregnancy, but following a difficult birth and consequent anaesthetics, her father had taken Ahad and secretly given him to Elyas to raise, allowing Jia to think she had lost the baby in childbirth.

By the time she'd come to learn Ahad was still alive, the baby had become a teenager. And for a while, Jia had been full of fury.

But life is complicated, and something had drawn Jia and Elyas into each other's arms once more. And Elyas considered the failure of their contraception a blessing, a second chance at what they could have had. But his life continued largely uninterrupted, and it was Jia who had to navigate the assumptions of men and the judgement of women.

Still, Lirian was here, and she loved him. And it was this that frightened her.

She'd named this baby 'freedom', because that was what she wanted for both her children more than anything else. To be free from the millions of voices that would dare to define them throughout their lives.

Jia pulled back the curtains of her bedroom.

Through the leaded windows, she could see the apple tree in the murky light. It needed to be cut down, a decision she wouldn't take lightly, but the tree had stopped giving fruit and a tree surgeon confirmed it was diseased. It might look healthy, but it was rotting inside and in danger of collapsing. It was time to plant new trees.

Every morning Jia would have two cups of tea, the first an ordinary builder's brew, the second an act of remembrance for a past where her father would be in her place, making chai with loose-leaf tea, milk and water boiled in a saucepan. She made it just as her father had taught her when she was a child, with cardamom pods from her organised spice cupboard. The chai would be cooked by the time she'd finished her cup of English Breakfast. It had been this way since she moved back, and she'd come to find comfort in such traditions. As she moved through the kitchen, choosing spices and inhaling the scent of tea leaves, it was as if the generations past were standing alongside her.

Seated at the kitchen table, she watched the ghosts of those she loved brush past. Her brother Zan grabbing a slice of toast, her father picking up his keys and offering to drive her to school. What she wouldn't give to head back to those teenage summers of ease and innocence. There were so many things she wished she could ask them both.

Jia looked out of the window at the manicured lawn, the hibernating flower beds, the trees naked without their leaves, standing sentry.

Something wasn't right. She wasn't sure what, but the small hairs on the back of her neck had lifted.

Her father's favourite swing chair was missing its cover, she noticed. And there was something in the chair, something bulky, a sight that drained her complexion.

There was a man in the chair, and he was facing her.

CHAPTER 6

Jia quickly flicked a light switch by the door frame, moving back to the window.

Whoever was in the chair kept staring.

She checked the security cameras, flicking through the images on the control panel in the utility room to see if she could get a better view of who it was, but the camera angles didn't offer much help.

She alerted the security guard, hitting the buzzer on the control panel as she wondered if he'd fallen asleep on the job. The voice that answered wasn't the usual man but he sounded awake. 'No, bibiji. I've been here all night, since Ishtiaq left. Idris jaan asked me to take over. No one has come in or out since 8.00PM.'

'Send someone over now,' she said, 'and…'

'Yes, bibiji?'

'Quickly.'

Jia unlocked the kitchen door, slowly pushing it open.

She should wait for the security man, she knew, or get Elyas.

Instead, she took the cashmere chador from the chair and threw it around her shoulders before stepping outside.

Jia was intimately acquainted with her demons, and the demons of others. Little frightened her, but as she walked across the patio and up the stone steps to the raised garden, her eyes on the figure, she made sure to look for any small movement that signified danger. She gazed all around to make sure she and the man were alone.

He was dressed in brilliant white, his head wrapped like a shaikh.

Then she stopped in her tracks.

Now closer, she could see the man was a member of her security team, Ishtiaq.

And he was dead.

The overpowering scent of camphor hit her as she edged towards him, and she realised it wasn't a suit he was wearing. He was wrapped in a sheet. And Ishtiaq's forehead was red, branded like a cow.

She'd seen this just the week before when Mark Briscoe, the police chief, had come to her, brandishing photographs. He knew he could depend on her discretion and had hoped she might be able to shed some light on the cases. But Jia was reluctant to get involved.

In person it was something else, and she shuddered.

She dialled Briscoe. He answered groggily, knowing better than to refuse a call from the Khan. Jia would not be ringing him this early if it wasn't of utmost importance.

'Send a car to my house immediately.' It was an instruction and not a request.

She was about to move closer to the body when she heard a noise. She spun around but it was too late.

Elyas was coming to her with Lirian in his arms. Barefoot, the little boy's golden-brown curls rested on his father's shoulder.

She tried to steer Elyas towards the house, taking their son from him. 'We need to go back inside,' she said.

'I saw you out here and...' He didn't finish the sentence as his eyes stared deep into hers. He didn't have to. Jia guessed what was on his mind. She had struggled with depression before, had a history of post-natal depression – did he think she'd been about to do something foolish?

Well, she had been foolish, but not in the way he feared. Jia knew she should have waited for the security man.

And then Elyas saw the body. He turned to Jia in horror. He'd been a journalist long enough to have seen some frightening things but never in his own back garden.

37

'He can't hurt us, Elyas, he's dead,' she said.

Elyas looked at the body again.

Jia pressed her hand on his shoulder, saying calmly, 'Let's go inside. Security will be here any second.'

Later, when Elyas thought about them all in the garden, the ease with which his wife had spoken bothered him.

'It's Ishtiaq,' she'd explained. 'Don't worry. It's going to be OK.'

Elyas recalled how collected she'd been, how practical, the two sides of her sliced cleanly in half. Because somehow in their life being dead now was OK. A dead man his wife had employed and been fond of sitting lifelessly on the lawn was nothing to worry about – that was her world now. And it really disturbed him.

The security guard arrived in a flurry. 'Tauba! Istighfar!' he cried, calling on God's forgiveness. 'We must call Idris jaan.'

'We have to speak to the police first,' said Elyas.

'They're on their way,' Jia said, handing back their son as she turned towards the house. She was relieved to see that Lirian was still sleeping soundly.

'Did you see his head?'

'That's why we need to go back to the kitchen. Now,' she said.

Inside, Jia locked the door and quickly tapped a message on her phone, and then stared once more at the dead man.

'How did this get past security?' Elyas's voice was shaky.

Jia pulled her eyes away from the body in the garden as she glanced at her husband. 'I don't know,' she admitted.

'Did you see his head?' Elyas asked again.

Jia nodded. The mark on Ishtiaq was shouting a message.

One she needed to take seriously.

CHAPTER 7

Elyas collected the mugs and placed them in the sink.

'Another round?' he asked. Countless cups of tea had already been drunk by the family around the kitchen table as they watched forensics from behind the glass doors.

Police officers had secured the perimeter and were heading out to question neighbours, the closest of whom was Idris, whose house was acres away. He was already here and was talking to two of them, making sure they had all that they needed and finding out what they knew. A forensics tent surrounded the swing, and people in hazmat suits walked carefully around the garden.

'An excuse to buy new garden furniture now, Mama,' said Benyamin, winking at his mother.

Sanam Khan furrowed her brow at him. 'Istighfarullah!' she said. It was what she said to most of his comments nowadays.

'Why do I need God's forgiveness? I haven't done anything,' he said, always ready to lock horns with his mother. She refused to rise to the bait.

The incident with Nowak had changed Jia's brother, she thought as she looked at him. It had fanned the flames of rebellion within him. With his father gone and his older sister in charge, he was navigating a new world. He'd wanted to make his mark on the family business, an empire that was run by men. Now that a woman was in charge, he was having to adjust and accept his own prejudices.

She turned to watch a black body bag being wheeled from the tent.

Feeling bad about his lack of sensitivity, Benyamin put his arms around his mother, an act that was as much for himself as it was for her.

Elyas placed his hand in Jia's, squeezing it gently. The last time an ambulance had been on the grounds of Pukhtun House had been the day Zan Khan had died, the day he'd argued with Akbar Khan and driven off in a rage. The eldest son of the family, Zan had been the glue that held everyone together. His passing had triggered a series of events. Afterwards, Jia had left Elyas and distanced herself from her entire family, only returning years later for her sister's wedding, then staying to take over the family business. Akbar Khan had had to die for this to happen.

Elyas had buried the details of what he knew about that particular matter. But there had been a letter he'd read, one that proved Jia had been responsible for her father's death. He'd been so distracted when he'd read it that later he couldn't fully remember the contents and tried hard to convince himself he had misunderstood. Having a small child and a teenage one left his mind little time to ponder the complexities of his life, Elyas told himself. But occasionally, like today, his conscience poked at him.

As the ambulance left the driveway and grounds of Pukhtun House, too much that was unsaid hung heavy between them. They shuffled around each other, until Benyamin broke the silence.

'Who do you think it was?' he said.

'We're about to find out,' replied Jia as Idris walked in.

Idris pulled off his thick down jacket and hung it on the back of the chair. His cashmere jumper, the colour of midnight, his white T-shirt, visible only at the neckline, and his black jeans were all pristine, leaving Elyas feeling shabby. He couldn't help noticing that even Idris's boots had that shop-bought sheen still. He felt decidedly second best in the presence of his wife's cousin, in part because Elyas knew Idris was the keeper of secrets.

Elyas glanced at his dishevelled reflection in the window. His pyjama bottoms were clearly slept in and his navy raglan shirt streaked with white marks left by Lirian's nose. He hadn't had a full night's sleep in days and was acutely aware that he was no longer a young man. Working in media and TV had made him prone to vanity, and he wanted to ask Jia to pause while he showered and shaved. But he was a grown-up and knew that none of this really mattered. That didn't mean there weren't days when it felt like it did. But he didn't dare say anything to Jia.

Idris turned the kettle on, taking out a mug and then locating the filter and filter cup with ease. He knew where everything was, having grown up in Pukhtun House. He treated it like his own home and no one expected otherwise.

Jia took him aside. 'What's happening?'

'I've called in all our men, and they've set up a perimeter around Pukhtun House alongside the police lines. We're not allowing anyone in or out. I've reviewed the security footage but there's nothing unusual.'

'He was marked,' she said. 'I didn't get close enough, but I think it said "Al-Haseeb".'

'You think someone is dispensing justice?'

She nodded. Branding the security man with a name of God, one that meant 'The Reckoner', and leaving his body on the lawn, was most definitely a message.

She said, 'Why the hell am I paying all those guards to sit at the screens of a state-of-art security system when someone can dump a body here? My son plays in that garden. Find out how this happened. And, Idris, I'll go to London alone. I need you to handle everything here – you know what to do.'

'Jia, you think it's wise to travel alone?'

A lesser woman would have been panicked, but Jia was used to running the family's affairs now, and heightened drama came with the territory. Blood ties had made her the Khan – and her ability to hide her emotions and her intelligence had kept her there. She didn't wallow in the highs and lows of running a crime syndicate; she always made sure she was the oil to calm the inevitable turbulent waters that came with living by your own law.

'Just do what I said, please.' Her look was firm.

Idris nodded. 'Yes, of course.' He put his hand on his stomach to stop it rumbling. He'd been called early and not yet had time for breakfast.

'Idris,' said Sanam Khan. 'Are you hungry, baita?'

'Sorry about that,' Idris said. 'It's a shame Chilli Chacha's away. I could really do with one of his parathas.'

'It was good of your father to take him with him,' said Sanam Khan. 'I'm grateful to Bazigh Lala for sorting out the new house and land issues in Peshawar. It's not something I could do, and Jia is so busy. Chacha arranged for his niece Hamsa to help us while he was away.'

Sanam Khan called over a young woman who had been standing in the corner. She'd been so quiet she was barely noticeable. 'She doesn't speak,' Chilli Chacha had told Sanam Khan before he left. 'You can talk freely in front of Hamsa, I promise.'

'I will make you a paratha,' said Sanam Khan. 'And Hamsa shall clean up afterwards.'

And before anyone could object, Sanam Khan had disappeared into the larder. Food was her love language, a way to make herself busy while looking after those she cared about, a practical sort of kindness. She returned with a black apron tied around her waist, carrying a large glass jar of atta and several packs of butter, along with a silver cannister of ghee.

'No ghee for me,' said Idris. 'I know "the coloniser" says it's a golden food now, but my taste buds are from the eighties when the doctors told us it was a heart attack in a tub.'

Sanam Khan poured the chapatti flour into the KitchenAid mixer, adding water and salt, measuring by eye. The machine began mixing and kneading the dough until it was soft and pliable, and she said, 'Benyamin, go and ask those outside if they are hungry.'

In the garden, fingerprint experts sprayed and brushed the garden furniture.

Jia watched as everyone played to type, her mother busying herself with cooking for her nephews and brother as they waited expectantly at the table. Sanam Khan placed the tava on the hob to heat, before forming little balls with the dough, dipping them in flour and then rolling them out into a snake on a worktop smeared with copious amounts of butter. Then she rolled the small snakes into a larger one, coiling it in on itself several times, before flattening it out and placing it on the hot griddle. More fat was added, and smoke began to rise, filling the air with the nutty fragrance of searing butter.

'The paratha patriarchy lives on. Even in our house,' said Jia Khan, surprised at how quickly her brother and cousins fell back into being looked after in the old ways.

During her childhood, she'd watched as women worked in hot kitchens, serving up deliciousness that the men, despite having made no effort, always consumed first. The aunts and female cousins had to clear up before they could sit down to eat, the men waiting for tea to be served. It had never occurred to anyone until years later that it didn't have to be done this way.

'Mama offered to do it,' Benyamin said defensively.

And there it was, the answer to why women remained subjugated in certain places and households: because some women were still willing to keep pandering to men.

Although change was happening all around as an inevitable consequence of Jia and her cousins being the children of two worlds, sometimes everyone reverted to the old ways.

Having lived with sisters, and more recently spent time in the company of Sakina, Benyamin knew he had said the wrong thing, and he started making chai to cover his mistake. Then he set the table, placing napkins beside each plate, before waiting eagerly for the hot, flaky parathas. He opened the large jar of pickled lime. 'Hey, Dris, try this,' he said, handing his cousin a knife and fork, the only cutlery at the table. Everyone knew Idris didn't eat with his fingers.

Jia could see how grateful the forensics experts were for the food Sanam Khan sent out to them, Hamsa silently carrying the loaded tray.

'Who has the balls to leave a body on our lawn?' said Benyamin as he tore pieces of the flat bread and dipped them in the lime pickle. 'Don't they know who we are?'

'What do you mean, who we are?' said Sanam Khan, turning from the stove at speed. 'We're just ordinary people, like everyone else.'

Benyamin laughed. He'd been at the harsh end of the family business and had only just escaped with his life. His mother had lived with Akbar Khan, presumably aware she was married to a criminal kingpin.

His mother gave him the side-eye as she said, 'Have you no shame? A man is dead in our garden. *Zama dae toba we!*'

'I told you, I'm not asking God to forgive me for something I haven't done. I'll leave that to you,' he said, standing up and wiping his fingertips on the edge of his mum's apron, before kissing her on the head. 'I'm going out.'

'Where are you going this early?'

'Gym,' Benyamin said as he left the room.

Sanam Khan turned to her daughter, exasperated. 'Sometimes he is so much like your father, I feel as if Akbar Khan has returned.'

Jia Khan couldn't reconcile her mother's words with her own experience of her father. 'Baba was always measured and respectful of matters of faith and religion. "In this house we respect Allah and we are loyal to his people" – remember how he would always say that as though drilling us in a basic tenet of faith?'

'Your father wasn't always the way you remember him,' Sanam Khan told her daughter. 'There was a time, before you were born, when he was a very different man. Time and circumstance changed him on the surface. Inside he was as gentle as a lamb – it was just the world expected him to be a lion.'

Not so long ago, Jia would have thought her mother naive for believing this lie – she had told it to herself so many times now that she couldn't distinguish fact from fiction. But Jia's own descent into the nefarious activities of organised crime had led her increasingly to wonder who Akbar Khan really was, and if the young man who came to London in the 1970s had any idea what his life had in store.

CHAPTER 8

1974

Akbar Khan had had low expectations of walking away with the job when he'd first stepped through the art deco revolving doors of the Pembroke.

'May I help you, sir?' he'd been asked by a suspicious doorman. He was assumed to be out of place without even speaking – the presence of melanin in his skin was enough.

Akbar Khan was led to the back of the vestibule, passing the potted palms, huge Grecian urns filled with fresh flowers and pale-pink marble pillars around which armchairs and tables were set for tea. He wondered if the spaces occupied by the moneyed were similar across the world. Very probably, he decided, and they weren't really a place for him.

He waited in the corner, tapping his right foot on the mosaic floor made from tiny black and white Victorian tiles. He felt sick with nerves. He'd been in the country four weeks already and he was worried they would run out of money. The landlady had been kind, but he knew that if they couldn't pay the rent, she would have to throw them out eventually.

He looked down at his feet, shoes polished to a high shine, borrowed from his friend. His own had become worn down from walking the streets in search of work. He had been to what felt like every accountancy office in London, each one turning him away. Now he was applying to hotels.

'I can do all these calculations in my head,' he'd said eagerly to the last hotel manager. 'You can test me. Ask me anything.' It didn't matter.

The manager was cold, and Akbar Khan read the judgement on his face as the man looked him up and down, eyes resting on the purple velvet suit he'd had made in Peshawar Market. 'I'm sure you can, but it is of no use to me if you can't write grammatically correct English.'

It wasn't the first time he'd been told this. Akbar knew his writing skills weren't nearly as good as his reading skills in his second language. He'd spent time learning to read, but writing was another matter. Literal translations from Urdu to English sometimes didn't make sense, and there were words that had no equivalent.

'Please. I need work. I have to pay rent,' he'd pleaded.

'I'm afraid we don't have anything. Unless you want to join our cleaning staff?'

Akbar Khan left that interview, red shame burning up his face. His brother had landed a job as a market trader, selling records and tapes on Carnaby Street, but Akbar had bigger dreams. He did not want to settle for being a rairree vaala. If that was his destiny, he could have pushed a wooden cart selling bootleg music in any city in Pakistan.

He had promised his mother he would do more with his life. She came from an established family and immersed her children in nostalgia for a life they had not managed to live. There was a time when her family had had money, and her father had been one of the first people to own a car. It had come straight from the National Motors plant in Karachi, where she grew up. 'We would go to the cinema in the evening with Baba, and then drive along Clifton beach,' she would tell him. The dissonance was a driving force in her life and in the idea of what life should be, and this she instilled in her son.

Despite the setbacks, Akbar's head was clear as he waited in the lobby of the Pembroke for an interview. He knew what he wanted and he didn't have time to feel bad, and he believed if he knocked on enough doors then at some point his luck would change and somebody would see his potential.

He watched the white men and women cross the marble floors, recline in the sofas, the soft furnishings seeming to adjust around them, as the world did for those with money.

And Akbar Khan knew without a shadow of doubt that this was where he belonged, where he wanted to be. One day his children would walk across this floor and be greeted with respect and elicit the same smiles from staff that the privileged did. Of this he was determined.

He had dreamt of becoming an accountant, just like his grandfather. Men who manage other people's money end up knowing how to make and keep their own. He'd heard that London was the place of opportunity, and while it hadn't been so for him yet, he still believed everyone had a chance to create their own life here.

He realised he was being watched from across the lobby. The man was probably the same age as Akbar Khan but blond and blue-eyed. He seemed unnaturally slim and his bell-bottom trousers kicked out ahead of him as he walked up to Akbar.

'That is a very good suit,' he said. 'Where did you get it?'

'I had it made in Peshawar,' replied Akbar Khan, surprised. This was the first time a white person in London had spoken to him in a respectful way, as if he were an equal. He liked the feeling.

'North-West Frontier Province? Ah, I travelled through Pakistan some years ago with my brother. I'm Henry Paxton,' he said, offering a handshake. 'Our father was in the diplomatic service, so we lived in India for a while. Until we started boarding school, and then the only time we were there was during the summers.' He paused. 'Your people have such great hashish. We had some great times smoking in secret in the pagoda at the end of the garden or with the maali.'

'You speak the languages of my land?'

'*Thori thori*,' said Paxton.

But a little was enough for the two men to feel a connection. Akbar was about to say something when he heard his name called from a doorway.

'I must go. I have an interview,' Akbar Khan said.

'Good luck,' said Paxton, nodding to Akbar and walking away.

As Akbar gave his suit a quick dust off, he noticed a fat leather wallet on the table. He picked it up and saw the pound notes furled inside it.

His stomach growled. With that much money, he could pay rent for a year and not worry about anything. It was weighty but small enough to fit in his trouser pocket. He considered his options. He could slip it into a velvet pocket and walk away from the interview.

But instead Akbar Khan hurried across the room and gently put his hand on the shoulder of the diplomat's son. 'You left something on the table,' he said, handing it to him.

Henry Paxton looked at the brown man standing in front of him, and then he removed a photograph from the wallet. 'This was my brother, Marcus. He died in a motorcycle accident.' A fleeting look of sadness swept across his face, one which Akbar Khan recognised.

'He looks like you,' Akbar said quickly, before hurrying off to his interview.

In the manager's office, Akbar Khan stood by the door, unsure whether to sit or stand. In Pakistan, employees stood in the presence of their employers.

The manager ignored him and instead made a show of looking down at Akbar's CV which, after weeks of rejection, Bazigh Khan had urged his brother to embellish. 'How will they know?' he'd said. 'No one will call Peshawar to check your references! Just write it down.'

They had been huddled around their friend Masood at his office. Everyone had gone home, and Masood had snuck them in at night to help Akbar make his CV look professional and type it up on decent paper.

It's what they did, these young men who were building a new life: they built it together. Masood wrote the best English of all of them, and he worked at a tailoring firm. He'd made friends with one of the young secretaries and she had helped improve Akbar

Khan's employment history and added a few more skills to the list of what he was proficient in.

These lies made Akbar Khan uneasy under the scrutiny of the man interviewing him and he shifted his weight from one foot to the other. The manager raised his eyes, peering at him from behind his glasses, and at last told him to take a seat.

'You speak English?'

Akbar Khan nodded.

'And why should I give you the job and not a white man?' There was something about the way he looked at him that made Akbar Khan shrink inside, like plastic wrap in a fire.

He considered his response carefully. He knew he was being deliberately shamed into discomfort and a hierarchy of ji sahib. Yes, he needed the money and the work, but there was a part of him deep down, a part growing slowly like a parasite inside him, that would rather die than let this man make himself his master.

And as he was weighing up the question and how much he needed to eat and survive, deciding if this reaction was ego or self-respect, the door behind him opened and the blond man from the lobby walked in.

'I hope you don't mind me interrupting, Martin, but I was rather taken by this chap's suit and wanted to enquire where I could get one made?' Akbar Khan stared at Henry Paxton as he went on, 'Does he work here?'

Akbar Khan was struck by the confidence with which he seemed to own the room. He glanced quickly at the man sitting on the other side of the desk, who now seemed wrong-footed. It was money, no doubt, that bolstered how Paxton spoke. But there was something else too. Perhaps it was the way he carried himself, his feet shoulder-width apart, making selective eye contact, seeming casual – almost disinterested in what was going on – yet very firm at the same time. It gave him an air of aloofness which made the manager desperate to win his attention.

And Akbar Khan heard the best words he could imagine.

'Yes, sir. He just started today.'

'Good! In that case let me take him away for a cup of tea in the restaurant,' Paxton said as Akbar heard the manager make a strange noise, perhaps a splutter.

***

'Martin was never going to give you a job.' Henry Paxton read the look on Akbar Khan's face and realised he'd not known that. 'He's a small-minded little man,' he added. 'Doesn't like – his word – darkies.'

'But why would you help *me*?' Akbar Khan asked, feeling cautious about what this man could want from him, experience having taught him that white men always demanded their dues, and sometimes those dues were more than the lives of brown men: it was their souls. 'Because I have nothing to give you.' Akbar thought he needed to be very clear about this.

'Why do you think I want something?'

Akbar Khan couldn't find the right reply. He'd been desperate this morning, worried about what would happen to him and his brother in a land that wasn't his own, where people looked down their noses at him.

But he had not liked himself in that meeting; he felt ashamed that he had altered his CV. He did not want to be afraid but he did not want to live under someone else's rules. This was why he had left Peshawar, to escape the place that society put him in. In London it was the same.

'Please, call me Henry,' the man said, putting a lump of white sugar into his tea. He stirred the cup thoughtfully and then he looked up at Akbar. 'I don't know why I helped you.'

'The suit – my friend can help you with that.' Akbar felt he had to offer something.

'What do you know about hashish?' Henry asked.

Akbar Khan knew plenty. Drunk as bhang and smoked as charas, it was everywhere and nowhere, depending on the circumstances of your life. 'In Peshawar, some,' he said. 'But here, nothing.'

'I have friends who would pay for the kind of quality merchandise I experienced in Pakistan. But I've had difficulties finding a supplier.'

Akbar Khan thought for a moment. He was not in London to become a drug dealer. His plans for life were bigger than that. 'I'm sorry,' he said with a small sigh. 'Although you have been kind to me, I can't help you with this.'

Henry said, 'I'm looking for a business partner. Someone who knows the lay of the land, who can help procure certain items for me.'

Akbar Khan stared at his tea as he shook his head.

***

'What did you say?' his brother asked that evening.

'I said no,' Akbar said, dropping a final spoon of the glistening shorba of the aloo gosht on to his plate. There was little in life that couldn't be solved with meat and potato, especially when the balance of the slow-cooked onions, tomatoes and garlic was just right. He didn't regret what he had said.

His brother stared, aghast. 'You didn't even ask any questions?'

Akbar Khan broke the potato with a piece of roti and put some sauce-coated chapatti in his mouth. He seemed to chew for an eternity, enjoying the first meal he'd had all day. He shrugged his shoulders. 'I don't know this man. Why should I trust him?'

Bazigh Khan stared at his brother. He had been on his feet all day, selling records and army surplus stock on his stall. His feet ached from the work, and he couldn't understand. 'You always said we just needed one chance to make it big.'

'I know.'

'But a chance is only a chance if you take it. Maybe this was your chance.'

'Eat your food,' said Akbar Khan. They finished their meal in silence, but Akbar Khan's mind was churning as if it were an ocean, its waves lashing against the sides of memory, experience and hope, and by the time their chai was served he was ready to explain.

He picked up the sugar pot, taking off its lid and showing it to Bazigh Khan. 'They want us to be like the sugar in this tea, invisible, dissolving into the background, sweetening the land but losing ourselves.'

'You just left him, this man with money and houses and cars who could help us. I know what you are saying but it makes no sense.'

Akbar Khan put his hand on his little brother's shoulder. He had their mother's eyes and their father's temperament, gifts that would have served him better the other way round. 'Relax, I've got another meeting with him in the diary,' he said.

'But if you don't like his idea, then why?'

'Because although I didn't like *that* business proposal, I thought he may have others, and I told him so,' he said. 'Remember, Brother, that not all boats need be burnt. We must rein in that Pathan fire in our bellies as it doesn't always serve us.'

***

Years later, he would offer his daughter Jia the same advice.

He soaked and steeped her in everything he had learnt, without revealing how he had come by many of the lessons, hoping she wouldn't have to endure the things he had.

Life had its own plans.

The playing field was nowhere near level when Jia Khan met Henry Paxton, but she was armed with her father's lessons and she had always been a grade-A student.

CHAPTER 9

When Jia Khan met Henry Paxton accidentally on purpose, she made sure to remember the lessons her father had taught her.

She'd asked the driver to let her out at Green Park, close to the Ritz, so that he could take her case and drop it at her apartment. She wanted to walk today. She had missed the sights and sounds of London and wanted to reacquaint herself with them. Going through her father's diary had made her see everything in a new light.

The city was lit for the winter season. She wandered past a shop with a giant pink flamingo in the window, huge dangling chandeliers behind it, a velvet chaise longue to the side. Money and taste didn't always go hand in hand in her experience, but it always brought judgement.

Jia wondered if the Indian soup at Cojean Berkeley was any good, and who was playing what at the tables in the Palm Beach Casino. The Sexy Fish signage read 'Fishmas', surrounded by red and purple baubles, as it prepped for the winter celebrations. She headed on to Annabel's to see what the designers had cooked up for this year's Christmas spectacular, wishing she had brought her father here. She paused outside the private members' club, staring up at the Christmas facade with its red and gold drapes, the pale-green lights and three flying unicorns that made up a carousel that covered the whole front of the building. Inside would be girls and boys who knew nothing of the lives their parents lived, just like she had known little of her father's work as a child.

It was Akbar Khan who had made her, Jia knew. He wanted her to have all the money, power and wisdom he had lacked when he came to England. He had poured experience into his children, paid with his soul and cold cash to propel them as far as he could in this life, but it was only Jia who had taken on board what he said about risk-taking diplomacy and how to play the hand you are dealt. 'You should play poker,' Elyas would say whenever he failed to read her.

Today, she was going to see what the deck offered.

Finding Henry Paxton in Akbar Khan's diary and discovering through Idris's research that Lord Paxton was one of the wealthiest people in the country was intriguing.

She walked past the Royal Embassy of Saudi Arabia and on to the Pembroke. She slipped in confidently through the revolving doors, hearing the words, 'Welcome back, madam.' These days men and women of varying skin hues were taking tea, dining or enjoying their drinks.

She settled herself by a pink marble pillar and waited. Henry Paxton didn't know her yet, but Jia had made it her business to find out that he would be here this evening.

She thought how women still had to abide by different rules to men, especially women of colour. But these were rules Jia could exploit.

Her friend Amal had spelt it out. She was only a few years older than Jia and came from an influential background. Highly regarded in her field, she had climbed the career ladder at speed. A partner in a private investment firm, and for some years the only black woman working at that level, Jia paid close attention. 'I come from old Cameroonian money,' Amal had explained, 'and I know how the game is played. It doesn't stop the racism but when people find out who my family is, suddenly everyone wants to please me.'

Amal was the kind of woman who made life look easy. She was like a swan, gliding through life, but Jia knew how hard she was paddling under the surface. Her lips were always rouged, and her cheekbones were as sharp as her wit and intelligence. She only dressed in high-end clothes, the kind whose cut whispered money.

'Listen, darling, our intelligence is construed as arrogance, and yet we are always seen as stupid,' Amal had told Jia in those early days of becoming the Khan. 'This is how men maintain the old hierarchy, simply by disregarding anything that disrupts the status quo. It's also why they assume that nearly all the interest we show in them is sexual. God forbid we might be interested in them as people. What does that tell you?'

'That we must learn to be comfortable with silence,' Jia had replied. 'Let people come to us. It's not about looking cool or saying the right thing or always landing the deal. It's about living one's life.'

She'd said as much to her son Ahad a few days after she and Amal had spoken. But afterwards she wished she'd warned him that living that way could be lonely and would make him feel weak at first. Striking his own path, particularly coming from a crime dynasty, would make most people too scared to stay close to him, and he'd be alone for a long time.

But she hadn't. Instead, she'd skipped to the part where you stop worrying about what everyone is saying.

As Jia waited for Henry Paxton, she wondered if her father had done the same to her, avoided telling her the truth about life so as not to scare her.

Still, it had all turned out all right in the end. She had faced her fears and then passed through the wilderness until she was surrounded by people who loved and respected her.

Now Jia was ready to see what came next. And, best of all, she didn't feel scared in the slightest.

CHAPTER 10

Leaning back in his armchair, round-rimmed glasses in his hands, pale-grey suit stitched perfectly to fit his broad shoulders, Henry Paxton looked every bit the aristocrat he was raised to be. Born into privilege, he would have fitted into the elegant rooms of one of London's most esteemed hotels at any stage of his life.

Jia studied him closely as he cleaned his glasses, his every gesture, his expressions, relaxed and open. And she wondered how it was that this English gentleman was connected to her father, a penniless Pakistani immigrant back when they knew each other.

Soon he was deep in conversation with an elegant woman in a black dress and pearls. Jia recognised her from her days at the bar – she was the Lord Chief Justice, the first Muslim woman to be made the Head of the Judiciary of England and Wales, and President of the Courts of England and Wales. She checked her watch, and Jia understood that this was a business meeting and not a drink between friends.

Jia had chosen a seat by the door, which meant it was virtually impossible for them to leave without passing her. She looked up from her laptop to see the woman smiling and walking towards her, Paxton a little behind. Jia stood to greet her.

'Jia Khan,' the woman said, kissing her on both cheeks. 'What are you doing here?'

'I was here for a meeting and decided to stay for coffee,' said Jia.

The judge turned to the man beside her. 'Lord Paxton, meet the distinguished Jia Khan,' she said. 'Jia and I are old friends. I gave a lecture at Oxford when she was a student. You'd do well to keep an eye on this young woman, I told myself back then, as she'll run the world one day.'

'You always were kind to me, Salma,' Jia said with a smile. 'Are you Henry Paxton?'

He nodded.

'In that case, I think you knew my father. Akbar Khan.'

Something flashed across Paxton's face and left a darkness lurking in his eyes, Jia thought. Though fleeting, the expression told her that the two men had had history, and that Henry Paxton still had strong feelings about it.

The judge interrupted, apologising for having to run off to another appointment. As she said her goodbyes, Jia could feel Paxton's eyes scrutinising her.

'And how is your father?' he asked when the judge had left.

'He passed away a few years ago.'

Another unreadable expression passed across Paxton's face. 'I'm so sorry to hear that. We lost touch such a long time ago.'

'Actually, I recently came across your name among some of his things, so it feels serendipitous to run into you. I'm doing some family research and so I don't suppose you'd have a minute for me, would you?'

He glanced at his Rolex a little too long. Jia caught a glimpse of its white-gold oyster band. Her father had had one of these.

'I'm afraid I can't,' said Henry. 'My wife is watching the grand-children tonight and I promised to help her with bedtime.'

'Of course. I understand,' said Jia, casually making sure he could see her Audemars Piguet watch with its simple blue face that had also belonged to her father.

Henry flinched. He said nothing, but it was clear he recognised it. He hesitated a moment. 'Although…I suppose that can wait. Why don't you join me for an early dinner. We can dine here?'

Jia was pleased her trick with the watch had paid off. She remembered Akbar telling her it had been given to him by a business associate back in the seventies. He can't have known many people back then with the funds to hand out gifts like that, so she'd made an educated guess who that associate had been.

Henry Paxton proved convivial company, although there was something slightly unsettling about him that Jia couldn't quite put her finger on, and he was adept at sidestepping any questions he didn't want to answer. But by the time they reached dessert, Jia thought she could bring the conversation around to her father. 'Akbar liked to bake with us when we were children. The kitchen would be a mess, and my mother would be livid, but that never stopped Baba doing what he wanted.'

'I can believe that,' Henry said. 'Although when I briefly knew your father, it was a different phase in his life and he was yet to be married. Tell me, what made you reach out to me after all this time? I don't for a moment believe our meeting was fortuitous. You don't strike me as a person who does anything by chance.'

'Rumbled. I have the same feeling about you,' she said as she nodded to show he was right. 'Why did you suggest dinner?'

'Curiosity.' Henry Paxton said this in a tone that closed off this part of the conversation.

'Tell me about your own business.'

'It's mostly weaponry. My family has been in the defence business for many, many years.'

As he continued to talk on the subject, Jia was surprised by his honesty. And clearly he was taken aback by her confidence. Jia could see why most people would be cowed by his money and position, all buoyed by an expensive education.

'Coffee?'

Jia shook her head. 'I don't drink it.'

'Tea?' And he ordered from a nearby waiter without waiting for Jia's answer or asking which tea she would like.

'Do you know how my family made its money?' he said, turning back to her. 'By doing what the British do best.'

'Colonisation?'

He laughed. 'I like you,' he said. 'Do you know, Ms Khan, I recognise my privilege, and I choose to maximise it.'

Jia didn't doubt this for a moment. And while his statement about his privilege may have seemed odd or heavy-handed to someone else, Jia Khan felt the same way about her own power.

'You know what the Brits are known for?' he asked as he began a second bottle of wine. 'Our manners, our resourcefulness, our reserve. That combination is our greatest export. Those who can afford our services know that if we can't make it happen, no one can.'

'The British are like a concierge service – is that what you're saying?'

He laughed again. 'I suppose we are. My company also moves and invests international money. We help open doors, grease the wheels of well-heeled society, so to speak.'

Jia nodded in encouragement. Lord Paxton might prove to be a valuable asset with his wealth of contacts, privilege, experience, not to mention money. She would have to tread carefully though. He was someone used to having the upper hand. If they were going to do business together, he would need to know who was boss.

***

Later, she video-called Idris from her apartment, the sounds of Alexis Ffrench coming from the speakers of the room's sound system.

'You look like you're having a good time on your own,' said Idris.

'Not enough of a good time that I don't want to check that no one else has turned up dead?'

'Not yet. You'll have seen the press is all over the story though. It's come out that those other murder victims were branded on the forehead too, which means the police might be dealing with a serial killer. And now there are panicked whispers in our community about destiny being visited on those who deserve it.'

'Whatever message the killer's sending, it isn't just aimed at me. Although whoever did this definitely wanted my attention by leaving a body in my garden. Any news on why Ishtiaq was targeted?'

'It's too early to say. But I'm looking into it. Anyway, how was Lord Paxton?'

'He liked talking about his money. And he was open about how his wealth is pretty much generationally laundered,' she said, 'and how the further up in society you rise, the more likely you are to dodge the consequences of your actions. Refused to be drawn on family-type personal details or much about how he knew Akbar, other than to say Akbar gave him back a wallet he once left on a table. Anyway, he wants us to work for him.'

'Do you trust him?'

'We don't have to trust him to do business with him. I'd never trust anyone with that much money. To be able to sustain such wealth, though – that makes me think I might be able to learn from him, aside from potential business opportunities. He was perfectly agreeable company but I can't say I took to him especially. Then again, I never expected to. He does have an odd aura.'

'I could ask Baba about Paxton, but he's cagey about the past at the best of times,' said Idris. Bazigh Khan, like most men of his generation, wasn't much of a talker.

'Maybe we'll ask him about it when he gets back. In the meantime, let's find out what we can through other means before we decide how to proceed,' said Jia.

CHAPTER 11

He had realised he was being followed at the bottom of Sycamore Lane. He had been checking the red streak at the front of his hair was still in place when he sensed he was being watched. The lights changed but the white man sitting in the blue Honda van in the next lane kept looking at him with unblinking eyes. The road was clear, the cars ahead gone, but the man's eyes remained on him. He looked back and swore at him, 'What the fuck you looking at?'

Then he'd noticed something about the way the man stared back, something cold and empty, that made him regret he'd said anything.

He'd pressed his foot down hard on the accelerator, tyres screeching as he pulled around the bend and on to the main road. He drove for thirty minutes, over roundabouts, left and right turns, along a bypass.

But every time he checked the rear-view mirror, there was the blue Honda. The van stayed with him constantly, maintaining distance and then pulling up beside him, as if toying with him.

It was 2.00AM and he'd been on his way to make a drop, although it wasn't drugs he was peddling but films he'd taken to blackmail women. His mates had left the shisha bar before him and as he left too, he looked forward to being home soon after that last drop.

He hit the motorway and sped up to a hundred miles per hour, the car's navigating system alerting him to the fact that he was going the wrong way.

He took the first exit, rejoining the motorway on the other side, heading back to where he was supposed to make the drop.

He turned on to a cobbled road, patchy grassland on one side and derelict mills that had once brought trade and wealth to the city ahead. The rusted wrought-iron gates of a textile mill hung off their hinges to one side as he drove through.

There was no one around, and he felt a shiver of fear. He got out of the car and headed towards a door into the sort of anonymous building on any typical industrial estate.

As he reached it, there was the noise of an engine and he turned to see the blue van pull up behind his car, the driver locking eyes with him as he switched the motor off.

He dropped the envelope he was carrying and ran into the building, footsteps behind him as he bolted up to the next floor, desperately pulling on the handle of the first door he found.

But it wouldn't open.

His phone began to ring in his pocket, but he ignored it and kept climbing, stumbling up the stairs, banging his knees on the worn edge of the steps.

In panic, he tried door after door on floor after floor. Each one was locked. But as he tired, the slow thud of boots below remained steady. By the time he reached the fifth floor, he was exhausted and confused – why was this man after him? What had he done?

When he wasn't working his day job, he was dealing with women in difficult situations, whose husbands had divorced them in moments of anger, fits of rage, and then regretted it. These were women who had nowhere else to turn, no money to build their life up again and who needed men to give them respectability. When the imams insisted they return to their husbands no matter what they had done, because 'of all the lawful acts, the most detestable to Allah is divorce', he was the one who made that possible for them. The sex tapes were just his way of earning a bonus on the side. He couldn't see how this man had anything to do with all that.

'What do you want with me?' he yelled down the stairway.

There was no reply, only the steady approach of heavy footsteps. With nowhere else to run, he tried one last door.

When it opened at his wrench, he fell through. And suddenly he was flooded with relief as he saw he was in a room full of women.

'Help! I need help,' he cried to these aunties, who seemed to be doing something with meat and vegetables.

A woman in shalwar kameez and a brown tabard was using a huge cleaver to cut the chunks from a carcass, her hair hidden under a blue net. Huge pots bubbled away on a stove close to him.

An elderly lady wearing a pink tabard that matched the chiffon dupatta that covered her hair, moved towards him as she said in Punjabi, '*Kee gal ai puttar?*'

His Punjabi wasn't good enough to explain, so he answered in English. 'Auntie, I think someone's after me!'

'*Kee kita hai tunai?*' the woman said, her chin raised.

Something within him shifted.

'I haven't done anything,' he cried.

When she spoke again, it was in English, without the trace of an accent. 'You must have done something,' she said. 'Or he wouldn't be after you.'

'Nothing! I haven't done anything,' he whimpered as he stepped backwards. 'I swear.'

He felt intimidated as every woman in the room was looking at him. He recognised one, a young woman in a grey silk hijab for whom he'd arranged a halala marriage.

Now they were forming a circle around him, a circle that was tightening.

'Come on, Auntie,' he tried, but he saw that none of these women considered him blood.

He glanced around, seeking another exit, but he couldn't see one. And then he felt a waft of air behind him as the door opened and the blue Honda man came in.

None of the women made a move. And he realised that there was no one there who would save him. He could see from the way they looked at him that all these women knew what he did, not just about the halala service but the secret films he sold and used for blackmail.

His phone was ringing in his pocket once more, and he reached for it with a shaking hand.

The old woman snatched it from him. She placed it on a counter and hit it with a mallet that another woman handed her.

'We are your mothers, your sisters, your aunts and your daughters. We will send you to Allah, and you can profess your faith there,' the old woman said as she took his elbow and walked him to the man waiting by the door.

What happened next was not filmed. The women had made promises they would do what needed to be done and they didn't need a record.

CHAPTER 12

The chief of police was worried. He had a rising body count on his patch and he needed help.

The bodies of three men had now been discovered around the city, each with his nails removed and his head branded with a name of God. The police had no idea whom they were looking for.

Mark Briscoe made sure to have dinner with Jia Khan regularly now that he understood her place in the puzzle that was this city and that he needed her. She maintained control and allowed him to be a part of that. That she was clever and charming made things a little easier.

For her part, it benefitted Jia Khan to let the police chief feel as if he had some grip on what was going on around him.

'Things are changing so swiftly,' he said as he looked around the upmarket restaurant where they were sharing a meal. 'It's not like The Karachi, is it? This is what my grandson would call "fancy pants".'

Jia nodded. 'People are well travelled and they have money to spend. The next generation are becoming comfortable in rooms that their parents could once only dream of.'

That the police chief was unaware of deeper changes in the city didn't surprise Jia. She knew he lived in a leafy village well outside the city.

'I got turned away from here because I didn't have a reservation,' he said.

'They don't need your business anymore,' Jia said.

Briscoe looked through the menu. Buttermilk fried chicken, boti tikka, seekh kebab.

'It's very meaty, isn't it?'

'Let me order for you,' she said. Pathans and Kashmiris liked their meat, something she'd realised when she'd moved back, and her vegan diet had fallen by the wayside.

He nodded and Jia ordered quickly on her phone.

'I need your help with this case,' he said. 'We have no idea who is responsible, but we do know that they are slick, smart and fast, and we can only guess at the precise motive. There aren't any witnesses. Clean-up is so thorough there's no trace of DNA and precious little other forensic evidence. It feels like a warning. The body left in your garden was moved from the premises of a samosa factory.'

'And no one saw anything?'

'We sent a couple of officers but with no joy. Can your men ask around, maybe put the squeeze on a few names if I give them to you?'

'You make it sound like I'm running the mob.'

'I mean, these are your people.'

Jia raised her eyebrows at him.

The chief of police saw he'd slipped into the old ways. This was a new world, one where women could be equals and women of colour at that. There were different modes of thinking, talking and operating now. Hastily he added, 'I mean your network. You're so well connected. Someone must know something.'

The waitress brought over a large round tray with a bowl of chaat smothered in creamy yogurt and tamarind sauce and a plate of freshly fried samosas. She placed it on a stand beside the table.

'Hmm,' Jia said, taking the bowl of crispy chaat, placing a spoon on the side and passing it across the table to her companion. Her distracted expression made it clear she was as much in the dark as he was.

And this put the fear of God into the chief constable. If Jia Khan didn't have any ideas about who was responsible, then this was even more serious than he'd thought.

CHAPTER 13

The gossip mill was churning, whispering details about the bodies that were appearing. Whether you called it biraderi, khandaan or family, the transmission of information between communities was always faster than high-speed broadband, irrespective of race and religion. The corpses were branded with the names of Allah, names like Al-Muhaymin, 'The Protector', and Al-Muzil, 'The Abaser', the rumours went.

'I hear he's a member of a Christian terrorist organisation, intent on making an example of Muslims, and that he's a member of some far-right group targeting brown people,' Khalid the pimp told Benyamin as they stood vaping at a car meet. Benyamin was cutting loose with his friends, drinking hot glasses of chai as they showed off their wheels and caught up. 'Brother, I haven't seen you for some time,' added Khalid.

'Business has changed since my sis took over. She wants me in the office more, and I'm down with that,' Benyamin said, ignoring Khalid's slightly raised eyebrow.

Under Jia Khan's guidance, the Khan family's business interests had expanded rapidly from red-light-district prostitution, street-corner drug deals and small-time racketeering. They still took a cut off everything, because giving anything up would risk power vacuums and land grabs, but their remit now was larger, as they'd moved into cyber-crime, darknet drug deals and laundering money through other means. They ran a secret online store for illicit items and, right alongside it, countless philanthropic efforts which shoved money into the mouths of anyone who might be inclined to talk smack about them. And, so far, nobody had felt inclined.

Benyamin worked from a plush office, his days of collecting from the 'bitch pitch' long gone, although he still stayed in contact with the pimps he'd dealt with back then. Street-corner information was far purer than any other kind in his experience. He was the little brother of the Khan and he enjoyed the glow reflected from her high status. But increasingly he found himself feeling protective of Jia in ways he didn't always understand.

He listened to Khalid respectfully though.

'One punter told me the killer's an ex-Muslim traumatised by internal colonisation, whatever that means,' said Khalid. 'I don't know what's gone on, but one thing is certain – guys are scared. They don't say it, but you won't often see anyone out alone at night now. Even driving around the city, they're together. Business has got tight for me.'

Benyamin thought about Khalid's words later. Whoever was responsible, they had managed to intimidate a city, and young Muslim men of colour walked the streets a little less brashly.

'Ironic,' said Sakina when he told her what he'd heard. 'I've never known men to be too scared to go out before. Women, yes, but men? Never.'

CHAPTER 14

'How many names of Allah are there?' Ahad had asked his dad on the phone.

'Ninety-nine.'

'Jesus Christ. Do you think this guy is planning on making his way through the list?'

'No, Son, I don't. You just keep your head in your studies and leave this to the police. They'll get it sorted. How are lectures going?' Elyas was fast to change the subject, but he was worried, and he had mentioned this to his wife when the police finally left.

The house had been swarming with them for days, gathering evidence, taking statements and trying to build up a picture of what had happened.

'Years of hard work ruined,' Jia had said when she saw the trampled flower beds. All those Sunday mornings she'd spent with her father, clearing weeds, planting bulbs and trimming rose bushes, felt sullied and violated. Jia hated this, as it was where she remembered him being most content.

'There's nothing like a garden to teach a believer how to keep the faith,' he would tell her. 'We bury our seeds deep, cover them with soil and the manure that the world hands us, and then we wait, hoping that away from prying eyes, tiny green shoots will appear. When they come, you protect the seedlings, like this.' He would take a plastic cola bottle and cut off the base, putting the cone over the plant. 'This will protect it from anything that will come for it.'

Jia still had his secateurs, the ones he would keep in his pocket as he taught her how to trim the rose bushes. 'A good gardener is not afraid to cut' was one of his favourite sayings, and even as a child she had known he was not just talking about the roses.

Since his death, under the guidance of the family gardener, who had been with them since her childhood, Jia had continued his work in the garden. It helped her think, organise her busy mind and plan the future for her family.

Now, it was covered with blue and white police tape. After more than a week of this, she took it all down and walked back to the house, locking the door behind her.

The police presence on the premises had made her men nervous, and Idris was on his way over to discuss ways of handling the Jirga's concerns.

It had been over two years since the new men had taken over from their fathers and uncles. They'd been quiet, almost tame, and eager to learn at first, but they were now beginning to show their teeth.

A toothless army was no good to anyone and so she was equally proud of their impending bite as she was of their patience. The city did not need to be run by a domesticated form of the Jirga. It needed strength, and she needed a Jirga that would go toe to toe with her for what it believed in – as long as they always kept within the bounds of respect. 'Surround yourselves with people who are smarter than you,' her father had told her.

The dead man, the Jirga and the garden filled Jia's head, leaving little time for much else.

But as well as being a leader, she was a wife and a mother. As she picked her way through the pile of papers and magazines that were strewn across the living room, she wondered how it was that she came to be married to a man who thrived in chaos. Elyas's style of working was in stark contrast to hers.

She felt her impatience build as she tried and failed to find her glasses. Sifting through the clutter, moving his laptop and countless books to reveal empty chocolate wrappers and stained coffee mugs, her growing annoyance felt like a ping-pong ball bouncing around inside her head.

She picked up the books, closing them and placing them in a pile. *Moneyland* by Oliver Bullough and *The Dark Net* by Jamie Bartlett caught her eye, and Jia thought she should probably read them.

And then she wondered why, if Elyas had these interests, he didn't interfere in her business concerns. Then again, the last couple of years had been full of sleepless nights, nappies and the endless itinerary of parenthood. Elyas was the active parent when she needed to focus on other things, and she supposed this could be the reason he kept out of her work matters.

Elyas had never tried to broach with her how she ran her kingdom, and his avoidance of the subject made her wonder if he was afraid. And, although she didn't like this about herself, the mere thought of this possibility made her respect him less.

Jia knew that what she rated in those around her was fire and frenzy, demands and justifications. Elyas was a nice man, but in her world, nice was easy. Nice people were neutral, they never upset the apple cart, they maintained the status quo. Nice people were compliant, easy-going. All the things Jia Khan was not.

Out of the corner of her eye, she caught sight of Elyas watching her from the doorway. She straightened up a little. He was one of the few people who got under her skin, even after all these years. And he was also one of the few men who had the courage to love her and to say so. Jia reminded herself of these things; they had to count for something as they were so rare in her life. Perhaps there was a different kind of strength to Elyas, one that at some point she should explore. Only not now, not before the killer had been brought to justice.

'Are you still not talking to me?' Elyas said.

'Why don't you clean up after yourself?' she replied, continuing to shuffle papers as she looked for her glasses.

'The baby was crying, and you were in a meeting.' He sounded annoyed that she only saw what he didn't do, not the hours he spent raising their sons. 'When will *you* have time for the other things?'

'I don't know.' She carried on searching, moving books and papers.

Elyas remained by the door, measuring up the best course of action: to step forward and help, or to call out her petty behaviour. He stayed where he was.

The silence grew around them and then began to change, filling up with the weighty, unsayable things people really want to tell the ones they love but somehow cannot. The things that would hurt them or make them think less of the other but were the truest bits of one's soul and, sometimes, a sign of love.

Elyas knew he had made himself vulnerable to Jia by nature of his love for her, and her to him (although she might not admit this), and now they held weaponry in their hands that could annihilate the other and everything around them.

She stopped and stood motionless in the centre of his work. 'Elyas, I know you think you are the measure of all that is good and decent.' She paused, and then said more softly, 'I don't know how to navigate this.'

'You just have to talk to me,' he said, stepping forward, about to take her in his arms, glad that she was opening up in an honest way at last. 'I've wanted to talk about this for such a long time.'

'I mean, I don't know how to navigate *this*.' Jia gestured to the mess around her.

He stepped back, his arms dropped to his side. The tone of her voice told him that she thought he was weak. But he couldn't agree, preferring to think instead he had the moral high ground and that his actions were good. This was the dance their marriage had become, a marriage punctuated by moments when Jia would remember why she had married him, or by his apologies when he was in the wrong – something she found difficult to do – or by him berating her about their children, as he was about to do now.

'What are you looking for?' he asked.

'My glasses. I've got to sign some papers for Idris. He's on his way over.'

'They're on your head,' he said.

'Not these ones, my reading glasses!' she snapped, as if he should be a mind reader.

Elyas assumed her annoyance wasn't about his mess or her glasses. He guessed it was to do with their eldest son.

'This is about Ahad, isn't it? You're taking it out on me, as if I'm at fault, but really it's about Ahad.'

'Well, whose fault is it?'

'It's no one's fault. This is just who our son is. Who he has always been. Stop being angry about something that nobody can change.'

Jia found her glasses, at last.

'I'm not angry,' she said. 'I'm…' The unfinished sentence hung in the air like an unexploded bomb. 'I'm tired, Elyas,' she said, sitting down in the middle of the mess, the papers all around her.

'It's going to be OK, Jia. Ahad is going to be fine. The world is different now. People are more understanding.'

But Jia wasn't convinced by Elyas's easy platitudes.

It wasn't her son's sexuality that frightened her, nor what that could mean for her; it was what it meant for him and others around him. She loved Ahad exactly as he was, but she was scared on his behalf. To be a young man with brown skin wasn't easy at the best of times; to be a young man with brown skin who was the Khan's son was more difficult; while to be a young man with brown skin who was the Khan's son in a world where it seemed a turf war was coming – and who was publicly queer – well, Jia didn't like to think through all the scenarios that might create.

Experience had shown her an ugly side of life, one where people hated for no reason, telling their own version of the truth, writing their own script, one that meant not having to take responsibility for themselves.

That this world might come for her beautiful son and ravage him terrified her.

The delicate balancing act of familial love and leadership was a tightrope as fine as a thread of silk. It was a rope that men rarely walked, because women took care of domestic affairs and propped them up without ego and consideration for self. Women were raised to be self-sacrificial, planets and moons to their menfolk's suns, orbiting silently, reflecting only the light they offered.

Jia felt that she had been the sun for a long time, that there had been nothing else other than her that shone so brightly – until motherhood.

There was no place where the Khan could be afraid, no space where she could speak of her fears without weakening her empire and risking the castle her father had built and whose keys she now carried. The responsibility on her shoulders was large and at times overwhelming.

There was no place for weakness, except maybe with Elyas. She looked at him, hoping he would say something reassuring, but he was busy tidying his papers.

CHAPTER 15

Before his birth, Jia's love for Ahad felt all-consuming.

While her father's crimes and her brother's death had made Jia Khan protect herself with a steely emotional armour, the feeling of Ahad having grown inside her was her weak spot, she realised the first time she held him.

And these days she found it almost impossible to reconcile the great love she had felt for her growing foetus with her terrible behaviour in the hospital after Ahad was born, when her conviction he was too perfect to live and that he made her vulnerable and petrified in ways she couldn't fathom became too strong to control.

It was only years after Ahad arrived that Jia understood she'd been gripped by undiagnosed post-partum psychosis, and this was in large part why Elyas had been so active in looking after Lirian when he arrived – although, as it turned out, Jia didn't suffer in the same way the second time.

Thankfully, Ahad hadn't come to harm, and Akbar Khan had bundled up his newborn grandchild, secretly driving him two hundred miles north to leave him in the safe care of his father, Elyas, even though he and Jia were no longer together. Jia had no contact with either of them for many years, not until Akbar Khan had died, and when she finally met Ahad, he was a teenager, and she had to live with the obvious fact that he was trapped between hating and loving her.

Ahad was at university now and things were going well, he said. Jia thought he seemed happy and that he'd found a place where he belonged. But she worried for him. Things might be alright for him now, but they wouldn't always be.

When she had overheard Elyas encouraging Ahad to open up to her that Friday night back in October, she felt a chill wash through her. He had been at university for about a month and had returned home for the weekend with a bag of washing. She braced herself for what was to come, fearing he had fallen in with a bad crowd and had landed in some trouble. It wouldn't be the first time, although he had seemed so much more settled since Elyas and Jia had got back together.

But her son had stayed silent the next day and Jia didn't press him. They spoke finally on the morning he was to leave.

Ahad was making breakfast, slicing and toasting bagels, sesame seeds spilling across the kitchen counter, when Jia walked in. She put her arm around him and kissed the top of his head, before reaching for a coffee cup. To a casual observer, it would have looked like an effortless interaction, but both Jia and Ahad knew how long it had taken them to arrive at this sense of ease, and Jia's heart warmed when she felt him lean into her, just for a moment.

'Would you like some coffee,' she'd asked, 'or are you still on that health kick?'

He'd raised a glass of green juice in answer. She couldn't help but notice how many faces of the people she loved he wore in his own. He was just a little older than her brother Zan had been when the police had taken him for questioning, and although they had released him without charge, the young man who came back home to them had been changed. She sometimes wondered if Ahad was a second chance for her family, a gift from God. Weren't they always told that Allah does not take anything from a believer without replacing it with something better?

'I want to bring someone to meet you,' Ahad said slowly, without looking up from his juice.

Jia felt a rush of relief then. This wasn't going to be the bad news she had imagined. 'You sound a bit nervous about this.'

'Kind of.'

'You don't have to be. I do remember what it's like,' she said, looking into his eyes, trying to reassure him. 'I was afraid when I introduced your father to my parents. Your father was my brother Zan's best friend. Did I tell you that before?'

Ahad nodded.

This conversation with her son had filled the room with memories for Jia, sore and sweet, the kind of wound you can't resist touching. She could almost smell the breakfast Chilli Chacha had been making the day she'd brought Elyas home. The way the dappled sunlight streamed in and hit the kitchen cabinets. Those oak doors of the old cupboards had been replaced with simpler French Grey panels and the dark-green laminate countertop was a now a much more beautiful pale granite.

But the house had felt warmer back then, Jia realised. Her father's presence had filled every inch and corner of it, holding up the edifice that was the Khan family in such a way that they felt safe, protected, and were oblivious to anything he might have been going through.

She knew now how brave it was for a young girl of her faith and family to bring home a man and announce to everyone that they had eloped, but back then it had felt simply like a matter of the heart. Maybe if she'd known the events that would unfold as a result, she would have thought twice. But she had been young and in love, the kind of love that you can only feel when you are inexperienced and the veneer of your heart hasn't been cracked and sullied by life.

She sometimes wondered what it would have been like if she and Elyas had not separated after Zan's death. Falling asleep in his arms night after night, waking up to his face, knowing that she was never alone and that she only had to ask for his help and he would be there.

Would she have looked at him now with the same adoration she had done before Zan's death changed everything? If he had been by her side through every ugly, difficult thing she had seen, if he knew about all the things she had done, the things she had hidden away deep inside of her, would he still love her?

But he hadn't been with her, and they had stood apart like two trees in the same garden, their roots intertwined. It had taken long years before their branches did too.

She looked at Ahad then and said she loved him.

'Mum, I'm queer,' he told her.

And Jia had blinked at him in confusion, as this was the last thing she had expected him to say.

Thoughts spiralled through her mind that she could never publicly admit. Jia wondered if it was her fault, if he would feel this way if she had stayed in his life. If she had been the one to raise him, maybe he would see the world the way she did, that life demands its dues. For her, those dues had been heavy, and she had paid so that he wouldn't have to.

She reacted badly.

'Everyone will reject you,' she had responded.

'Who is everyone? All the people who rejected you for marrying Dad? Why would you care what they think?'

'I don't care about what they think. I care about you being on your own. Everybody will come for you. Don't you understand? Every side. You think queer white men will accept you because you're queer too? Trust me, they will not. Life is hard, Ahad. It is hard and it is heavy and it bears down on you until it breaks you. Can't you...?' She stopped. She was handling this poorly and she knew it, and so did Ahad, judging by the look in his eyes. Self-control was strength, and calmness required mastery, but when it came to her son, both failed her.

'Can't I what? Just like girls?' he said. The look on his face had been anger and upset and heartbreak. It was as if she had slashed him open from head to foot, his own mother. 'How can you tell me to hide who I am when you have been telling me to be honest and authentic ever since you came back into my life?'

She didn't answer. And then she did the worst thing she could do. She turned away.

And she was ashamed, ashamed that she gave to everyone, but when her son reached out to her, she had nothing.

No one could have hated her more in that moment than she hated herself.

***

Later that same day in October, Elyas had stood by the open fire in their bedroom, his face lit up by the flames. But his voice was cold as ice as he said, 'You told him to pretend. Our son cried in my arms on the way to the station.'

This had made Elyas angrier than he had ever been before. He had raised Ahad from a newborn to a man alone, with affirmations and kindness, with an open heart and an equally open mind. For so long it had only been the two of them, and he had assumed it would have been easier if Jia had been around. But he'd been wrong. What kind of mother was she to make her own child feel that way?

By the time he'd returned to Pukhtun House, his head hurt. He'd changed into running gear before pummelling the pavement to work off the rage simmering within. He felt it was time to leave this city, and Jia Khan. He had loved her unflinchingly for decades and he would forgive her for anything.

Except the betrayal of his son.

He'd rounded the corner, running up a steep incline, his breathing getting heavier, his thighs feeling the pull of tiredness. But the truth was that he couldn't leave. There was a second son now, one Jia would not give up easily. Extricating himself from Jia for one son would mean losing the other, and Elyas knew he couldn't do that.

After his run, he'd stood in the shower, letting cool water flow over him for a long time. Eventually, he'd stepped out and dried himself, and walked out of the bathroom.

She was waiting for him.

'You told him that he should live a lie because it would be easier for you,' Elyas continued. His arms were folded and his voice was level, but he didn't know for how long.

You hurt my son, you cold, fucking bitch, is what he'd wanted to say. He'd wanted to shout and scream, but Lirian was asleep in the other room and his mother-in-law only a few doors down.

'Are you homophobic?' he said. 'Because I need to know if you are.'

'I'm not homophobic, Elyas.' Her voice was quiet, tinged with sadness, and it deflated him. He'd been ready for a fight, but she had already put her fists down, and now he had nowhere to go. 'I just told him to play his cards close to his chest. Honesty and authenticity don't mean telling everyone everything about your personal life.'

'It's Ahad's life. Not yours, not mine. It's his, and he must make the decisions about how he wants to live it,' said Elyas.

He'd moved towards her then as she sat on the edge of the bed. The thought crossed his mind that he was always the one to make peace, as much for himself as for their marriage. She never apologised.

His mind brushed over the letter he'd found detailing her father's death. The one he'd read but never spoken about, the one that had told him that Jia Khan had had her father killed. There were days he swore he could sometimes still feel the warmth of the fire as he'd tossed the paper into the flames. It had all happened so suddenly, and it was the same week he'd found out she was pregnant with Lirian – which was in part why he didn't say anything. Although the bigger reason was that he didn't know what to say. But now those questions were growing, and starving them of sun would not make them disappear.

Elyas picked up his favourite pillow and Jia knew he was going to sleep in the nursery, and she doubted he would want to make up with her in the morning.

'You're not going to make our son pretend to be something he's not,' Elyas had said as a parting shot. 'There's no way back from that for any of us if you do.'

After he left, Jia remained where she was, running through all the things she had said to Ahad that morning, maternal guilt coursing through her veins.

As she sat alone in their bedroom, the darkness descending outside, she thought about her husband.

Elyas's loyalty lay with the truth, no matter who was telling it. He was the kind of man who would fight for the rights of those he did not agree with just because it was the decent thing to do.

It was why she had fallen in love with him, and why she had married him. It was why she had come back to him, because she had been like that once.

But circumstance had changed her, and the responsibility that came now with being the Khan meant that much of her loyalty lay with maintaining the family business, and the nature of the business meant her interpretation of truth had become fluid, depending on who was telling it and to whom. But this attitude was not good in any way for family life and harmony.

She justified her actions to herself. It was the only way she knew to survive. The Khan family was a house of cards, with her at its centre.

But she knew that Ahad's revelations would not be taken well by her men. Men did not know what it felt like to be physically tied to one's child the way a woman is to her baby. They knew only possession, and taking, and demanding.

Her Jirga was all men.

It was then she'd picked up her phone to call Ahad, to make sure he'd arrived back at university safely and, perhaps, in some small way, to try to make amends.

But she'd heard the front door and voices coming from downstairs, and Jia decided that she would have to call her son later.

CHAPTER 16

It had been a month since the body had turned up in the garden of Pukhtun House, and Jia and Idris were sitting in her study at the antique desk that once belonged to her father. The room was exactly as it had been when Akbar Khan was alive, its secrets kept by the walls, loyalties protected and bound by blood and honour, an honour that was now, for the first time, in the hands of a woman.

After her father's death, Jia had encouraged her mother to redecorate the house, hoping it would give Sanam Khan something to keep her busy. Her mother had thrown herself into this, choosing paint palettes, having floors restored, rugs cleaned and paintings put into storage. Other paintings were brought out of storage and hung once more in the house.

But Jia had insisted her father's room remain the same as it had when he was alive, knowing the Jirga needed sight of the old to be able to move with the new. Diplomacy would help in the coming years as she nudged them towards modernity in the hope that one day all their business interests would become legitimate.

Idris inserted the memory stick into the computer and then turned the laptop towards Jia. He had been looking into the background of their security man Ishtiaq, and specifically what motive someone could have had to kill him. He had found a video he wanted to share with Jia.

As he set it up, he said, 'Henry Paxton called. He wants to talk to us about possible business interests. I hear he's been sniffing around for investment opportunities up here.'

'Find out about that for me, and let's not rush in until we know more,' Jia replied.

Information on people was easy to come by in the world they lived in, especially since they ran a highly successful tech company, one that was not afraid to break a few laws and manipulate a few others.

Money brought power, but information about powerful people brought leverage. Together, power and accurate intelligence made the Jirga the force it was. It spun an intricate web that made drugs, guns and women easily accessible, and just as easily untraceable.

Information could also be weaponised, especially when that information was other people's secrets, often handed over freely without their knowledge.

'So tell me about this video,' Jia said, watching it on the laptop.

'That's Ishtiaq,' Idris said, pointing at the grainy image on the screen. 'And that's a young, unmarried girl.'

The clip was explicit, a couple caught in an intimate moment, the young woman clearly unaware she was being filmed, the older man staring straight into the camera enough times to make it obvious he did know.

Jia closed the laptop, her hand resting on it. She paused for a moment. 'It looks genuine. Why was our security man doing this? This doesn't look like a home video,' she said.

'Blackmail. We've uncovered quite a collection of these. Mostly young, unmarried women, but not all. We think Ishtiaq was part of a syndicate arranging halala marriages to divorced women who wanted to get back together with their ex-husbands but couldn't until they'd married someone else and that marriage ended. It looks like he was using them as further blackmail opportunities. We men will monetise anything – and if it means getting sex in the process, it's a double win.'

Jia fell silent. The thought of a man she'd employed taking advantage of vulnerable women like this filled her with rage.

Then she opened the laptop again, the image of the young woman frozen in front of her.

'And this girl's family knows, I presume. That is very difficult,' she said in a clipped voice.

She considered how easily this could have been her, and how she had only just got away with it by coming back a married woman. Not much had changed in the years since then.

Well, one thing had – smart phones and social media. Life was so complicated for young people today. Mistakes were literally recorded, uploaded and tagged. There was no room for error and no place for forgiveness in a society that could drag up decade-old mistakes. University had once been a place where you could butt up against your ideals, test them, see where the line was and cross back. You were expected to be radical; you were expected to blur the lines. Not anymore. Reputations could easily be tarnished for ever. Izzat was hard to hold on to. And this young woman's izzat was probably now strewn publicly across mobile phones, laptops, anywhere there were screens. Digital keystrokes lasted for ever somewhere in the electronic ether.

'Her family has remained silent,' Idris said. 'Like all the other blackmailed families.'

Except that Ishtiaq was dead. He'd been sacrificed, offered up as a sign to any other man who would put his pleasure above a woman's honour.

'This might explain why Ishtiaq's body was left here,' Idris added. 'Maybe somebody blames us.'

'He was one of our employees. We should have known what he was up to. Still, would any of those families risk disrespecting us in this way?' Jia thought for a moment. 'When will people stop celebrating virginity like it's some great prize for men?'

Idris nodded and was about to speak but a noise from outside the room stopped him. He got up to check what it was, opening the door. Lirian was standing barefoot, clutching his stuffed lion with one hand and rubbing his eyes with the other. Idris picked him up and carried him back to the desk.

'Hello, big man,' he said. 'What are you doing up?' He put the boy in his lap and started playing peek-a-boo with the lion, hiding his face behind it and popping out. Jia watched as Lirian laughed with glee, envious of the ease with which Idris played with her son, an ease she could never find within herself.

'Idris, it might be time to address the lack of women in the Jirga,' she said.

Idris turned to her with surprise. 'OK,' he said. 'Well, we did discuss Meera Shah at one time. She knows all about being a woman in charge of many people.'

'That woman who runs the catering company?'

'Yes. I know our last meeting misfired, but her business has expanded since then. She's highly regarded and she's interested in joining us.'

'I'll think about it. If we do set wheels in motion, it will have to be quietly.' Jia was aware that they would only have one chance at getting the approval of the Jirga. 'If we screw it up in any way, it will be a long time before the men agree to another woman being given a position of trust.'

Idris sighed. 'Are we still that old-fashioned?'

'The Jirga like money and I've helped them make a lot more of it than Baba did. But I doubt they treat their wives better than they did before,' said Jia.

She was under no illusions about the Jirga, the city or the culture in which she had been raised. Her place at the head of the organisation did not mean that women were being treated better or given opportunities they hadn't previously had.

'Besides, we must never forget that there are women in our community too who do not like that I am the Khan,' Jia added.

'But why?'

'We don't always like ourselves. When society treats you badly, you begin to assume everyone who is like you is worthless. We're subliminally sold ideas that keep us in our place, and that place is at the feet of men. Indebted to them for choosing us, supporting us, letting us live.'

'This is some messed-up shit.'

Jia wasn't surprised that Idris was blind to the ways society betrayed women, and all the ways in which good men were complicit in the stripping away of a woman's self-respect and self-esteem, celebrating women who backed them, holding down the women who questioned them.

'Society places value on us according to our gender, race and sexuality, but our own self-respect comes from deep within,' she said. 'It's a bit like social media, "likes" on Facebook, Instagram followers, retweets, all signifying how important someone is. And to get more and more of this validation, people will betray themselves. But self-betrayal destroys self-worth. Compliant women are valued by society but that compliance strips self-respect. And if you don't like yourself, you don't respect others like you. Especially the ones who rock the boat. They are thought of as troublemakers.'

'And so they don't like anyone who upsets the status quo?'

'Exactly. But we need the women who believe in themselves and me, those who want to take their sons and brothers with us.'

She didn't know if Idris understood what she was saying, or if the men would be onside, but she had to find a way to make everyone understand that the best society was one where everyone was valued properly.

The branded bodies that were mounting up fast were a sign. Another victim had been discovered in the past week. The police read the situation as the actions of a madman, a reaction to men who were taking advantage of women and using the threat of the 'honour brigade' to blackmail them for their missteps.

But the message that Jia was hearing instead was a clarion call to arms.

She needed to know who was responsible, and what it was they wanted from her.

CHAPTER 17

'I'll be back in a couple of hours,' Elyas said to Sanam Khan as he kissed Lirian goodbye. 'I hate to do this but my contact is only free this morning.'

The little boy was playing happily with his toys on the rug, and Elyas thought of how easy it was to raise children when one had help. He'd raised Ahad alone. Navigating work as a single father had not been easy. He'd needed emergency dental work when Ahad was six months old, and at the time he hadn't known which had been more painful, leaving his screaming son with a newly recommended sitter or the root canal treatment.

That experience made him more accepting of his current situation. The extended family with whom he and Jia lived felt mostly a privilege and a blessing, even when things were tense within their marriage. Seeing his son play happily with his nani gave Elyas a feeling of warmth.

'Take your time,' said Sanam Khan. 'See some friends, you need a break. And don't worry, my beautiful grandson and I will be just fine.'

Elyas climbed into the blue Volkswagen Golf GTX Jia had insisted he upgrade to after Lirian was born. He'd been reluctant at first, but she'd stated her case, using the baby's safety as her primary concern, and he'd relented. Benyamin had picked it out, chosen the features — Elyas's only condition being that the car was electric — and arranged for it to be dropped off. Elyas knew his previous car was old and shabby, especially compared to the plethora of gleaming vehicles in the Pukhtun House garage, but part of him liked that this had separated him from the Khan family.

Climbing into his comfortable car and turning on the heating in his seat, Elyas admitted he was pleased with the upgrade. But it made him uncomfortable that Jia had paid for the car. He wondered what that said about their situation. He owned a flat in London that he rented to a couple looking to get into a school catchment and this income more than covered the mortgage, while the rest was accumulating in a savings account. And, of course, he had his journalism, although this had wound down somewhat since Lirian had been born. He wasn't exactly a kept man, but something about the set-up made him uneasy. Elyas wondered if it was because of what he knew about Jia's business dealings, or just old-fashioned patriarchal feelings of manhood.

What he needed was a good story to write up. He entered the details of where he was going into the sat nav.

The state-of-the-art autopsy facility had opened a few years earlier, funded by investment from Malaysia. It allowed 3D scanning of the body without carrying out intrusive post-mortems. Muslim burials were swift, usually taking place within three days of death, and this speeded things up. But regardless of religion, the bodies of murder victims still had to undergo traditional post-mortems.

The medical examiner was waiting for Elyas. And his old friend John, also a journalist, was with her.

'Mahboobeh, meet Elyas,' said John, introducing the two of them.

'Thanks for doing this,' said Elyas. 'I know you must be busy.'

'Step this way,' the pathologist said, placing a surgical cap over her highlighted hair.

She walked them down a long, well-lit corridor and into a cold, windowless room. Pristine white tiles ran from the floor to the ceiling and spread to two other walls. There were five identical doors on the fourth wall. Elyas assumed that behind each of these were the remains of deceased people.

A body was laid out on the examination table, covered in a white sheet. Mahboobeh led them over, pulling back the sheet to show them her findings.

John moved forward. But Elyas felt like the eggs he'd had for breakfast might be making a comeback. 'We don't really need to see him,' he said, holding up his hands swiftly. 'I'm just interested in hearing your report, and your opinion.'

'Sorry, John always wants to see everything,' she said, quickly readjusting the sheet. 'I just assumed you did too. I forget what it's like to have normal people in here, who aren't police or doctors or crime writers.'

John laughed nervously, as if he'd been found out.

'I'll just get up the file,' she said.

Elyas studied the photographs of the deceased that came up on a screen attached to the wall, along with detailed information about the incisions and wounds inflicted on him. The information was no less gruesome than seeing the actual body. He'd seen a lot in this life, but there were some things he'd chosen not to get used to. He'd watched far too many people become desensitised to things that no one should get comfortable with, things that slowly stripped them of their humanity.

'The nails were removed at the bed using some kind of pliers,' said the examiner, pointing at the images. 'The scrotum and penis were amputated here. It looks like it was done by someone with medical knowledge and skill. That person knew how to wield a scalpel,' she said. Her tone suggested she was impressed with the killer's handiwork. 'The tongue was removed, with clean incisions again. The other bodies shared this characteristic.'

'Talk about brutal,' said John. 'I get the feeling there is pure rage behind this.'

'That's for psychological experts to confirm,' said Mahboobeh. 'But, in my opinion, not every violent crime is perpetrated by people who have lost control. There seems to be a high degree of care taken with these amputations.'

They left the building, Elyas deep in thought, renewed concern for his family flaring, jarring against the puzzle of why someone would leave a body on their lawn. Jia had business interests that rubbed some up the wrong way, but he couldn't understand what she could have done to attract the attentions of a killer, let alone one who now seemed on a campaign. And if this killer was a dispenser of vigilante justice, would Jia be on the list? Maybe there was another reason behind it all, and for an instant there was a glimmer of an idea, but it dissolved before it crystalised.

Elyas could only sigh.

CHAPTER 18

Jia opened the wardrobe and looked at the rows of neutral-toned clothes. She had long ago put away the vibrant colours of her youth, but she remembered them fondly. The parrot greens, maroons and fuchsia pinks had added warmth to her face and drenched her body in colour.

She didn't know exactly when she'd stopped buying patterned dresses and opting for simpler cuts and unobtrusive shades, but now that was all there was in her wardrobe. She no longer knew if it was the dulling of the senses that came with age, or whether she was losing herself to her Western sensibilities, taking on the navy, grey and black of white society.

She took a kurta from the cupboard and placed it on the bed beside her chador. She loved the feel of starched and crisply pressed cotton, cashmere shawls and jumpers and freshly laundered linen.

Jia looked closely at the white-on-white embroidery of the kurta, pleased that the laundry had managed to get a couple of spice stains out.

Pakistanis liked to display their wealth in a way that Jia felt posh white society considered crass and would describe as gauche. Those with this sort of opinion were, in her experience, usually longing for mummy and daddy to die so they could inherit, the moneyed-in-waiting, the sort of people who assumed immigrants and their children to be poor.

Having lived on the edges of so many cultures, never wholly ensconced in any, Jia Khan understood these nuances well. Life had brought experience to her door, and her own privileges had made an observer of her. She'd been reminded of how invisible she was the last time she'd flown to New York. She'd been waiting to check in to business class when a blonde in penny loafers had brushed past her, heading towards the desk at some pace. Jia knew the type well, having been here before. She'd watched as the woman placed her passport expectantly down on the desk, tapping the desk and clearing her throat to get the flight attendant's attention. The attendant looked up and smiled. Then she nodded and reached out to take Jia's travel documents.

The woman's confusion was apparent, her irritation obvious. 'But I'm in business class,' she said. Her voice was clipped, like ice chips.

'I'll be with you in just a moment,' the attendant told her.

'Isn't Economy over there?' the woman said.

Jia made this trip often, and she had made it her business to know almost everyone who worked the route. This was something her father had instilled in her, how to wield her intelligence with kindness. 'You are cleverer than most people,' he'd said. 'But that doesn't mean you can be unkind. Be patient, be understanding, baita.'

Jia had smiled at her father back then, as she did at the flight attendant. 'How is the family, Louise? That baby of yours must be coming up to a second birthday?' she'd asked, putting her travel documents in her bag. She handed the flight attendant a small gift bag. 'I brought a little something for him. I hope you don't mind?'

'Ms Khan, you are always so thoughtful,' said the flight attendant as she reached for the stuffed white bunny poking its head out of a gift bag.

Jia made sure to display her Birkin as she turned away. She could feel the eyes of the rude woman assessing her anew as she took in Jia's expensive navy blazer, palazzo pants and box-fresh trainers, as if trying to make sense of a mathematical equation.

Jia had never been bothered by women like this, but she knew that her exchange with the attendant, delivered in clearly spoken English, and her handbag and clothes would have hit home. The rude woman would have expected her to speak with an Urdu accent. They always did, for despite her expensive clothing, Jia was invisible to white women. Until, that is, they found out what she did for a living and where she'd gone to university, and then they wanted to be her friend. Jia walked towards the lounge, waiting for her flight to be called, hoping that the woman wouldn't find her for a chat, which she inevitably would. They always did.

Once she would have been irritated, but she had more compassion now. Jia knew the woman trying to check into business class ahead of her was desperate to be seen. She too would have been lied to, been promised the world, told she could do anything, be anything. Having once been prized for her youth and beauty, something to be won and adored, a prime vessel for the next generation – because only white women can make white babies – the shifting sands will have taken her by surprise.

She'll have discovered that women had a shelf-life, one linked to their biological clocks and ability to give birth. These women found themselves having to make sacrifices at the altar of society, convinced it was for a short time, until the children were older and living on promises that they would then be equal beneficiaries in what was to come. Some willingly gave up high-flying careers, while others were pushed out as men built empires without having to compromise.

These women had been loyal. Their husbands may have bought the bread, but it was they who laid the table, set the crockery and polished the silverware. But in all those years she would have failed to notice that there was ultimately no seat at the big table for the unpaid labourers who formed the bedrock of society. They were the invisible workforce, and she had joined them.

As Jia stood in her bedroom, getting ready for her meeting, she thought of all the precious time she had lost thinking about people who sought to control her. The loss of time and loved ones in her life pulled everything into sharp focus.

She moved her hand over the Saville Row suits that hung still in her wardrobe, the polished shoes and the smart shirts. These days she favoured silk kurtas and denim jeans, her chador drawn over her shoulders or on her head, depending on whose company she was in. There were those who underestimated her when she dressed like this. But power suits, Rolexes and designer labels were for those who needed to announce their money.

Jia Khan needed no introduction, and in circles that didn't know her, she was happy to fly under the radar. Being underestimated was powerful, and Jia Khan had weaponised her invisibility.

Today her men were waiting for her. Tensions in the city were starting to simmer, in part because of wild and growing rumours about the serial killer and whom he was targeting, and in part because of the way her organisation was altering things. She was the only one who could do what needed to be done.

She applied mascara to her top and bottom lashes. She liked what she saw in the mirror. Her financial privileges had allowed her to invest in her skincare routine since she was a child, and so now she needed little more than tinted moisturiser, blush and lipstick. There was also a lot to be said for genetics.

She finished getting dressed and looked out of the window to where Michael, the son of one of her father's favourite employees, was waiting to drive her to the meeting.

He was home for a few days from university, and she'd asked him to drive for her while he was in town. She was glad he'd agreed as she liked his company. It was rare to have someone outside the family circle who was completely trusted. For his part, he needed the money, but more than that, he too enjoyed being around Jia Khan. She filled up the gaps in his confidence. There were few places he could be his whole mixed-race self, and when he was with Jia it felt like a place of psychological safety. She was smart and she was strong, and she made others feel that way too. As if anything was possible. As if change was in the wind, sun-kissed days were around the corner and success was inevitable.

'Which car are we going to take?' asked Michael as she opened the front door.

'One with a car seat,' said Jia, emerging from the house into the late-winter sunshine with Lirian at her side. She crouched on the step to zip up his jacket. 'Elyas has an appointment today, so this little man is coming with us.'

'I'll get the Range Rover. The one that was modified last year,' said Michael. He liked fast cars, but as a medical student there was no way he could afford one. It would be years before he could own vehicles like the ones parked in the Khan garage. Each was unique. Some of them had modified music systems, they all had bespoke interiors, and the sports cars were clad in body kits specially designed according to Benyamin's taste.

A minute later, Jia strapped Lirian into his car seat and climbed in beside him. 'Will you be here for Eid?' she asked Michael.

'Planning to be. I hate the thought of Dad spending it alone, and I'm grateful to you for looking out for him. I'm hoping to get a job close by this year. I've been away too long.'

'I'm glad,' she said. 'Even though it will mean we'll have to make an appointment to see you.'

Lirian pointed out of the window, spotting cows and sheep on the way. 'Moo,' he said very clearly, and then, 'Baa.'

'He's speaking!' said Michael. 'The last time I saw him he was babbling.'

'He's clever, all right,' said Jia. 'He's also a handful.'

They pulled up to the gates of a purpose-built sports and leisure complex. The Khan family had owned this land for years, and Jia had decided to turn it into a luxury spa. It had proved an excellent way to launder money.

It was early morning, but the car park was already lined with a complete row of cars. They'd chosen to park beside each other, as if each Range Rover was trying to outdo the other. The Defender, Cabaro and Huntress, each one's alloy wheels different to the next, but at the centre of each was the symbol of the company they kept, the orange 'K'.

'We do like our cars,' said Michael, parking up beside the army green Huntress. 'All these flash wheels, like the queen's funeral.'

Jia laughed. 'Did you go and see her lying in state?'

'I did,' said Michael. 'To make sure that she was gone, after decades of walking around in other people's jewels, spending other people's money.'

Jia smiled. 'The Koh-i-Noor?'

'Indeed,' he said, turning off the engine. 'Do you have strong feelings about Elizabeth II, Queen of the United Kingdom and other Commonwealth realms?'

'Not really,' she said. 'I don't have the luxury of seeing life in black and white any longer. I'm sure people will say things about me, that I was cold and hard, that I did things I shouldn't. But after losing my father, and now seeing his legacy, I've come to understand that when one takes a stand, one splits public opinion. We do the best we can at the time, but others will probably feel differently about what we've done afterwards.'

'How can you defend what was done by the empire? We're still paying the price for what that family did, what it took, from millions of people.'

'I'm not defending it, not in the slightest. They plundered and stole from nations, like all empires. They raped our women and our land, and then told us they were there to civilise us. The white man's burden is that he thinks he knows better. But I don't have time for the past, and I don't know better, and I cannot alter history. All of that is for people like you to consider, and you should. I work to make sure the future is strong, that what is to come looks different from the past, and that no one dares take from us again.'

'So, what you're saying is, we can mourn her death while acknowledging she was the head of a violent colonial apparatus?' said Michael.

'Didn't F. Scott Fitzgerald say, "The test of a first-rate intelligence is the ability to hold two opposed ideas in the mind at the same time, and still retain the ability to function"? Sometimes people are bound to the sins of their fathers, but to unravel those sins while making sure everyone who profited from that machinery is still fed just isn't as easy as we'd like it to be.'

'I didn't have you pegged for a monarchist.'

Jia laughed as she got out of the car. 'I'm not a monarchist. I don't have the privilege of being one thing or the other. I am a survivalist. And I work to ensure that people like you get to see life in black and white.'

'I'm glad I'm not you,' said Michael.

'You are very wise,' said Jia, unclipping Lirian from his car seat and lifting him out. It was a cold day, and she fastened the buttons of her slim black overcoat, before taking her son's hand.

Idris was waiting for them. 'Hello, little man,' he said to Lirian, picking him up and carrying him into the building. He turned to Jia. 'What are you two discussing?'

'The queen,' said Michael.

'Is that what we're calling Jia now?'

Jia ignored Idris. 'Let's get this party started,' she said.

'Cake?' said Lirian to Idris.

They walked through the entrance towards the back of the building, past a room containing state-of-the art treadmills, an equal number of rowing machines and various other exercise apparatus. Another room had red and green weights piled high on a stand, alongside lifting machines that were polished and waiting. They stepped into a courtyard that housed an athletics track, and a sandpit to one side. Lirian pointed excitedly at the sand, desperate to be let out to play.

'I'll stay with him if you like?' said Michael.

Jia nodded, grateful not to have to take her son into the meeting. He was at an age where he needed constant interaction, and this would have made controlling the men in the room difficult. She also knew that the sight of a woman with a child automatically placed her somewhere else in their minds, hardly conducive to running a crime syndicate.

She knelt down on the newly laid rubberised surface of the running track and looked at her son. 'Uncle Michael is going to play with you in the sand pit, OK, baby? If you need anything, you tell him.' She handed Michael a backpack. 'There's snacks in there,' she said. 'Give him whatever he wants. Call me if it gets too much. I'm not going to lie to you, I've got the easier crowd.'

Michael laughed, and then looked a little cautious. 'What is this part of the gym complex?' he asked. 'I didn't know this was here.'

'It's the women's section,' said Jia. 'I had it added recently, but it's not open to the public yet.'

Lirian began throwing sand at Michael.

'Let's go,' Jia said to Idris.

She tapped in a code to a door in the wall and they strode across the glass-fronted corridor to a second door, where Jia tapped in another code.

The men were waiting in a room that would be used for yoga, talking as they sat in a circle. Near the window part of the circle was Jia's cousin Malik.

Sakina stood silently at one side of the room. She'd been the one to let them in.

The men fell silent at the sight of Jia, but the atmosphere in the room was tense.

'What's happened?' asked Idris.

'The police pulled me over. Again,' said Malik. He ran his fingers through his thick black hair. He was in scrubs and needed a shave. 'I was on the way home from a double shift – I'd been on call,' he said.

'We need to tell them who you are,' said Idris. 'Get you on the no-stop list.'

'That's not good enough,' said Malik. 'You know how I feel about that list. And I shouldn't have to tell them I work private practice plus a day job for the NHS, and that's how I pay for my wheels. What about every other brown kid who's driving a nice car?'

'They think we're all drug dealers,' said Afzal Khan. He was the only one in a suit. His Rolex glistened as he talked, oversized on his bony wrists. 'I mean, I know we are, but we're not like the rest. I do what I do so my kid brother can finish his degree and get a good job. One where he doesn't have to worry about HMRC. But what's the fucking point if they're still going to assume we're all the same? You've done time at medical school, Malik, and you still get pulled over? Nah, man!'

Jia had heard this conversation numerous times. It ran through their people like an artery. Car culture was inherited from their fathers and uncles: it gave them freedom, creativity, and it brought a sense of pride. Cars didn't cause racism, but they allowed decades' worth of embedded stereotypes to surface.

Revving boy racers, speed demons and money-laundering was what the police thought when they saw a brown boy behind a modified top-end car. A Defender parked in Belgravia was a sign of success. Parked in her home city, it was assumed to be ill-gotten gains.

For Jia Khan, this was troubling as well as problematic. She was trying to bring change while dabbling in the very things that she wanted to escape from, but what choice did she have?

She could feel time running through her fingertips like the sand in an egg timer, faster and faster. She looked at her cousins and felt a tug at her heart. History must not repeat itself, and if they didn't clean up things, it would.

It was something her sister Maria talked about all the time.

'Who these kids see thriving in the world teaches them how to see themselves, how to think about their value, how to dream about their futures,' she had said.

As Jia worked to change things in industry, her sister was shaping young minds.

'We keep taking the fish out of the water, cleaning them, and then putting them back in the toxic water. Last week, I was talking to one of the nine-year-olds. You know what she said to me? She said, "On my phone I can make more money than someone with an education. I'm gonna look better, my car is gonna be better, my house is gonna be better, I'm gonna smell better. And everyone is gonna want to be me when they see my posts." What am I supposed to say to that?'

That was one of the reasons Jia had called the meeting, to talk about the future.

'Why are we meeting here, Jiji, rather than where we usually do?' asked one of the men.

'To make a point.'

'I don't understand.'

'The point is that none of you knew this place existed. You're the eyes and ears of the family business, and yet not one of you knew where you were going to be, or how to access it.' She paused. 'You need to do better.'

'Why should we be interested in what the womenfolk are doing? Making biryanis and babies isn't men's work,' said Afzal Khan. He looked at Sakina. 'Not you, love. You're different, you're not like the others.'

Sakina remained expressionless, but Jia noticed her eyes blaze for a split second and saw that Afzal Khan noticed too. He knew he'd crossed a line, one he wanted to retreat from immediately. But he was in it now, and there was no way out.

'Afzal Khan, I understand you've invested in a chain of pharmacies?' said Jia in a casual voice.

Afzal Khan shifted forward in his seat. He'd run the idea past Jia in the last meeting, and she'd told him to hold off. 'We're cleaning up in things like diazepam, nitrazepam, tramadol. Also, you know how many middle-aged, middle-class white women are after testosterone? A lot,' he said, as if his high turnover would make up for him ignoring Jia's instruction.

'What do they want testosterone for?' asked Razi Khan.

'It's for menopause, guys,' said Afzal Khan. 'I know you wanted us to start reining things in, Jiji, but it was too good an opportunity to pass up on. The front end is clean. Untraceable. The books are squeaky clean.'

Jia watched her men looking at each other with deep respect, as if their mutual approval was all that mattered and they deserved a star on a chart, like the one Elyas had pinned in the kitchen for Lirian.

Afzal Khan, puffed up and preening, was like a rooster in a hen house. And Jia could almost feel Sakina's eyes rolling out of her head.

Jia Khan had always surrounded herself with people who were smarter than she was. She looked at her closest cousins, Idris, Malik and Nadeem. They had served her well, but many of the others were troubling. She had gone to war the first time with the army she had, but now she needed to rebuild.

But each of these men was powerful in his own right, and so getting rid of them wasn't an easy option. That didn't mean she would back away from the problem.

'I'm wondering whether it's time for you to retire, Afzal Khan,' she said. The sentence was spoken in almost a whisper, so softly that it forced the men to lean in. 'You don't seem to value my opinion,' she said, her eyes like knives, locked on Afzal Khan.

He floundered, deflating like one of those waving-tube men placed in the car-wash forecourts where they used to launder money before Jia Khan took over. Now, the money ran through countless shell companies, none of which Afzal Khan understood, but his cut was larger than before and it was in his interests not to ask questions. That was the thing with money: the more you had, the more you needed. And Afzal Khan was clearly thinking about what retirement would mean for his income.

It was how Jia Khan had controlled them: she'd made them richer than they could have imagined. She'd done it by giving them legitimate business interests to hide behind, and that had given them access to circles where even the white people talked to them with respect. No one wanted to lose that.

But they were standing on a rug, and Jia Khan was holding the edge of it. One tug and their empires would tumble, and Jia wanted all the men to understand this.

The room was silent, waiting for Afzal Khan to respond. Jia Khan had, very quietly, put a bullet in a man's head right in front of them. Being cut loose from the family business meant being frozen out of every deal, money-making opportunity and dinner in the area that fell under Jia Khan's jurisdiction. She had silently solidified her father's business interests and controlled virtually everything.

In the last few years, she had made it her business to know every member of the operation by name, and she knew their wives and their children. She sent them cards on Eid, baskets of mithai, gifts of money for the little ones in small paper envelopes, each one handwritten.

Being blackballed by Jia Khan meant your neighbours would shun you, your son's marriage proposal would most certainly be rejected and even your wife would stop speaking to you. The doors of the mosque would not be closed, but the other worshippers would give you a wide berth, to the point that you'd eventually stop going. It was a slow and insidious grinding down.

Afzal Khan was one of the few men who remained from her father's Jirga. Most of his contemporaries had been gently nudged into retirement, replaced by their sons. These old men now stayed home and played cards, gardened and annoyed their wives.

Afzal Khan was still young, and he was not one to step away from a fight, even one that he was sure to lose, except when it came to Jia Khan.

He tried humour at first. 'Check yourself, cousin, don't wreck yourself,' he said.

He swallowed audibly when she didn't respond. He was used to smiling women, and those who didn't frightened him.

This was Jia Khan's power. She didn't behave the way she was expected to. She had no honour to lose, and she gave no credence to the value others placed upon her.

'I'm sorry if I have offended you,' he said at last. 'I didn't intend to go against your wishes. I should have waited, exactly as you advised.'

He looked chastised, and Jia held him in a long stare to drive home her dominance over him, and over all the other men in the room.

After an endless minute, she glanced away, and immediately the atmosphere lightened.

'Do you know any more on who's killing those poor bastards and leaving their bodies all over the city?' asked Razi Khan. 'Two of them were my men. They were coming up the ranks fast, and the others are worried.'

Everyone chimed in with their concerns. After a quiet month, a fifth body had been recovered from a parking lot. Each of the victims had connections to people in the room.

'There's a lot of rumours flying around,' said Razi. 'Someone said it was a guy from over Ben Rhydding way. Some guy who don't like brown dudes cos his wife left him for one of us.'

'Some kind of spurned white supremacist. That's what I've heard too,' said Afzal Khan. 'But it's making me concerned for the safety of my soldiers.'

Despite the topic of conversation, the mix of local accents in the room was strangely comforting to Jia. From broad Yorkshire, to desi patois and Idris's King's English, everything about the voices felt like home.

'I'll get in touch with Mark Briscoe, see what else he knows and what his officers have turned up. In the meantime, I suggest you look at why someone would want those men dead. I mean, it could have been any one of you. So why them?'

There was a chill in her voice that ran through the men and made them more afraid than they had been before.

Her phone buzzed, and she asked Sakina to open the door.

Lirian ran in and into his mother's arms. She kissed him gently on the cheek. She wondered what the little boy would make of his mother leading a meeting with this roomful of men. Would it register with him, the way memories of her father's Jirga did with her?

'I think that's all from me for now, gentlemen. We'll reconvene next month. Idris will send you the location. I suggest that you don't leave your houses after dark, and that your foot soldiers work in pairs.' She turned to Lirian. 'You want to go for a swim?' He nodded vigorously. 'Let's do it.'

She got up, and then stopped, looking at Afzal Khan. 'I give you advice based on evidence, not ego,' she said. 'Make sure you receive it the same way.'

Sakina followed her out of the room.

'I have it on good authority that the police are going to raid his chain of pharmacies,' Jia told her when the door had closed behind them. 'At that point, I'll decide what to do about him.'

'He's a big, moody man-baby,' said Sakina.

Jia laughed. She'd forgotten how nice it was to have a woman's opinion.

Her men had become weak, and things needed to change. That her men were unaware of everything happening in the city was troubling. If they didn't know about the new women's gym, what else had they missed?

Their blind spot left her vulnerable. It wouldn't have mattered before, but now her children needed her, especially Ahad. He was living in a London-bubble, and a small, woke one at that, but Jia knew the rest of the world would always be like this for him.

She wanted to surround him with great, billowing swathes of privilege and protection. The Jirga was her army, but if they were forced to go to war as they were, they wouldn't win.

CHAPTER 19

'One needs a goose-down parka to sit in your room, even in the spring,' said Idris as he walked into Jia's office. He pulled the collar of his coat up around his ears.

'The Northern wind and the central heating were ruining my complexion,' said Jia, pulling off the beige cashmere blanket she had placed on her lap and getting up to close the window. She handed the blanket to Idris.

'Why are you always barefoot?' he said.

She looked down at her pedicured feet, her toenails painted a blood red. 'Habit, I guess. I can never find my slippers.'

Idris noted how comfortable she was in her father's office. It had been hers for almost three years. Her books now lined the shelves, and on her desk there were always flowers that changed with the seasons — daffodils, sunflowers, lilies and the occasional rose.

She looked tired. Those years had taken their toll. 'Come, sit down,' she said. 'How have you been, Idris?'

'About as good as can be expected.'

'That sounds ominous,' she replied. 'How are things with Layla?'

'We broke up.'

'I'm sorry to hear that,' she said.

'It's actually a good thing,' he said. 'She didn't want to have children.'

Jia was surprised by the revelation. She hadn't considered her cousin to be the marrying and fatherly type. But then, they'd never discussed personal matters deeply.

'I didn't know you wanted to be a dad,' she said.

'I didn't either, not until the choice was being taken away. But at the end of the day, family is all we have, and why else do we do all the things we do?'

Jia nodded. Some days, she understood Idris better than she understood her own husband.

Idris changed the subject. 'How did things go with my brother?'

'A bit like your relationship – as well as can be expected under the circumstances. He's glad we're finding work for the families Nowak left behind but he wants us to go further. I know you suggested Meera Shah might offer a solution. Her business interests are expanding fast, with her mango business and restaurants, but I want you to look at what else we have. My understanding from Sakina is that she doesn't pay her workers fairly, many of them women.'

'I don't think we should be surprised if she's cut-throat when it comes to business. She's probably had to be to get where she is. That's why she might be a good Jirga candidate too.'

Jia thought for a moment. 'I will meet her to honour you, but I don't trust a woman who sells out other women, and it sounds like she does exactly that.'

'You don't trust anyone.'

'You sound like Elyas.'

'I should stop then,' said Idris. He was unsure how much gunpowder was behind the trigger he'd just brushed.

He and Jia were good at working together but not so good at the social niceties of normal life. The silence between them felt heavy, filled with things unsaid, thoughts that Jia wasn't ready to share, and wounds Idris didn't feel ready to address. Work was easy, work was a known place and did what it was supposed to, in that it made them feel whole and successful. In short, work was worship.

'Did I tell you Henry Paxton was in town recently?' he said.

'What was he up here for?'

'The opening of an art gallery in Leeds. He's the patron. And then he had dinner at Meera Shah's restaurant, Hujra.'

'And he didn't let us know,' she said carefully, her mind then deliberately setting the thought aside like a jigsaw piece that is not ready to be placed.

'Idris, I need you to look after Sakina for me,' Jia said next.

'You have plans for her?'

'I do. I'll share them when I'm ready. But for now, keep an eye on her,' she said. She turned to her desk and picked up her father's 1974 diary, flicking her way through. 'I still don't know what happened between Baba and Henry Paxton. Baba never mentioned him to me, and Paxton has never given any indication they were close. But I don't know – the fact Akbar appears to have had a number of meetings with him in 1974, as well as with this *Mary*, whoever she was, seems to suggest otherwise, no?'

'Not every strong relationship lasts,' said Idris. 'Sometimes the people we trust the most, the ones we think will never cross us... do.' He paused, watching his cousin at her father's desk, the moonlight falling on her and making her look younger than her years. He knew that to be her greatest power: she was everything and nothing, all in a split second. 'You of all people know that,' he said, gently waiting for a reaction, some flicker of acknowledgement, but nothing came.

'Stop by the kitchen on your way out,' she said, without looking up from the book. 'Mama has some haleem for you. You know how she likes to fatten her children. She might even have a rishta for you now you're not with Layla.'

Her teasing took him by surprise, and he laughed out loud at the suggestion of his aunt's matchmaking, before getting up to leave. 'Jiji,' he said, pausing by the door. 'Elyas...he's wrong.'

Jia looked up from her papers. 'He is?' she said.

'You used to trust people implicitly – I remember those days. Remember when you made us spend Christmas Day at the soup kitchen when we were sixteen?'

'That was the year when the snow was really heavy and came up to our knees.'

'I know. And you made us take the bus, because you didn't want us turning up in our fancy cars and making people feel bad.'

Jia cast her mind back to those easier times, before Zan was arrested, when life was simple and warm. Snowy boots in the hallway, soup on the hob, aunts by the fire drinking chai, uncles in this very study discussing business, whose details she now understood deeply. 'It's not like we've had a normal life, is it?' she said.

'I don't think it's bad to start from a neutral position and let someone prove or disprove themselves,' Idris said.

'You're right, and sometimes I forget. That's why I need you here. To remind me I'm not crazy.'

There had been times since she came back to this city, and to the fold of her family, that Jia had wondered what it would have been like if she had followed tradition and married Idris.

'Do you have a thing for him?' Maria had recently asked her outright. 'I mean, white society would never understand, but I would.'

Jia had laughed at the idea of having 'a thing' for anyone at her age. She was so far gone down the road of practicalities that her mind had little time for such frivolity. 'How quickly the English forget their own heritage and the lineage of their royal family,' Jia had replied.

'It's just that people do it, don't they? Close off from outsiders, never have to explain the nuances of anything or navigate familial quirks,' said Maria.

'In answer to your question, no, I don't have a thing like that for Idris, but he gets me and I get him.' She had paused. 'And sometimes I think that it would be nice to be understood, without question.'

As Jia now took back the blanket Idris was offering, she said, 'I think we need to consider what Paxton might have to say – we can't overlook how useful it could be to have an investor with his connections. If he has an offer for us, it could be the thing we've been looking for to break into the establishment. Have you mentioned him to Bazigh Lala at all? Paxton says they were friends when Baba and Lala lived in London.'

'I was going to wait until he got back, but he's had to extend his stay in Peshawar.'

'How is he?'

'He misses Akbar Khan, not that he says that out loud. The changes in the Jirga have been hard for him. He needs something to do, something to be part of. Choosing marble floors and bossing workers around on the site of the house he's building is doing him good, I think. But it's only a few more months away from being complete, and then he'll be back home.'

'In that case, you'd better crack on with getting him some grand-children,' Jia said.

CHAPTER 20

What Meera Shah lacked in height, she made up for in personality, and the six-inch heels she teetered around on added to the impression she was taller than she was. Her face was smooth and plumped, like her pride, courtesy of Baby Botox, which was all the rage in Lahore. She always paid for the best services whenever she returned there on her yearly visit.

Idris Khan had called to say his cousin would be coming to the restaurant. It was clear from the way he said it that this could be a precursor to the business meeting Meera had been wanting for so long. She was being offered a second chance.

She'd been patient, biding her time, building her business, and she was more than ready to put her ideas forward to Jia Khan.

She stood at the front of the restaurant kitchen, surveying the heart of her empire. Rays of morning light bounced off the empty stainless-steel counters. In a few hours the tiled floor would be teaming with workers in white, their hair tucked away under nets, their hands in latex gloves. Some would spend the day making savouries for frozen orders, while others prepped meals for hungry customers looking for a taste of home cooking. The counters would be packed with produce, the fragrance of sautéing onions and tomatoes vying with that of the charcoal grills.

And the restaurant would be abuzz with gossip. Meera Shah knew everything that went on in this city, including the building of Jia Khan's new women-only gym.

She needed everything to go well today. The restaurant had only recently reopened after a refit, the idea being to attract more high-end customers with its stylish update. It was not so long ago that she had been struggling. Her husband's car accident and the loss of his legs had left him unable to provide for his family, at least in the way that Meera expected.

Meera had had a brainwave. And now, stacked-up silver tiffin boxes were a common site in the city. Quickly they had become her signature after she'd started the Lunch Club, delivering hot meals to the workers at offices nearby who had had enough of sandwiches, both plain and artisan.

Her husband's family and her friends in Lahore had judged her for taking on what they felt was menial work. But the bank had been threatening to seize their home, and she would die before going into rented accommodation.

As she'd made samosas and patties, chapatis and daal, she'd thought about those friends, the ones who were attending kitty parties and living off inherited wealth and wearing outfits made by people like Deepak Perwani and Sania Maskatiya, while she was in a shalwar kameez from Poshak Palace, folding triangles of pastry.

Once, she had wanted to be a singer, but women from her family went to medical school or became wives. She'd met Parvaiz at a friend's mehndi in Lahore. He was visiting from England, but was so taken with her, he had found out where she lived and arrived at her home with his parents. He'd promised her a life of excitement, free of small-minded judgement, and moonlit walks by the river Thames. That was what had led her here. He had been everything she wanted, until his accident. She deserved better, she had expected more, and when things became difficult, she'd taken things into her own hands.

Now here she was, edging towards fifty. For a long time she had cooked mince with spices, peeled and chopped up potatoes, boiling them in great vats of salted water. They had managed to scrape by.

'It was when I found ways to help other women,' she'd told Idris. 'That's when things changed.'

They'd met that first time in a neighbouring city, an hour's drive from the restaurant. It had been Meera's suggestion. She was reluctant to be seen in another local eatery and hand over even a penny of her hard-earned cash.

Idris had listened, impressed by her ideas and her generosity when Meera made it clear she would pay for the meal.

'There were many women who needed work. They were stuck, thinking they had nothing to offer, but they could cook. I'm an educated woman, but even I was judged when I first set up. So I built the business up with these women. Eventually, I was asked to tender for meals with a supermarket chain and I needed money to invest in my business to help it grow. I heard your uncle might be helpful to a woman in business, a rare thing in this city, but he was killed before we had time to meet. I was at the funeral, but it wasn't the right time for Jia Khan to speak to me.'

The next time the two women came face to face, Jia had taken over as Khan. The land was soaked in rumours of what had happened between Jia and Nowak, of how ruthless she was in defence of her people. The hills that surrounded the city absorbed her secrets, standing in loyalty beside her, like sentinels.

Meera felt she had been helping the women of the city for years, while Jia was pandering to the men and the old ways of the Jirga, simply stepping into the legacy left by her father. But now she wanted in on Jia's inner circle. If that didn't happen, there was a ceiling on how well her food empire could do.

***

'What does she want to discuss exactly?' Jia had asked Idris that day as they waited for Meera.

'She has some business she needs help with and ideas she has been developing.'

Jia checked her watch. 'I've only got an hour until my hospital appointment.'

Idris knew Jia was preparing herself to be edgy about time to assert her dominance over Meera. 'She's just running late. Give her a chance.' He'd been thinning out the diary so that Jia would rest, as she was pregnant with Lirian.

'Why are you so eager to help her?' Jia asked.

'She's not had it easy,' said Idris. 'We should have more visible women in the Jirga. You hear how some of them talk about women – what was it they said? – "bringers of babies and biryani"? They need more exposure to clever and determined women with good business heads.'

But by the time Meera arrived, Jia was stepping out of Pukhtun House and into her car. Jia Khan waited for an explanation or an apology, but Meera said nothing. Jia was no stranger to difficult conversations. She let the silence grow into discomfort between them. She was tired, her feet were swollen, and the baby inside her had kept her up all night. She was at that stage of pregnancy when she was hungry all the time but the size of the baby meant her stomach was squashed up so small that everything caused indigestion.

This was a battle she didn't need today. 'I'm afraid I can't stay,' she said to Meera at last. 'I have an appointment. Idris can make new arrangements if you're amenable to it?'

Meera was used to getting her own way. She was a wealthy woman, and people rarely said no to her. She took Jia's words as an affront and recoiled.

She looked from Jia's pregnant belly to her face. 'Should you be working in your condition?' she said, a cutting edge to her voice. 'I wasn't that big even at the end of my pregnancies.'

Jia was not in the mood for this and so she just gave Meera a hard look.

Meera turned to Idris. 'Maybe it is for the best? Let the men make the decisions at this time.'

Idris looked uneasy. 'I don't make decisions without the say-so of my Khan,' he said.

The three of them stood in awkward silence, Jia waiting for Meera to leave so she could give Idris instructions, Meera refusing to budge just to be tiresome, Idris waiting for his Khan and unsure at that moment how to speak to either woman.

There was something about pregnancy that made Jia feel powerful and weak at the same time. It laid bare the biological division of the labour of life, and the need for sisterhood.

She sensed Meera felt differently. Meera's refusal to budge, her hardened eyes and her softness towards Idris spoke volumes.

Jia decided that Meera represented a feminine attitude that assumed survival was based on an allegiance to men, in which you forced your will on other women and the hammer was the only tool in the toolkit. Jia had little time for this attitude.

'We will be in touch,' Idris said to Meera finally. His tone snapped her back to reality. She was in the grounds of Pukhtun House – this was Jia Khan's territory, and Idris was her consigliere. That she had thought for a moment she could manipulate that had been a fallacy, one she had never experienced before.

Jia looked at Idris once she'd left. 'You misjudged her,' she said, her eyes cold.

Idris had shivered as Jia had driven away.

And Jia had felt her body relax as she climbed into the back of the Range Rover beside Elyas. Her husband had taken her hand in his, and she'd closed her eyes, just for a minute.

She'd thought she could trust Idris's judgement, that the empire would be safe under his watch. His misstep with Meera had rattled her, making Jia wonder if she had made a mistake.

CHAPTER 21

Sitting back in the car, on her way to the hospital after that first aborted meeting with Meera, Jia had been glad to have some semblance of normality in her life. Even if Elyas and she disagreed on many things, she knew him to be a good man.

She'd smiled in the car as he held her hand.

'What's funny?' he said.

'Just thinking of my father. "Beware when a good man goes to war," he used to say. Do I need to beware of you?'

'What, today? Maybe some,' he'd said, kissing her tenderly. He took her phone from her hands and put it in his pocket with a 'You'll get this back once we're done.'

This drive from home to hospital, with someone else watching the road and her husband watching over her, felt like a well-earned break. She wondered how long she had before it turned to shit again.

She had until they pulled into the car park.

Elyas always saw the best in people, even if it was a speck of goodness, and it meant ignoring the obvious. 'Meera seems harmless,' he said. 'Sounded like she was concerned about your well-being. Couldn't that be it?'

'I've met women like Meera before. They only care about themselves.'

'You always start from a position of distrust,' he said. Despite his gentle tone, Jia only heard judgement in the words.

He helped her out of the car and she reluctantly accepted his hand as they made their way to the ultrasound department.

The familiar hospital smell hit as the double doors opened. It was both comforting and alarming. This was a place of joy and anguish, of soaring hope and endless hopelessness. The men and women who worked here delivered life and death sentences, often on the same day. Jia knew a little something about that, but in her case, she was the one doing the sentencing.

Elyas knew he had said the wrong thing. He wished he could now make it all right again.

Jia waddled as she walked, her body changing shape to accommodate his child, and something about her made him want to take care of her forever. It was rare for Jia to show vulnerability, and in this condition she was all vulnerability without saying a word. His feelings for her seemed to run deeper than ever before. Between the time they had first met and now, she had evolved into a hyper-independent creature, the kind of woman men are in awe of but too afraid to approach, her self-reliance a defining feature. As the elder sister, she had always been the responsible one, the one everyone else turned to, but the death of Zan had embedded autonomy deep into her bones.

Elyas knew that Jia had been failed by those she loved, her ability to trust systematically worn down. His wife was a warrior, and she still carried with her the tools that had once served her survival. That he was the one at whose feet she lay them down meant there was nothing he wouldn't do for her.

As she lay on the hospital bed, gel on her pregnant belly, the sonographer searching for a heartbeat, Elyas felt a sense of renewed purpose. Lesser men would have felt intimidated by a woman in Jia Khan's position. She looked after everything and everyone else. She was steeled, armoured up, and she was brave. To the point that the world forgot she was human, and sometimes even she forgot that she was made of flesh and bone like everyone else. Elyas never forgot. He knew who Jia was at the start of her adulthood, and he was the one who looked after her. And she had chosen him, not once, but twice.

'Your age makes the baby more susceptible to placental failure,' the consultant had said at her six-month checkup. She looked through the notes in front of her. 'You're not cousins, are you?' she said, flicking from one page to another.

'No, we're not cousins,' Jia said, doing her best to remain calm.

'We get a lot of cousin marriages,' the doctor had said without skipping a beat.

Jia took a deep breath, for the sake of the baby. The consultant's assumptions about Jia and Elyas were based on ethnicity. Nowhere was one safe from microaggressions, it seemed. 'It's in the initial report,' Jia said crossly. 'Along with my profession. And my husband's profession. He's a journalist and I'm a barrister.'

She had felt Elyas's hand on her arm. Afterwards she'd said to him, 'I couldn't tell if you were trying to reassure me or stop me hurting the consultant. You know that microaggressions like that have the same effect as smoking a packet of cigarettes a day?'

He did know, because Jia reminded him of it whenever he stepped into situations like this. 'I'm worried that one day your mean left hook will make contact with the face of one of those microaggressors,' he'd said.

The consultant had looked nervous. Journalists were dangerous people, and allegations of racism could end her career. 'Good. Good,' she'd said, reaching up to calm her twitching eyebrow.

***

When the baby finally came, Elyas had been ready.

Jia had woken up with strong contractions and called for him. He almost forgot the bag and left the car engine running while he rushed to get it. She was silently holding his hand as he drove, only the crushing of his fingers between hers told him how close she was to giving birth.

They made it to the hospital, and the midwife, who knew they were coming, quickly ferried them into a delivery suite. 'I'm afraid there's no time for pain meds,' she'd said.

Jia had looked at Elyas. 'I've changed my mind,' she said. 'I don't want to do this anymore.' Shuffling off the bed, on the cusp of giving birth, the contradictions of womanhood were never more apparent to Elyas. Childbirth made women behave in ways they wouldn't otherwise. 'I definitely can't do this,' said Jia, her lips speaking words that Elyas knew she would never utter in ordinary life.

He'd looked into her eyes. They were warm, and frightened, like pools of chocolate, and he knew she was making him privy to her secrets, to her most intimate self. He could see she was unafraid of the world but terrified of losing those she loved, even those who were yet to enter the world.

You can do this,' he'd said, taking her face in his hands. 'You've done it before, and I'm here this time.'

Later, her body took over, doing what it had to do. She screamed in primal pain, and just moments later her cry was joined by another.

'Well, Jia Khan,' said Elyas, looking at their baby son, 'that's the second pair of balls you've grown.'

The midwife placed the baby on Jia's chest, and she gazed down at him. He was as beautiful as she was broken. She was everything and nothing, powerful and powerless. When he had been inside her, she had some kind of control, but outside of her body, this newborn was vulnerable. She knew the world to be a violent and mercurial place. The love her parents had given her was the only thing that had saved her, and even that had come with a price.

She asked Elyas to take him, and she watched as he sat in the chair, holding his son. She marvelled at her husband's ability to be unsullied by the world, to step anew into love each day. If it weren't for all the years between them and the evidence to the contrary, she would consider his innocence foolish. Whatever it was, he brought balance to her life. Perhaps his naivety was a kind of strength, and one that she needed in her life.

'I never understood why people are told to grow a pair of balls.' Elyas was still sitting in the chair by her bed, holding the weighed and wrapped baby, when she awoke. 'I mean, my balls could not handle the level of pain you just went through. A person has literally come out of you. This person,' he said, smiling at their son. 'Do you want to hold him?'

Jia shook her head. 'Soon, but not now,' she said. She closed her eyes again, hungry for sleep, safe in the knowledge that Elyas was better at this than she was.

Two weeks later, against all urging to the contrary, Jia was back as the Khan.

CHAPTER 22

The restaurant was busy the evening Jia and Elyas ventured out into the world. It was to be expected: it was a balmy Friday evening. Most people finished work early after Jumma prayers and went home before heading out with family.

When Hujra had first opened, it quickly became the place to eat. Now, sumptuous green velvets covered the seating and hung from the floor-to-ceiling windows, and Jia wondered if the actual hujras of her ancestors had been like this. Oversized crystal and bronze chandeliers hung from the centre of ornate rose mouldings in the high ceilings of the private dining room.

Meera had no taste for such things, but what she did have, thanks to investment, was money, and she had used it to hire someone who knew what they were doing. 'I want something that Umrao Jaan would perform at,' she'd said. 'Brocades and silks, velvet – whatever is the most expensive, I want it.'

The designer had tried to explain that silk and brocade weren't the best choices for high-traffic areas, but Meera had disagreed. 'Is it your money? No, it's mine. And I want a stuffed peacock.' The designer had relented, drawing up plans and invoicing a hefty sum for her trouble.

Meera made it her business to check the reservations a day ahead, and as she had skimmed her finger down the list to find Jia's booking, she had paused on Elyas's name.

'What kind of woman doesn't change her name after she gets married?' she'd said to her husband. But she had made a point to get her hair blow-dried especially. She was wearing her best red shalwar kameez, her hands hennaed, and she had had one of the girls who worked for her smooth dark shades of eyeshadow over her eyelids, deep into the sockets of her eyes. 'You look like a jinn,' her husband had said, watching her from the safety of his wheelchair.

'When you pay the bills,' Meera replied, admiring herself in the mirror, 'then you get to have an opinion.' She'd added a diamond brooch to her shirt, pinning her dupatta in place, before walking away. She turned the lights off as she left the room, leaving her husband alone in the dark. There was no one home today, and he'd have to fend for himself. He'd find his way to the light switch but only after fumbling in the dark.

She'd arrived at the eatery at seven, as was her habit.

She hovered around the restaurant, waiting for Jia. An electrical current ran through her when she saw Jia arrive. Although dressed simply in black jeans, a white shirt and a cashmere jumper, there was something imposing about the way she held herself, even Meera had to admit. Everything about Jia Khan irritated Meera, especially the way she spoke to men, as if she was better than them.

'Society works well when men and women know their place,' Meera Shah was often heard saying to her sons, oblivious to the irony of her own judgement.

'Why is there security at this place?' Elyas said to Jia as they walked in through the double doors. He was carrying Lirian with one arm, the leather Storksak nappy bag slung over his shoulder.

Jia shrugged. They were here partly because Elyas had suggested they needed to get out and partly because she'd agreed with Idris to meet Meera once more. Enough time had passed since that meeting at Pukhtun House for Meera to understand that she needed Jia much more than Jia needed her. 'Jia Khan gives everyone a second chance, but never a third' was what was said about her. This was the credence of the Khan, fed to babies with their milk. That she would meet Meera again was a test for Idris, and he knew it.

So with Hujra having recently reopened, Jia decided to take the opportunity to see the public face of Meera's business ahead of a more formal meeting. It was long past Lirian's bedtime, but Sanam Khan wasn't feeling well and wanted an early night without having to check on the toddler, and so they had bundled him up and brought him along. It wasn't out of the ordinary for children to be up late in the city. Their parents came from a country where siestas were common and timings fluid.

Jia looked young this evening, her hair tied back in a ponytail and her make-up minimal, and this was how Elyas remembered her when they first met.

Meera studied the couple. It was obvious that Jia's husband loved her, and that he was happy to hold the child while his wife ate, unconcerned his plate of food was cooling.

Slowly Meera worked the room, stopping at each table to check on customers, make small talk and shake hands. She had come a long way since the early days of folding pastry into triangles, stuffing them with filling and then deep-frying them. Jia saw that customers enjoyed her banter, her knowledge of food; she knew that occasionally they would ask her to sing, probably the real reason she was here night after night.

'Idris Khan mentioned you would be here. I hope you enjoyed your meal,' Meera said to Jia Khan.

'Thank you,' said Jia as she asked herself why Idris had said she was coming. She had made sure the table was booked in Elyas's name.

Meera was used to being gushed over. People from all walks of life came to eat at Hujra, travelling from far and wide. They complimented her cooking, her clothes, the restaurant's interior. And Jia Khan's silence niggled.

'You poor man,' she said to Elyas.

He looked up from Lirian, surprised. 'Excuse me?'

Meera turned to Jia. 'Look, your husband, bichara, he hasn't eaten anything. His plate is cold.'

Jia was slow to respond. She was tired; her mind was filled with Ahad, the work that needed to be done and all the rest.

Jia smiled wearily. 'My husband is a grown man, and he loves to take care of his son. I don't like to tell him what to do.' Her voice held the tiniest hint of steel.

'Of course,' Meera replied. 'Now I must oversee dessert for the large party in the corner.'

Few words had been said but both women knew a boundary had been set in place between them and that neither thought much of the other.

Elyas looked at Jia as Meera walked away. 'She was just being polite.'

A sigh of exasperation escaped Jia's mouth and Lirian turned quickly to stare at her, his attention caught by this unexpected sound his mother had made.

Elyas's desire to defend the indefensible was becoming tiresome. He was always vying for the other side, looking for the good in the other person, while Jia knew that sometimes people were just plain mean, or had lost touch with their humanity through drugs, drink and illicit sexual encounters.

Jia and Elyas sat in silence. People came and went, starter plates were cleared, and a bright yellow and white biryani was being placed on their table when a loud crash came from the kitchen. It was followed by shouts. An old man and his wife emerged, clearly upset. The woman's clothes looked wet, as though something had spilled on them.

The whole restaurant watched as the elderly couple were nudged towards the door by the burly security guard.

'Rasmalai for everyone, on the house,' cried Meera, bursting from the kitchen, and the servers rushed out behind her with dessert dishes filled with soft balls of cottage cheese covered in saffron and cardamon and soaked in sweetened milk.

Jia and Elyas looked at each other.

The elderly couple were outside now, the old lady's shalwar soaked through and clinging to her legs. Throwing some notes on to the table, Jia got up and followed them, but the couple were too upset to make much sense when she asked them what had happened. All she could gather was that it was something to do with money and that they were scared of losing their home.

Jia helped them into their car and watched them drive away slowly. Idris's judgement had been so wrong about Meera Shah, and not for the first time.

She continued thinking about him and the couple well into the night. She lay awake for hours, planning what she would do.

Idris was her adviser, her right-hand man, and until now she'd trusted his judgement implicitly.

She picked up her phone. Elyas stirred beside her. 'What are you doing?' he said.

'Sending a work thing.'

'Does Idris not mind getting pinged at this hour?'

Jia flicked through her phone book, stopping at Sakina. She typed a message and hit send before putting the phone down. 'He's used to it,' she said, turning on to her side.

'I can't stop thinking about that elderly couple,' he said. 'Sometimes I wonder who helps people like that. What do you think?'

He looked over at his wife. She was now drifting off to sleep.

He pulled the blanket up over her shoulders.

He was going to lean over and kiss her cheek, but something stopped him.

CHAPTER 23

Elyas was having dinner with his friend John. After what happened with the old couple at the restaurant, Elyas had started looking into Meera's business, and John had pulled up some information.

'Do you know how she funded her business? She smuggled cocaine into the country in her bra. Each cup held a kilo, £10,000 worth of white powder. Delivered it in tiffin boxes across the city. So they say.'

'How do you know this?' Elyas asked.

'Sources that wouldn't stand up in court. A few years ago, she started having financial troubles. Around the time Akbar Khan died actually. Some new guy had taken over the drugs market and wasn't allowing anyone else a share.'

'Nowak?'

'Possibly, but even after his death, she never really recovered that side of her business. Until recently that is. But the word in the dinner queue is that she has an investor. Someone from out of town.'

Elyas looked down at his plate, his appetite smaller than it used to be. Time had dulled his senses and nothing tasted the way it did when he was young. Even his feelings for Jia felt dimmed since her conversation with Ahad.

'Remember when we used to come to this place and eat kebabs late at night?' he said to John.

'It wasn't late at night,' said John. 'It was the early hours. Nowadays, if I eat humous after seven, it repeats on me.'

John had left the paper and, thanks to Elyas's contacts, was now working as a nonfiction editor for a publishing house, although he still freelanced a bit on the side. His speciality was crime.

'How are things with you?' he asked.

'I don't know,' said Elyas, pushing his food around on his plate.

CHAPTER 24

The old lady took her place beside her husband at the dining table.

'You really shouldn't have done all of this,' said Jia, gesturing to the platefuls of foods that lay between her and the couple.

'It's how we do things,' said the old man. He offered Jia some papri chaat. Jia thanked him and spooned some of the chutney and yogurt-covered chickpeas and potatoes on to her plate. They were covered in the crispy fried papri and sev, made from flour. The sweet and savoury flavours, the softness of the potato and crunch of the papri, took Jia back to her childhood days, when a steady stream of guests would fill Pukhtun House. 'Our hospitality is the best of our ways,' he said. Jia could not help but agree.

'Tell me what I can do for you,' she said. 'My cousin Idris tells me that you have lost money in a financial scheme.'

The old man opened his laptop and showed them a website. 'Meera told us, and countless of our friends, that we could make a lot of money through a currency scheme. We have known her for many years and we trusted her. But now that we want our money back, she refuses. I call the number on the website and nothing happens. My son has spent days trying to help but nothing. He's an investment banker in London, and he's upset with us. We thought we would surprise him, being the big noise with our crypto currency. But I think that Meera has been fooling all of us and filling our heads with lies. There are hundreds of us. We are older, this was our pension, our retirement money. We hear that you help people get justice.'

'Uncle, it is a sad situation, but I wonder if justice would bring you happiness,' she said carefully.

'Our money is gone,' said the old woman. 'We worked hard for years and saved our money so we wouldn't have to rely on our son, and here we are being forced to turn to him.'

Jia Khan understood the old woman's feelings. She looked around the living room. It was covered in photographs of a life lived: a black and white picture of the old woman when she was a bride; the couple dressed in wide lapels and flares, holding a baby; a toddler on a beach; the child grown and in a cap and gown at his graduation, flanked by his parents.

The old woman walked across the room and picked up the wedding picture, handing it to Jia Khan.

'You were a beautiful bride,' said Jia, admiring the photograph. The bride had large kohl-rimmed eyes, a moon-like gold teeka hanging on a string of pearls in the centre of her forehead and a choker of gold, pearls and gems at her throat. A delicate hand above a bangle-filled forearm was holding the edge of her dupatta.

'I hoped to give this zevar to my son's bride, but I worry that we will now have to sell it. I had it valued yesterday,' she said, her face speaking a thousand words. Her husband took her hand in his to comfort her. He was equally distressed.

The admission hit Jia Khan hard. Wedding jewellery was everything to Pakistani women. It was the gift many parents would save for from the moment their daughters were born and then give to them on the day they left the family home. In a world where women did not always have financial freedom, it was security. Zevar was handed down from generation to generation, and only sold as a last resort.

Jia had come here knowing the couple needed help, but that the situation was this dire took her by surprise. Meera had crossed all lines of decency by stealing from her own people; worse still, she had targeted the elderly and vulnerable. Meera did not have the skills to have pulled this scheme off alone, of that Jia was certain.

She felt angry, but she would hold this in until she knew exactly what and who she was dealing with. Only then would she dispense justice.

Right now, she had to help the people that Meera had stolen from.

'Auntie,' Jia said, 'leave this matter with me. I may have a way of giving you what was originally promised to you by Meera. In the meantime, keep your zevar safe. You will need it for your son's wedding.'

***

The sunlight was fading fast by the time Jia got home. The sky was turning shades of red and orange, a sign that a cold morning was to follow.

The day had been as warm as northern climes would allow, and Jia was sitting in the garden, thinking about how it had gone. She'd woken with knots in her back, and they had tightened as the day had progressed.

After spending a couple of hours with the old couple, she'd headed to her next appointment, which was a garden party.

Nadeem had arranged for her to meet with the families who'd once been looked after by Nowak. Nadeem had been taking care of them since he handed Jia a list of their names outside Costel's house.

They were men and women who had believed Nowak to be their salvation. Like him, they were from Eastern Europe. But from many he had extracted heavy payment in exchange for food, shelter and assistance. Indebted to him, they had had no choice then but to pay, since rumours as to what might happen if they didn't hardly bore thinking about. So, to these people, Nowak had been both villain and saviour.

As Jia had shaken hands and kissed babies, she'd wondered if they considered her the same way.

The line between good and evil, criminal and legal, was thin, blurred and, at points, even non-existent. Where she fell in relation to that line depended on who was making the judgement, she guessed.

Nowak's means of making money had hurt her people, certainly, but he'd siphoned that cash off to help his own. What he'd demanded in return was between them and him. He had shared their heritage, understood their ways, spoke their language. All these things had lulled them into his life, like rabbits in a poacher's trap.

And Jia knew that the fact she had killed him to save her own people did not fill their Eastern European bellies or put a roof over their heads.

She'd watched the children playing hide and seek, swinging from trees and searching for sticks, the way she once had at parties like this with her cousins. Their skin was paler, and in a few generations these families would have assimilated to invisibility; but for now, their soul was like hers, caught between two worlds.

Nadeem had seamlessly slipped into a kind of humanitarian ambassador role with them on behalf of the Khan. He'd helped find these families work, assisted in enrolling them on to courses, covered the costs of school uniforms and paid off rent arrears. He was wiping the blot from his soul.

It was what the Khans did – they helped those in need. It was as it always had been. Their elders had forever been sending money to schools in Pakistan, collecting for charitable causes or easing the way for some distant relative here in England. It was a part of their faith, to be trained in the art of charitable giving.

'Charity increases sustenance and protects wealth,' Nadeem's father would often tell him. 'It is written in countless hadith that the person who lends to Allah a good loan will receive many times more.' He'd said this the first time he'd given Nadeem money and encouraged him to place a part of it in the mosque's collection. And now, giving away wealth came easily to Nadeem. Easier than organised crime.

The transfer of loyalties hadn't been troublesome. To those on the breadline, money was not dirty, ill-gotten or sullied by its origin. Jia Khan and her men had helped to elevate those families beyond mere survival. The future was beginning to fall in line with their dreams, and so today had been a day for celebration. The leader of the Jirga had milled around, making small talk with the men and women. From a distance, Jia Khan could have been mistaken for a politician.

'We are more alike than people might think,' she'd said to one of the women. 'You came to this country in search of a better life, much like my parents. They often talked about the difficulties of giving up the familiar so that we, their children, could have a better future. I know that you will find what you were looking for here, and your children will have the future you want for them.'

Nadeem had picked the right day for a barbecue, as the weather had been warm but not too hot. A cool breeze had danced among them, wafting the smell of pork sausages, hamburgers and hog roast around the park.

Although the salads, breads and chips were the same, the aroma had been very different to that of other Khan barbecues, one that was difficult to stomach for those not used to dining on swine. It was for this reason Nadeem had given Nowak's former families everything they needed to run the party themselves, from grills to awnings and coolers. He couldn't have asked Jia's men to cook haram food and hand out cold beers, but he hadn't wanted to force Muslim values on to non-Muslims in a heavy-handed manner either, and so he'd handled the arrangements and left all the cooking to them.

Speaking to each family and taking note of their needs had left Jia depleted. The smell of roast hog had unsettled her stomach after a while, and so she'd made her excuses and headed home. She was becoming increasingly aware that her energy levels were not what they used to be.

Now, she sat back on the outdoor sofa, sinking into the oversized cushions. She scrolled through messages, switched from Spotify to podcast to radio, longing for the days of zero internet. Everything she tried merely exacerbated her feelings of exhaustion.

A swim would have helped, but the club felt too far away. She pondered another of her father's old plans, the one to build a pool in the grounds of Pukhtun House. It was a good idea, and Jia smiled as she saw how she was slowly taking on more and more of Akbar Khan's ways and wishes.

Indeed, she had run the idea of an indoor pool past Maria last week. 'Feels like another stone on the path to you becoming a recluse,' had been her sister's reply. Jia knew Maria was teasing, but there was some truth in what she said.

This new life was getting heavy, each day bringing greater responsibilities and more mouths to feed. Although the business was thriving, Jia occasionally doubted her abilities, wondering whether she was up to the task, doubts that a man in her position would never have. She'd lived long enough and read enough books, from Mary Beard to *Hood Feminism*, to know that men were propped up by structures and systems from the day of their birth, and that in the race to the top, women like her started a hundred miles behind their male counterparts, having to run through undergrowth and swamps, while the guys took a leisurely stroll with their pals. Race and religion added obstacles, of course, but not as many as those faced by just being women and mothers.

The hourly news bulletin began, and Jia turned the radio up.

'We're coming to you live from the press conference where police have confirmed the body found in Queensbury Cemetery is the latest victim of the person tabloids are calling the Kismet Killer...' The reporter began speaking to spokespeople, locals and experts. Each had an opinion, an experience, but nothing new was added to the story, except that the body count was mounting.

Jia looked up to see Elyas walking across the lawn, his long, lean strides closing the gap between them. He smiled, the dimple in his cheek bringing with it nostalgia, and for a split second she felt the overwhelming urge to take his hand in hers, the car keys in the other, and just run. She could leave this life far behind. Her cousins would take care of the family business – they'd probably be better at it than she was anyway. She could ditch the responsibility of making money, maintaining control, attempting to go straight, and the mental load that came with all of that, right by the flower beds at this minute, and drive out of the front gates.

She hadn't asked for any of this. It had been built on Akbar Khan's life, and it was far from the life she had wanted, planned or pined for even. She could survive away from this house; she had done it before and she had done it well.

Jia was lingering on the thought of her departure, her fingers tracing the growing line on her forehead, when the news switched to familiar songs. Stevie Nicks's powerful and vulnerable voice put a sharp pin into her plans, yanking her back to the here and now. Decades ago she had tapped her fingers innocently along to 'Landslide', not really taking in the lyrics, but now she was older, she was left looking at the exposed sinews of the song.

Jia Khan knew there was no more running to be done. She didn't have it in her these days.

Elyas wordlessly read her unsettled state of mind. He lifted her feet and placed them in his lap.

'Where's Lirian?' he asked.

'My mother took him out to the park.'

'That's good. Did you manage to rest at all? After your thing?'

She shrugged. 'Not really.' She moved her feet from his lap, tucking them under herself. 'They've found another body. An imam this time.'

'I heard,' he said, taking off his cap. His hair was greyer than it had been a year ago, his face thinner, thanks to parenthood.

'They're calling the man responsible the Kismet Killer.'

Elyas raised an eyebrow. 'I wonder which sub came up with that one... I'm so glad that phase of my life is over.'

'You used to be such an ambulance-chaser,' Jia said.

'I don't think I could chase a kid's pedal car now, let alone an ambulance.' He was trying to lighten the mood, and she was grateful for it.

'Remember that one time we'd gone to celebrate my birthday, and you parked up because you'd seen police tape and an ambulance?'

'Which time?'

'Ah yes, because there were countless!'

He laughed deeply, and somehow it was she who felt the catharsis.

'God, we were ballsy, weren't we?' Elyas said.

'That we were.' She paused, wondering if that hunger had left their veins or if they were just too fatigued by life to chase anything these days, including stories, ambulances or the truth. 'Do you ever miss it?'

'No, not really. It took a while to detox. But once you've climbed that hill a few times there's nothing to see. You wake up to the sensationalism. Salacious details, digging for information, death knocks, and for what? A scoop and a breaking-news strapline.'

His revelation surprised her. She'd known him to be ambitious his entire life, but as they talked, she wondered if this was what it meant to grow old with someone, to be aware of their follies and flaws, to witness them become different versions of themselves, familiar and foreign all at once. Even his eyes were changing colour, a thin blue circle developing around the brown of his irises. Her father's had been the same, and so had Elyas's father's. Jia realised they were the age her parents had been when Jia brought Elyas home. How fast that time had flown, and how quickly this too would pass.

'Are you done for the day?' he asked.

'Yes,' she replied. The day had been full of information, ideas and revelations. She brushed aside the Kismet Killer and all the theories that came with it. She had other concerns. Between the old couple and the Eastern European additions to her business, there was much to consider. She took her work seriously, both in terms of the safety of her people, and in terms of serving justice to those that needed to pay heavily for their wrongs.

CHAPTER 25

The cousins were at Pasha's shisha bar, catching up on the last few months.

Jia leaned back into the cushions that lined the uneven chalky walls, her legs folded beneath her. The glow of Moroccan lamps, with their red and yellow stained glass, softened the room further. The sounds of Carnatic violin filled the air, enhanced by the bubbling hookahs and intimate conversations. The sweet scent of shisha surrounded them.

This may have been the spot for mocktails and milkshakes, but it was no place for children. Young men and women in sharp threads flirted gently, and in some cases openly.

Hijabistas wore their head coverings with panache, some high, piled atop their heads, others pinned around their faces. Jia watched as a young woman effortlessly brushed her long hair away from her face with her hand. She was in deep conversation with a friend with an elfin cut, their faces identically made up. This was the place of beautiful people, a land where YouTube tutorials meant everyone knew how to apply, shade and blend their make-up to perfection.

'I'm starting to wonder if we're too old and underdressed for this place,' Jia said. She was in black running shoes and a hoodie, her hair tied back, her face covered only in CC cream. How grateful she was for Maria and her Korean skincare advice.

Nadeem, Malik and Idris nodded, all three in agreement.

'But where else is there?' said Malik.

'Maybe we need our own private members' club,' said Nadeem. 'Our own Annabel's or Soho House.'

Jia's inner coterie of cousins had come to be known as the Verdict since taking over the Jirga. Only they knew that the name, along with the takeover, had been Zan's idea to begin with.

They had each grown into their roles, taking on more and more responsibility. They were a private members' club; they just didn't have a sign above the door.

'Tell us about the hedge funds,' said Nadeem.

They were here to discuss the last wave of chaos they had created deliberately. It was a test to see how the world would react to their power. It had gone a little too well. The ingenuity of the scheme, its untraceability, its scale, the power that it gave them long-term, made a heady concoction.

'Bringing Costel in to work with some of the brightest in our tech and finance companies paid off,' Jia said. 'His team developed a short-selling strategy that messed with the banking system.'

In other words, Jia's organisation had taken on the hedge funds and won. The reverberations were still being felt.

'Can someone explain short selling again?' said Malik. 'It never quite sticks with me. I'm afraid they missed it off my medical school curriculum.'

'Short selling is a bet that a security is going to go down in value,' Idris explained. 'I borrow stock from you and sell it for £10. The stock goes down 20% and I buy it back for £8. When I give it back to you, I've got £2 in my pocket, and you've got your stock. But if the price goes up and I have to buy it back, I have to pay the difference before giving it to you. Hedge funds work by hedging their bets.'

'Right, so how did we skew the system?'

'Our team used all the socials, you name it. We had some information about a stock everyone thought was going down, and we planted a few seeds that encouraged ordinary people to use the investing apps they have on their phones to buy the stock. The seeds grew so fast and high that they pushed the price into the stratosphere.'

'Can't they trace it back to us?

'No. And it was a good buy for those people who did invest.'

'But what's the endgame? Those hedge funds feed NHS pensions, teachers' pensions and ordinary folk. I don't get it,' said Malik.

Jia felt Malik was right. Capitalism was embedded in all parts of society, and there was no getting out of it until someone created a better system. But they needed to look after their own. That's what this had been about.

'Look,' she said. 'It was a project that did better than we expected, and it could be a regular thing. Remember, there's no change without chaos,' said Jia. 'And the advantage is that we have their attention now, and they're afraid. Respect brings you power, and power can be used to make money, but until we have their respect, we'll have to work with fear.'

Malik looked to Nadeem, hoping that he would see sense and explain to Jia and Idris that they were falling fast down the rabbit hole. But Nadeem wasn't the saviour he expected, simply shaking his head instead.

'I thought we were going to go straight?' said Malik. 'Wasn't that why we did all this shit?'

'In time, Malik,' said Jia. 'It was always going to be this way for a while.'

'I get it, I know that it's very difficult to be right there within the bullshit, trying to improve it, without becoming part of it. All this gangster stuff, all this rogue trading, it might earn us respect in the end,' said Malik, 'but it is changing us and I don't think I like what I'm seeing.'

Nadeem said, 'There are kids in this city who are desperate to be seen and have their voices heard.'

'I know it's a myth,' said Malik. 'I know that white people are like kids with stabilisers on their bikes and the rest of us are here on our penny farthings and unicycles, and we are still catching up with them. I see it at the hospital all the time – who makes consultant first, who gets the best job. But I also know that they're afraid, and that this is a last grab for power for them. What we have to decide is whether the new systems will support just us or everyone. Are we like the white people we see around us or are we better?'

Jia Khan listened. She wanted to justify herself, to tell Malik he was wrong, but she couldn't because she didn't think he was. The truth of it was that they were becoming more and more enmeshed in the family system that was much closer to aspects of the old ways than Jia wanted. Something that had started out as selling drugs and sex was now built on massive amounts of fraud. Their legitimate business interests were growing too, and flourishing, but nowhere near the speed of all the illegal interests, and of course not everyone could partake in that. There were still kids on the streets who thought their only chance was dealing drugs, and elderly and vulnerable people out of pocket because of what Meera had done to them, not to mention the vacuum left by Nowak that had hit so many hard in their pockets. The money needed replacing in all these places, and those lives had to be protected.

Jia felt the weight of responsibility on her shoulders. She had no idea how she was going to change things for everybody. Perhaps she had lived away for just too long and had lost grip of what young and old people needed, and what they were interested in. She needed someone, who knew the landscape upon which her empire sat, to guide her. For the young people, she needed Maria, but she was also reluctant to get her sister involved.

Jia's phone buzzed. She looked at the notification. It was a message from Henry Paxton.

Before she could read it, Idris interrupted. 'Jia, you need to see this,' he said, handing her his tablet. It was a bulletin on the hedge fund they'd hit the worst. It was Lord Paxton's.

Somehow that didn't seem like a bad thing to have happened. Jia wasn't sure why she felt that way, just that for her, Henry Paxton was an itch she didn't mind scratching.

She opened the message on her phone.

'You won't get away with this,' it said.

CHAPTER 26

When Adam Diaz called, she knew it had something to do with Henry Paxton. It was too much of a coincidence to be any other way.

'I fly into Heathrow on Tuesday, but I'll come to you if that's easier?' he'd said, always eager to simplify life for her. He was a successful financier with intimate knowledge of the workings of crime families, because he came from one.

Jia had been on an evening walk across the Yorkshire Dales with Maria when he'd called. She'd taken to walking after Lirian was born as it helped soothe her mind. The Dales were home to the darkest skies in the country, and with memories of Zan's love of stargazing, it felt like he was with them. This was the land of waterproof jackets and hiking boots, things that gave gun-owning a respectability, things she didn't possess.

Even with the lengthening summer days, darkness had caught them out, the unpolluted night sky so clear that the sisters could see the Milky Way. They were far from the sights and sounds of urban life and were happy to head back to the car in silence.

Jia's phone vibrated. The timing of Adam's call left her considering whether this was a sign from God; or was it because the devil always found his people in the darkness?

'Who was it?' said Maria after Jia had ended the call.

'An old friend. He was an American attorney and money person working for big-name tech companies. Last I heard he was working for an investment bank. Something to do with fraud.'

'Did you date him?'

'Not really.'

She couldn't admit to Maria what she'd never admitted to herself, which was that although she and Adam had been friends for years, when it looked like the relationship was moving towards something deeper, her fear of even the slightest commitment with anyone other than Elyas had paralysed her.

'We offer creative counsel for high-stake matters,' he'd told her during that first dinner party fifteen years ago. She found herself seated beside him, thanks to meddling friends who always needed an extra to make up numbers.

'That sounds fraudulent,' she'd said. She was bored by small talk and had zero inclination to make new acquaintances. She shouldn't really have been there, and she knew her unfriendly attitude wasn't fair on her hosts or the other guests. But when his laugh took her by surprise, she'd reconsidered. And he'd leaned over and quietly said, 'The best lines are the grey ones. That way there's no guilt about crossing them.'

She'd been struck by his immense mass of hair that parted to one side, gleaming and black, and had assumed they shared the same heritage. She also guessed that he was a bit of a player. Wrong on both counts.

Circumstances brought them together again one Sunday morning, when she bumped into him in the café of the National Gallery.

'I wonder how many times we've been in the same room and passed each other by,' he said.

'I would have remembered you. I remember everything.'

'I must come clean,' he said. 'I did my due diligence after we met, and I've discovered we are quite alike. Our families are in the same business.'

She was taken aback by how forthright he was, and honest. She had never spoken about her father's business interests as openly. He told her he was in London to leave an old life in the States behind, and Jia had understood exactly what that was like – how it left one exposed, like raw nerves, with the kind of pain one feels compelled to touch over and over again, even though it brings no relief.

***

When Tuesday came, she found herself watching him before he noticed her, standing in the doorway of the café. She'd picked a place in North Yorkshire that was close to a station, somewhere easy to get to but quiet and out of the way, wanting to keep a clear distance between past and present.

She touched the nape of her neck, surprised by her own hesitancy. She was older now, she'd become a mother again, and her familial responsibilities left her feeling less pleasing on the eye than when they'd last seen each other. She was surprised by her need to feel attractive.

But he smiled and kissed Jia on both cheeks, and she relaxed. The old warmth was still there. They laughed at the fact that they were dressed almost identically. Both in a navy hoodie, denim jeans, trendy trainers and a dark peacoat.

'How have you been?' he asked.

'Good, I've been good.'

'I came back and you weren't in London any longer.'

'Did you expect to find me waiting around for you?' There was a sparkle in her eye, and it felt good to be outside her countless circles of responsibility. He laughed his raucous laugh she remembered well, and they slipped easily back into how it used to be between them.

'My father died,' she said. 'I'm guessing you already know.'

He nodded.

Adam understood what a father's death meant for people from their worlds. He often thought of Jia Khan as he went about his daily life. She was a touchstone to him, their lives connected by an invisible thread across time and space.

'You've rattled cages, Jia Khan, and you need to know that. That hedge fund you hurt, its portfolio holders were some very powerful men, including the arms dealer Henry Paxton.'

'I know he's not happy with us right now. Are you visiting on behalf of all these portfolio holders? And there's me thinking you were here to see me.'

He reached out and took her hand. She let him, just for a moment, before taking it back. Their lives were different now; there were other people involved, serious relationships.

She glanced out of the window at the green of the fields stretching up to the fork in the road, the drystone wall lined with telephone poles and a bus stop in the distance, the signs of a modern life fading into obscurity.

Their relationship had been the drop-in-and-drop-out kind. Adam had told himself that it was because he had been too young to settle down, but really it was because he always felt Jia could undo him. There were times he'd thought that their relationship would be devastatingly beautiful, and at other times just devastating.

Perhaps if they'd met before Elyas and Ahad, when Jia hadn't been ravaged by loss, things would have been different, and Adam had known that, even during those years away from her husband, Zan's death had made anything between them totally impossible. But he'd understood, too, that even if none of that had happened, the reality was that Jia would have grown into a different kind of woman, one that he might never have been drawn to. Even now, Adam regarded the cracks in her soul to be filled with golden thread. Kintsugi, the Japanese called it.

'Remember those events and classes you used to make me go to? The ones in Borough Market, Spitalfields and the V&A, where we masqueraded as normal people?' she said. 'They are nice times to remember.'

'You always were an early riser, and someone had to stop you spending your weekends running or working.'

It was true, and she had enjoyed having someone arrange things and send her the details, so that all she had to do was turn up.

Once, when they had been talking about their fathers, Jia remembered Adam confiding, 'You know whose name came across my desk last year? The leader of the posh boys who made my life hell at school. He heads up the hedge fund that his father built. Turns out, my own dad wasn't the only one doing all kinds of illegal shit. We take the guy to court, he swears under oath that a document, one that's key to our case, never existed. Last week I found the notary who witnessed the signing of it. Among the 8.6 million residents of New York, like a needle in a haystack, I found him. And it feels like dynamite.'

'What are you going to do?' Jia had asked.

'That's the thing. I haven't decided yet. One minute I want to withhold the evidence as leverage, with the threat of passing it to my dad. And then I tell myself to do what all those law-abiding lawyers would do and declare it.'

'That only shows you're human,' she had told him, 'like everyone else.'

Those Saturday mornings were a lifetime ago to the Jia Khan and Adam Diaz who sat together now.

'Why are we here?' said Jia.

'It was a lot easier to sit in judgement back in the good old days in London, far from the families who relied on my father's interests. Things are different now. Jia, this failing hedge fund is affecting my family's interests.'

Jia understood. 'I'm not proud of what I do, but I am not ashamed either.'

'I know,' Adam said. 'But you should know that these guys are watching you, and they are bigger players than your father was and bigger than you can ever be. I've grown up with these guys, and now they're telling me you may understand their needs better than some of the bankers and accountants they currently use.'

Although Adam's words were mild, Jia recognised the threat at their heart.

'And if I don't want to work with them?'

'You know the answer, Jia. We always knew, didn't we? Deep inside. You and I might have entertained the idea of getting out in those less responsible days, but I think we both recognise now that the chances are neither of us will get out of this alive.'

Adam was one of the few people who saw her clearly and saw her world clearly too. There was something about the way he looked at her, as if he could see into her soul. She knew he was right. She would either have to get into bed with the plutocrats, or she would have to destroy every single one of them. Neither choice was appealing.

'Your husband, what's he like?' said Adam, changing the subject.

'My husband is an honest journalist. The kind of man who writes about people like us. I did try and tell him a long time ago, but I don't think he really wants to recognise the whole truth of who I am.'

'Maybe he loves you. The Hollywood kind of love you always scorned when we watched a romcom.'

'Yes, I think maybe he does. Or did. These days I feel the scales are beginning to fall from his eyes. I think he's starting what will become a long process of leaving me.'

Adam was surprised. This was quite an admission on her part. 'What will you do?' he said.

'I don't know,' she answered. 'Maybe my sons are better off without me. I can't seem to get things right. It's why I work all the time. People are grateful, but not my children. They don't understand what I do for them. Lirian is beautiful and funny and clever, and I know that he will grow and want to go out in the world and do things that are frightening and dangerous, just like his big brother. These children do not know what it was like for us, how we have fought to be accepted, how many doors we have opened for them.

The older one, Ahad, has no idea what it is like to be rejected and alone. He thinks he does, but he doesn't. He wants to show up in the world in all his authenticity, and I just want him to thicken his skin slowly before he does. And I am the last person he wants to listen to.'

'Remember I'm always there. If none of this works, or even if it does,' Adam said, and Jia felt her heart lift at the idea of a different possibility.

The ringing of her phone broke the spell, and she knew duty was calling her home and with the Jirga. She closed her eyes for a moment, and then answered the call.

CHAPTER 27

'I'm losing my faith,' the imam admitted.

Jia had needed counsel, advice about Ahad, from whom she felt estranged, life and other things to do with faith. As it turned out, so did he.

They were sitting opposite each other in the centre of the prayer room, as their fathers would have done, under a stained-glass dome made of intricate geometric patterns in various shades of blue and green. Shafts of coloured light fell on to the maroon carpet.

'Not in Islam, so much, but in an omnipotent creator, maybe,' he went on. 'So much of what I see doesn't sit right and the more I try and untangle it, the more the knots tighten.'

Jia related to the imam's sentiment. But his life was built on the foundation of being an imam: to lose his faith would mean the dismantling of all of that.

'I see injustice around me, and I'm at a loss. Even the work that you do, Khan sahiba, I hear things...'

'Speak plainly,' she said.

'I am not judging your work, as it makes sense to me. But perhaps that's the rub. If it didn't, then everything would be fine, as I would know what was wrong and what was right.' He paused. 'Faith is hard, but religion is harder. Our scriptures have been interpreted in so many ways.'

Jia listened carefully. She needed him in her Jirga. Her people needed belief in the world to come in order to live in this one, for good and evil only balanced where an unseen afterlife existed. She couldn't advise the imam about his faith, but she could show him his place in her world and his importance to her. She brought the conversation back round to her problems.

'My son, I don't know what to say to him,' she said. 'He has his whole life ahead of him. What do I tell him? We were raised in a world where he is regarded as an abomination. When I lived in London, I became friends with people who were gay, or queer as Ahad described himself. I loved those friends as my family, and I questioned and rejected what I had been taught. But I don't know what to tell my son about all of this, because while I can live with a fragmented idea of my faith, I cannot pass that on to him.'

Jia could see the sadness and understanding in the imam's eyes. His face was soft, his unlined hands sat in his crossed lap. He had never done a day's physical labour in his life, and yet here he was, trying to shore up the edifice of community. He was bright, brilliant and honest. But some would see their conversation as a danger to the status quo of society.

Jia needed men like him behind her though.

Disruption required one to stand in the wilderness of faith and family, to risk losing it all, while daring greatly. People like the imam were rare; men like him were rarer still. She hoped he was strong enough.

He finally spoke. His words came slowly, as if he was tasting something new, trying on something untried. 'In the Quran, there is no word that explicitly describes homosexual or transgender persons. The Arabic terms were invented after the Quran's revelation by jurists and journalists, doctors and social critics. Islam was never supposed to be about organisations, but that's the side effect of success, I guess. A lack of unity means that, unlike the Catholic church, we aren't answerable to one person. We don't have a formal movement, and so all change is gradual. But it does impact our immediate families, our friends, the people we work with. The question is whether, without a word, there is anything wrong. Not all the things we believe to be law *are* law. They are interpretations, ideas handed down from generation to generation.'

'Then where are the sermons saying this?' Jia asked. 'Why aren't you preaching this at Jumma prayers?'

'For those whose hearts and minds are sealed, they don't hear me. But this doesn't mean they won't one day.'

His phone buzzed and he rejected the call, saying, 'That was another journalist wanting me to comment on the serial killer and the Muslim connection. They'll leave a message. Makes a change, I guess. Do you know what most calls from journalists I get are about?' Jia shook her head. 'Why Islam oppresses women. No one asks the real question, "Why is it that Islam has produced seven women prime ministers and heads of state, but Europe less than that?" It is the lens through which we see the world that makes the difference between jannah and jahannam.'

'I need you to speak louder, imam sahib,' said Jia. 'I need you to talk about things that concern us here in England, not only about what concerned people in the old country. That is not our country any longer and we belong less there than we do here. We are seeds, planted here by our parents, that means we belong here. We have to make it work for us.'

'Chapter forty-nine, verse thirteen of the Quran tells us that difference is part of God's plan and should be celebrated,' he said slowly.

Jia knew he was doing what he could to help her. But she knew too their conversation would remain private and the challenging ideas they were discussing would not be repeated at the pulpit.

'Imam sahib, I would say preach the truth as you see it, especially when the masjid is full and the worshippers are listening. I trade my soul for theirs every day and you must do the same. If there is a God, He or She will understand. We all need to be braver. And we must remember that one day we will all be called to account.'

'Speak to your son,' the imam told her. 'He will need his mother.'

CHAPTER 28

It took a lot of investigating and looking at protocols to understand precisely what Meera Shah had done.

It became clear that a large number of people had been duped by her, and that some very smooth talking must have been done to tempt such a volume. Some had been plain greedy, that was obvious. But mostly these were ordinary people, many of them retired, with meagre resources. The only thing they were guilty of was naivety, and Jia felt sorry that they were now terrified of the unexpected debt they had ended up with, a debt that threatened to drown them.

While the money earned at Henry Paxton's expense would help her cushion the blow for some, Jia knew a long-term strategy was a priority.

'They deserve what they got, no?' said Benyamin.

'You need to broaden your mind and put yourself in the shoes of those who were persuaded by this woman. Perhaps you'd be more charitable about them. You and I come from a world of plenty – we mustn't think others are like us. It serves no one to let this thing collapse, remember.' Jia thought again of the anguish of the elderly couple from that night in the restaurant and the way their plight had touched her heart so.

She went to the gym, glad to be alone with her thoughts. Soon her shoulders ached, a good kind of ache, from jab, cross, upper cut, rear upper cut. The rhythm of each punch when executed perfectly gave her a sense of purpose and completion.

She'd spoken to Ahad after seeing the imam and he was coming home for the weekend. She had promised to put aside her fears and listen to him.

Mo's turmeric-coloured delivery van drawing into the gym car park was a welcome sight as she left the building. Printed in fading purple ink on the side of the vehicle were the words 'The Chai Guy – Karak'. Jia wondered if Mo would let her pay for a new fleet of vans. He was an honest man, and she wanted to invest in him, support his venture. She watched as the van slowly crawled all the way around the empty lot until he pulled up in the centre.

Jia waved at him, but he didn't respond. Something felt different. The van edged closer, the driver's face coming into view. Jia recognised him from somewhere. She couldn't quite place the face, but it wasn't Mo.

He was staring straight ahead, his eyes fixed on an invisible point, his jaw clenched.

Something was off. Jia took out her phone and dialled. 'Idris,' she said. 'I'm by the martial arts club. In the car park. I'm in trouble.'

The driver's face flashed before her, and she knew where she had seen him before. She knew what was about to happen. She knew it deep in her gut, the way she knew when one of her children was ill, even when they were far from her. She thought about Ahad and how she'd hoped to be at his wedding, of Lirian, whom she'd hoped to raise in a different way, free from his family's criminal past.

She had planned to be present throughout everyone's lives and was suddenly hit by the prospect that it might not happen. Who was she to make plans? And Jia thought for a second of Allah and the lesson he was teaching her.

But she wasn't ready quite yet to roll over and die without a fight.

Her heart raced as she weighed up her options. That van was a killing machine.

Aware of the blood rising to a roar inside her, she saw the serving window of the van open and the barrel of an AK47 gun emerge.

She thought of her sons and Elyas, of her father and Maria and Benyamin, all the people she loved merging into one. She dived behind her car just as a volley of bullets sprayed the side of the Aston Martin, the tinted windows shattering to reveal Lirian's car seat and his stuffed toy taking a bullet.

Jia glanced around, desperate to find some shelter, somewhere to stay hidden until help arrived. And then she saw a ray of hope to the left of her.

Close to the door to the gym were two huge metal bins. They might just save her life.

On the other side of the phone line, Idris held his breath. He was in his car, racing towards the car park, the car speaker relaying the volley of shots as the bullets hit metal, followed by the blare of a car alarm.

He needed no more information to know that gang peace was over.

Jia weighed up how long it would take her to make it to the bins; it looked too far for her to run without getting hit.

Instead, she clicked the button to unlock her car door and, slithering in, pressed the starter button. The car purred into life and she released the handbrake as she put the car in drive. She wouldn't be able to go far like this, crouched down behind the dashboard, and she didn't want anyone else getting caught in the crossfire.

As she was thinking what to do next, she heard another shot and the sound of the van's motor revving, its tyres screeching on the tarmac. Her foot slipped on to the accelerator, slapping down to the floor. Her ears rang and there was blood – so much blood – pouring from her head into her eyes as the car shot forward.

With an enormous jolt, Jia Khan felt the front of the car crumple up like a concertina as the air bag exploded. The steering wheel was digging into her chest, where she had been crouching. The bins beside her provided some cover, but she didn't know where the van was now. The gym was a safer bet.

How she crawled away from the wrecked car and stumbled through the door into the gym, she didn't know. The next thing she was aware of was lying on the floor, covered in blood and sweat. She was cold, so very cold, and she began to shiver.

Her father's voice was in the distance, getting closer and closer. Jia was twelve years old and messing around outside her father's study, listening as she waited for him to finish talking with Bazigh Khan. 'Death does not divide us. Life divides us. Death unites us,' she heard him say over and over again.

'*Inna lillaahi wa inna ilayhi raaji'oon*,' Akbar Khan said to his daughter, quoting the Quran. '"To Allah we belong and to him we return." You were lost and now you are found.'

Jia saw his face and his hand held out to her, his hair long, parted to one side, sweeping across his face, and she smelt his V-neck wool jumper with its mix of old cigarettes and cologne. The Akbar Khan in front of her was young again. She felt her father's embrace, and the glow of her mother's love, and Zan slipping his hand into hers. It felt like bliss.

But then she saw Ahad's face, and Lirian's too, and Jia Khan knew she had business to finish.

The door in front of her opened slowly, warm sunlight streaming in. She held up her hand to shield her eyes from the glare. A man stood in the doorway, looking down at her. Everything was out of focus but she saw him lift his rifle and point at her.

She hadn't expected to die this way.

CHAPTER 29

Ahad picked up his bag and got off the train. He had been pleased when his mother had called and asked him to come home, and he had boarded the first train north.

The last seven months had been rough. Up till then, everything had felt incredibly surreal – getting to know Jia, seeing his father happy, spending time with his baby brother – like the dreams of his childhood coming true.

He had been nervous about telling Jia about his boyfriend, but he hadn't expected her reaction. Her stonewall of silence felt worse than anything else she could have done, as he couldn't read it or understand what it meant long-term. He had assumed the worst: that his mother judged him, thought him bad and could no longer love him. And so he'd avoided going home, making excuses to his father on the phone, throwing himself into university life and his new friends.

Although Elyas was a kind and loving father, there were times growing up when Ahad had longed for a mother to read him a bedtime story or cheer him on during football matches, like his friend's mothers had. Instead, his childhood was marked by her absence and his father's reluctance to talk about her. And these two things felt like a cruel rejection. But if he tried to speak with Elyas about how this made him feel, the sight of his father not knowing what to say to make him feel better hurt too. So Ahad had taught himself early on not to think about Jia Khan if he could help it. As a strategy, it worked to some extent, although Ahad had never been able to convince himself that he wouldn't want to make her proud some day.

Ahad looked around the platform but couldn't see his father. Elyas had said he'd pick him up but had WhatsApped to say he was running late.

Ahad decided he'd wait in the mall where it was warm and quickly sent a message. He headed out of the station towards the tunnel walkway to the shops. That's when it happened: a sharp blow to the back of his head. Ahad reached up and felt his hair dampening with liquid. And then his body hit the pavement, hard.

He flowed in and out of consciousness after that, half aware of being bundled into the back of a van, a bag over his head, the rumble of the motor as he was driven away. It was the woman's voice that would stay with him forever, the things she called him each time her heel connected with his body.

When he came to, he was in agony, his arms twisted behind him and tied, unable to see due to a blindfold. He thought he heard the scurrying of rats nearby, and beyond that, the sound of dripping rainwater and occasional traffic. He tried to move but couldn't. His arms and legs were tied to a ring in the wall in such a way that he was lying prone, and the more he wriggled the tighter his bindings felt.

Ahad rubbed his head on his bony shoulder and was able to dislodge the ill-tied blindfold a bit. Blurrily, he peered around and realised he was probably in an old, empty factory or industrial unit. The windows were smashed and those that had survived were covered in grime, and he shivered when he felt cold wind gusting through a broken pane so sharply it felt like a knife. His head hurt, and the bit of himself he could see was damp and covered in dirt. He felt claustrophobic in his bonds, his body trembling, terrified of what was to happen to him.

'Hello?' Ahad called a couple of times. His voice sounded shaky and up and down in the way it had when he was going through puberty.

Nothing.

And then Ahad thought he probably shouldn't make too much noise, so he just lay there. Alone, and cold, panicky and petrified.

After a long wait there were approaching footsteps and a quiet babble of voices. He tried to turn over to look, but he couldn't.

He strained to listen and after a while could make out that the voices were all female and there had to be four or five of them.

'Help!' he cried. 'Help!'

A group of women meant rescue was at hand. They would let him go.

'He's just a kid,' said one of the voices.

'What is going on?' said another woman. Her voice was young and she sounded horrified. 'What is he doing here?'

'He's her son. He deserves everything he gets,' said a third voice that made Ahad tremble. He recognised its flinty edge as the voice of the woman in the back of the van.

'Jia Khan's son? You're going to get us all killed.' It was the first speaker, and there was panic and shock in her voice.

A door opened and a figure appeared at the other end of the room, in Ahad's blurred line of sight.

A white man was heading towards him, and he was holding something.

'Cut his fingers off. I'm going to send them to her one by one,' said the woman with the flinty voice.

A machine was turned on, loud and heavy sounding – perhaps a drill or a chainsaw. Ahad gave an involuntary whimper and began to struggle in his bindings.

The man stepped forward, looming over him with his machine, and Ahad screamed.

There were other cries. One of the women shouted something unintelligible. But whatever this was made the man turn his machine off.

'Stop!' cried the voice of an older woman. 'This boy hasn't done anything wrong. We work by committee and we honour a code. We punish the men who take advantage of us. What I see before me, this isn't right.'

'He's a khusra,' said the flinty woman. 'He's going to be teaching your sons all kinds of haram things.'

'No one teaches our sons anything they don't want to learn. What difference does it make to you what he does? This is not who we are. We're not paying this man to hurt innocent children.'

'You're not the one paying him – I am!'

Ahad was finding it hard to follow what was being said, as he couldn't see any of the women. The next thing he heard was the sharp beep of a phone. There was a brief pause.

'That boy's mother – she's dead anyway,' hissed the flinty woman.

He thought he had heard correctly but struggled to make sense of her words.

Was his mother – the Khan who terrified people – the person who had died? That couldn't be, Ahad told himself. Everyone knew the great Jia Khan was invincible.

And then it sounded as if the woman who wanted his fingers gone was stomping away, still speaking to the others over her shoulder as she added, 'So this apology for a child is not needed now. Matthias, dump him on Smith Lane, close to the hospital. That way people will know to fear us but respect us too for the mercy we've shown. We need them onside.'

There was a rush of air as a door slammed behind her.

There was a long silence among everyone else, and Ahad lay as still as possible, barely daring to breathe in case they changed their mind about what to do with him.

At last, the older woman who had stood up on Ahad's behalf said, 'I'd heard rumours about her. I should have believed them. If she's killed Jia Khan, she's a dead woman too as she will have to pay a blood price. She's not one of us. She's broken the code and deserves everything she gets.'

The woman crouched down in front of Ahad, taking off her shawl and wrapping it gently around his shoulders, untying his wrists and rubbing them to bring the blood back. 'Please leave the blindfold on for now. You're quite safe with us.' She called for water, helping the boy take a sip. 'Slowly,' she urged.

He rested against her, tired, less afraid for his own life and now concerned for his mother's. 'Who are you?' he said. 'Is my mum dead?'

There was a pause as the woman deliberated. Then, finally, she answered.

'My name is Bano. We didn't have anything to do with this,' she said, helping him stand. 'I wish I could have told your mother that.'

CHAPTER 30

The shots were still ringing in Idris's ears when he arrived at the car park.

The call with Jia Khan had gone dead straight afterwards. He'd dialled 999. 'There's been a shooting in Grayson Square by the martial arts club,' he'd shouted.

'Has someone been hurt?'

Idris didn't know the answer to the question. All he knew was that he needed to get to his cousin. He'd made errors in judgement, and now these failures might have cost Jia her life. He hated himself in that moment. She'd told him not to trust anyone.

'Sir, can you hear me? Is anyone hurt?'

'I don't know,' he sobbed and rang off.

He didn't know whether Jia had been hurt. Nor what had happened, who else had been there, or what was to come, but in his gut he knew Meera Shah was behind it. He should have listened to Jia.

He made himself think of practical things that needed to be done. News would spread quickly and he needed to get the Jirga together, even if one of them had been responsible for the shooting.

He called Nadeem. 'Brother, I think Jia might have been shot. I'm on my way there now and will let you know what's going on. But right now I need you to get Benyamin and Malik to the house. Elyas too. No one else. Not until I say. And if anyone asks, tell them Jia is at home, working. Got it?' He didn't say much more than that.

He couldn't afford to. Words started wars in this city, rumours started riots, and his priority was getting to Jia. Idris ran through a thousand scenarios, thought of all the things he hadn't said to her. All the plans they hadn't made. This could not be real. He pushed these thoughts aside.

Nadeem had known better than to ask questions, the tone of Idris's voice telling him all he needed to know. Something was unfolding, his cousin was in trouble, and Nadeem would find out what it was soon enough.

But both Idris and Nadeem understood that whatever was going on, it was personal.

Idris raced through the city streets, desperate to get to Jia. The centre was just starting to come to life as the morning commute began: children in school uniform boarding buses, parents walking the smaller ones to school, men and women in suits crossing roads or parking cars. It seemed like any other ordinary day.

But for the Khan family things had changed dramatically. In an instant, everything was about to come crashing down.

Idris had seen more than his fair share of these moments. When his mother had died, he had been angry. He'd looked at other children, wondering why they got to hold their mother's hand, smell her perfume and fall asleep in her arms. Jia's mother, Sanam Khan, had sensed his pain and saved him from disappearing down the well of rage that he'd been digging. If it hadn't been for her, Idris knew his life would have turned out differently. That Jia's sons might experience what he had, reignited his rage.

He cursed the traffic, the red lights and the pedestrian crossing. He needed to get to the club to see for himself, to hope against hope, to make sure Jia was alive, breathing, and that his world had not collapsed once more.

The phone rang. It was his brother. 'Salaam,' Idris said, and then he made a sharp intake of breath at Nadeem's words. 'Ahad?' said Idris. 'What do you mean, missing? From where? ... Where am I? I'm turning into the car park at the martial arts club. It looks deserted and quiet. I can't see anyone, but her car is here. I'll call you back.'

Ahad was missing, Jia had been shot – what was happening? What should he do?

Idris felt dizzy, and then he told himself to focus; he needed to focus. He began to bargain with God. 'Allah, if you get us out of this and save Jia's life, I swear I'll go straight. I'll be at masjid praying Tahajjud every night, I promise.'

Up close it was clear that Jia's Aston Martin was badly wrecked against the wall of the club. Idris's heart fell and the life left his limbs. He mustered what strength he could and went to investigate.

There was glass and broken body kit everywhere. But Jia's car was empty. He saw blood, a lot of blood, leading to the doorway.

He darted towards it, grabbing the handle and yanking the door open, praying that he'd not see what the evidence around him suggested.

But that's when Idris found Jia.

Her body crumpled in a heap as if she were a rag doll, her hair soaked in blood.

CHAPTER 31

1974

Akbar Khan looked at Mary. She was more beautiful than any woman he had ever seen. The girls in his city were kept away from prying eyes, wrapped in shawls, their heads covered and eyes lowered, and he knew always to maintain a respectful distance. His mother had raised him this way.

But Mary was sharp and strong, uncovered but still modest. Where his skin was pale, hers was dark; but her eyes were as large as his and, also like his, glistened with flecks of gold.

The first time Akbar Khan saw her was at the Legal Help Centre. He'd pushed the door open, stepping out of the cold wind into the warmth of the office, and seen her immediately, sitting behind a desk across the room. He had wrongly assumed she was a secretary, and later this was something she would tease him about endlessly. She was wearing a polo neck the colour of caramel. It sat high around her neck, and even from a distance he could see she wasn't like everyone else around her.

'Excuse me, I need some help, please,' he had said, looking into Mary's eyes, hoping for some kind of connection. Then he'd caught himself, his gaze a second too long, and abruptly turned away.

She'd smiled, and he'd told her about the problem with his contract at the Pembroke.

'You don't sound like the other Jamaicans,' he said later, when they met for a coffee in a café close by. 'My neighbour Errol is from Jamaica. He used to live in Clapham South, but now he lives in Brixton.' All the dark-skinned people Akbar Khan had come across in London so far said they were Jamaican, and so this seemed a safe thing to say.

'I'm not from Jamaica,' she replied, giving him a firm look as if she expected better from him. He felt like a man who had caught a magical fish but had let it slip away because of his stupidity.

When Mary had inquired across her desk in the Legal Help Centre if he was Pakistani, he'd asked her how she knew – most people assumed he was Indian. She'd told him it was on his paperwork. And all Akbar Khan could think to say was, 'Oh.'

Her face softened, and hope surged in Akbar's heart. Sitting in that café, he knew already that he wanted her.

'My grandfather was in the textile business. He owned mills across India, but after Partition, he fell on hard times,' he said, hoping his ancestry of lost generational wealth would impress her.

'Partition?'

'When the British split India and made Pakistan. We lost everything, almost everything. My parents weren't used to working – they'd been waited on all their life. They didn't handle it well. Much of that responsibility fell to me, and I missed out on a lot of my education.'

She'd smiled at him, and he'd felt seen, even as he realised by the curve of her mouth that she knew perfectly well what Partition meant.

People seemed to look through him, and not *at* him, in this frosty, inhospitable country. Mary made him feel as if pieces of him were coming together right in front of her eyes, making something rare and beautiful.

'I grew up in Cameroon,' she said as she sipped her tea. 'My family are political, involved in industry. I'm the daughter of my father's youngest and favourite wife. That is why I am able to be here, and to study, instead of getting married straight away. My mother fought hard for me.'

He nodded. He knew a little about the battles that women so often lost. He'd witnessed them in Peshawar, and occasionally in London.

'What is it like, in your country?'

'Not that different to here,' she said. 'Maybe a little warmer. And the people are kinder. Sometimes.'

Something passed across her face, and he recognised the look. It was homesickness mixed with the knowledge that things back home weren't necessarily better. They were different, that's all.

***

It wasn't long before Akbar Khan and Mary were spending virtually all their free time in each other's company. Walking through the falling leaves of Tooting Common, eating doner kebabs on Tottenham Court Road, listening to music on Mary's record player – it didn't matter what they did, as each minute together was perfect, each time they met like a homecoming.

Mary's ferocious intelligence was intimidating to Akbar Khan at first though. He wasn't used to women being so forthright. But his London self meant he could adjust his view of the world more easily than he might have done in Pakistan.

Mary had been in London for nearly two years longer than him, and so she naturally became his guide as an immigrant.

And when Akbar Khan's brother, Bazigh, was arrested, it felt natural that Mary was the first person he thought of to ask for help.

He had run through the rain across town in a panic, clutching a newspaper over his head as protection. The doors to the Legal Help Centre were closed and locked, but through the blinds, he could see Mary putting on her camel-coloured mac and tying a scarf around her head. He rapped on the door hard, and then went back to the window in desperation, banging his palm against it.

She looked up, fear in her eyes, and then relaxed, seeing it was only him. She came to the door. He heard the various locks and bolts open, and then the red door was pushed open.

'Please, Mary, my brother, he has been arrested. I don't know what to do.' Akbar was out of breath because he wasn't used to running, and so his words were wheezy.

She hadn't asked any questions other than where Bazigh Khan had been taken. Later, when they knew each other better, he asked her why she had put herself out to help him that night. 'I am a good judge of character,' she said.

That day, standing by her desk as the rain poured down outside, she'd picked up the clunky handle to her red phone and dialled a number, each turn and whirr and click of the dial an eternity. What was it about this woman that made him trust her, Akbar wondered. It was in the unsaid as much as the said; it was in gestures and, like love, in the eyes, he decided.

'Hello? ... Yes, it's Mary. I need your help with something. Can you come now? ... Yes, I know it's raining, but you have a car, don't you?' Her manner was direct yet somehow warm.

When she finished the call, she turned to him. 'That was an old university friend. He's going to meet us at the police station. He's rich, he's white, he's connected – and, well, he knows how to handle the police.'

She led him out on to the street. 'You need an overcoat, Khan,' she said.

'Not Akbar tonight?'

'Khan is better.'

She took off her scarf and wrapped it around his neck. It smelt of her, of perfume and the body lotion she covered herself with every morning. He was grateful for the warmth and the fragrance. He had never been this close to a woman before. It was an effort to turn his mind away from her towards Bazigh.

They arrived at the police station, and Akbar saw his brother standing outside with his hands deep in his blazer pockets. Beside him, offering him a cigarette, was a man in an overcoat with a briefcase. As they got closer, Akbar noticed the cut of his shoes, the shape of his chin.

'There's Henry,' said Mary, waving at the man. 'A modern Machiavelli.'

And Akbar recognised Henry as the man from the hotel, the one with the wallet.

Bazigh dropped his cigarette and crushed it under his foot, pulled his collar up and dipped his head as he ran across the road. Something about the way he moved made him look older. The brothers embraced, Akbar Khan glad to see his little brother alive and free. The bruises would be visible in the cold light of day.

Months later, while in bed with Mary, Akbar Khan told her how at that very moment he knew things had changed.

It wasn't anything Bazigh said; it wasn't the bruise on the side of his face, his hair crusted hard with blood from where the police officer had hit him with his truncheon. It was something about the way he carried himself. He was different now, as if he'd splintered into two distinct people. There was the Bazigh who didn't want to be noticed, who disappeared into the background to avoid calling attention to himself, to avoid causing offence. Then there was the other Bazigh, the one who walked with swagger, who pulled himself up to full size so that anyone who considered messing with him would think again. It was a change that would last forever.

And some germ of that experience found its way from his brother deep, deep into Akbar Khan's heart, and from there it reproduced and grew.

CHAPTER 32

1974

The men were on their way to the Scotch Club, tucked away behind the luxurious Fortnum and Mason emporium. London was lit up with the warm glow of Christmas lights, but the men lifted their collars against the chill in the wind. They looked up at the department store's clock as it began to chime. Two little, male clockwork figures moved out, one in red, the other in green, and bowed to each other.

'William Fortnum was a footman for the royal family,' Bazigh Khan said, pointing at the figurines and then to the decorated shop windows. 'They liked new candles every day, so he started taking the old ones and selling them.'

'Sounds like a swindle, Brother,' said Akbar Khan.

'Sounds to me like good business sense,' Bazigh replied.

Akbar smiled at the way working on a market stall had made his brother streetwise.

Watching the wealthy of London go about their business at the Pembroke always left Akbar Khan thinking too, and he knew he was learning a lot of things that one day he was determined to put into practice.

'Every empire is built on a crime,' he said now.

It was late and they were meeting Henry at his favourite drinking establishment. Henry helping Bazigh out and Akbar knowing Mary had greased the wheels of their friendship – and of course neither Henry nor Akbar had forgotten that moment with the money-stuffed wallet.

The plush club wasn't the kind of place Akbar Khan usually frequented, and Bazigh Khan's wandering eyes could not get enough of it. The sheen of Akbar's green suit against his glossy hair made him look like he belonged here as a customer, alongside the musicians, artists and young and wealthy elite who were hoping to monetise their talent.

'Have you heard of the Grosvenor diamond?' Henry asked, taking a sip from his glass.

Akbar Khan shook his head.

'It's a 45-carat diamond,' said Henry. He leaned back against the purple scallops of the private booth, swilling his drink, making the ice clink.

'Is he a lawyer or a jeweller?' Bazigh Khan said to his brother in Pashto.

'I am a lawyer,' said Henry, and both brothers realised they must be careful what they said in front of him. But Henry smiled then, and added, 'I'm interested in the gemstone for personal reasons. And I need your help to procure it.'

'But surely you have enough money to buy this yourself?' said Akbar.

'I do. But the owner of the store and I had a disagreement, and its value to me is that I want to teach him a lesson.'

'Buy a different one. Why do you have to have this one?'

'Because it belonged to someone I loved. Someone I met when I lived in Lahore, in the old part of the city.'

Far away from their land and the homes of the ones they'd loved, to hear mention of their motherland from the mouth of a white man sent an electrical current through each of the Khans.

Akbar asked, 'What would a man like you be doing in the old part of Lahore? It is a place for prostitutes and conmen.'

'Not everyone who lives that life chooses it – you know that. Besides, aren't we all just exchanging services to survive? My tailor sells his tailoring skills, you sell your numeracy, your dependability, your people skills, while Bazigh here sells his charm. Tell me I'm wrong,' said Henry.

'We don't have any money.'

'I don't need your money, Akbar. I need your help.'

'Ask someone else,' said Bazigh. 'One of these gorai,' he added, pointing to the bar.

'I need someone I can trust,' said Henry, running his hand through his blond hair, his eyes as blue as his shirt. 'Not a gora, but someone who looks the part. A man who can pass as a rich Arab.'

'Why would you trust us?' said Akbar Khan, his whisky untouched, the ice melting slowly.

'Because you returned my wallet. I've tried that out on people before. Most are willing to sell their souls for a few quid. But you didn't. And that interests me.'

'My soul is worth more than ten pounds,' said Akbar Khan.

He looked at the white man who had tested his honour. While he hadn't seen through the trick in the moment, Akbar Khan knew how to act. And later he'd suspected it had been a test, one that he would use on somebody himself one day.

What Henry was suggesting had possibilities, Akbar Khan decided. The arrogance of rich and powerful white men was their weak spot. That they assumed themselves cleverer than everyone else while they pretended not to be liars and cheats never failed to surprise him.

'To be clear, you're asking us to steal for you?' said Akbar.

'This isn't about money. Nor theft, eventually. I'll pay him once I have the diamond,' said Henry. 'This is about love.'

'Ah yes, love is a thing worth giving up both this life and the next for, or at least that is what poets would have us believe,' agreed Akbar Khan, not that he really believed this.

Henry took out his wallet, the one Akbar had handed back to him. He pulled out a photograph, just as he had that day in the hotel. But it wasn't his brother. It was a sepia-toned picture of a young woman in uniform, her dupatta folded flat into a 'V' over her chest, reminiscent of college students across Pakistan. She was drinking from a tall ice-cream glass, her eyes downcast, her lips almost touching a striped straw.

The Khan brothers exchanged a look, unsure what they were supposed to say, but Henry Paxton didn't notice this, being so intent on staring at the photograph.

'She was a girl I was at boarding school with.' His voice had an uncharacteristically dreamy quality. 'As we got to know each other, I fell in love, and she told me about the Grosvenor diamond, how it belonged to her family but had been lost when they fled India for Pakistan after Partition. I was young and made rash promises. I vowed to return it to her, and she agreed to marry me. Needless to say, it didn't last. My father convinced me of the futility of such a marriage, and of course, women aren't always what they claim to be. But I've never forgotten her, and I was always intrigued by the story of the diamond. Recently, I got news that it was here in London. It has found its way to the Knightsbridge jeweller, who is clearly a thief.'

'Who was this girl?'

'No one you would know. She came from a long line of courtesans. Or that's what I heard.'

In the background of the club, women drifted about with glasses in their hands, wearing knee-high leather boots and short skirts, and feathered hair atop their haze of purple, orange and brown shirts.

Akbar Khan considered how easily men categorised women into good and bad, virtuous or of ill-repute. He thought of Mary and the depth of his feelings for her, and how indefinable she was. For Henry, clearly lineage was more important than love, and the worth of a woman was measured according to the decisions that those who came before her had made.

Henry must have caught this thought in Akbar's eyes, as he added, 'All women are the same, whether they're in Whitechapel,

Lahore or Lagos. They like sex as much as we do, but they don't want us men to know this. They play different games to get what they want.'

Akbar felt that what Henry was hiding was that it suited him to see women in this shallow way, as it was how men like him lived with themselves.

'Anyway, I want that diamond,' said Henry. 'And you're going to get it for me.'

***

'His family is steeped in the blood of Hindustani and Pakistani women,' said Bazigh as the brothers headed home, discussing what they should do, adding, 'All those trains full of bodies of women, their breasts removed, that arrived at stations in both countries. The "colonies", what a quaint word for thievery, bloodshed, rape and enslavement. This pale-skinned man and his ancestors masqueraded as friends, and then carved up nations according to their own palate, taking things they regarded as delicacies and leaving the rest to rot.'

'You have a point,' admitted Akbar Khan. 'But ultimately this might be an opportunity to better ourselves, one that won't come our way again.'

The men talked about the way Henry held on to the love story because it made him feel like a romantic hero – and because there was treasure involved at the end. He would probably never acknowledge that he had very likely broken the girl's heart with his empty promise.

In the world Akbar came from, a promise was a promise, and loyalty lay with a woman. To betray her was an act of dishonour.

But there was a deal to be made if they wanted it, albeit with the devil. And one can learn much from the devil.

As they talked, Akbar Khan decided he wanted money and power like Henry Paxton had. He wanted it because he was certain he could make better use of it serving others than a spoilt man like Henry ever could in his determination to indulge his every whim.

***

Henry's plan wasn't clever or complicated. But it left Akbar Khan marvelling at the audacity that came with Henry's whiteness, the ease with which he demanded things, asked for assistance or simply spoke his mind.

The world was made for white men, who built castles for themselves and cages for brown men. And when brown men got hold of the keys and tried to escape, they found the locks twisted, bent out of shape. And even when they escaped one cage, they'd find themselves in another, and another, and for the man who escaped all the cages, the outside was the last, most difficult prison, the one that he had unknowingly locked himself in.

'The prison that we put our own selves into, that is the one we need to escape from,' Akbar would tell his children years later. 'The key is figuring out whether the bars are real or a figment of our imagination. Never let anyone else define you or tell you who you are.'

'You'll need a tailor to make something like this,' Henry said, handing over a photograph of two men in robes and a headdress. 'I know you're not Arabs, but you can pass as such.'

Bazigh Khan listened quietly. He lit a cigarette, took a deep drag and blew out a cloud of smoke that joined the cloud already round them. He could relax in a way that Akbar Khan could not. He was the younger brother; he'd always had someone to protect him. From the moment he was born, his brother had been there, like a wall between him and the world.

The pubs in southwest London were not like this one. They were filled with working-class men with calloused hands and hard faces, although the brothers had found their hearts to be kind. Akbar Khan sensed the opposite was true of the men here. The velvet jackets and long collars covered hardened souls. These were men after money, adoration and fame, things that ate up empathy as a snake eats its young.

'What kind of people come to this place? Are they like you?' asked Akbar.

'A lot are musicians and actors, and of course businessmen. Some have money, some don't. But everyone is acting as if they do.'

Akbar Khan thought of his and Bazigh's childhood, playing marbles outside the paan shop, music drifting from the old radio out on to the dusty streets. The white walls inside the shop had been papered with advertising for cigarettes, soaps and powdered milk – the red, yellow and green tin of Nido, the deep mustard – yellow of Lu biscuits.

The walls in this smoke-filled room were earthy tones, burnt oranges, yellow ochres and browns. The atmosphere was mellow, and Akbar thought of the lives of these people, the ones who could chill and hang and not worry about paying rent. Or maybe they did and just hid it well.

Henry's plan was that Akbar and Bazigh would walk into the shop and simply walk out with the thing he wanted.

'Henry, we get followed around shops by security guards,' said Akbar Khan, shaking his head. 'And a diamond like that will be closely watched.'

Henry lived how he pleased, but Akbar Khan's life was tailored according to the perception of others. He knew what they saw when they looked at him. His accent, his skin, his deep-set eyes and his jet-black hair marked him out as different. As someone not to be trusted. The more time he spent with Henry, the more he under-stood that this country would never accept him otherwise.

Where people handed Henry drinks when he walked into a room, they offered Akbar their coats. Watching the way people bowed and scraped and contorted themselves into strange animals, just to let the rich pet them, was changing Akbar Khan, he realised. His colleagues at the Pembroke were adept at making the wealthy feel important, fulfilling their whims, bringing them everything they asked for.

But Akbar wanted that for himself, and for any family he might have. He was smarter than many of the people he waited on; he was certain he was much cleverer than Henry. But what Henry had was power, and that came with money.

Henry rolled out a sheet of pale-blue paper on the table in front of them. He took their three glasses and placed them on the corners of the sheet to stop it furling. For the fourth corner, he went for something in his pocket, but changed his mind and reached for a heavy cut-glass ashtray.

Both Akbar and Bazigh had glimpsed the gun Henry's fingers had skimmed in his pocket, and they glanced at each other, their eyes rounded.

'It is easy to get weapons here?'

'My family is in defence. We sell arms,' said Henry. 'My father likes the money it makes him.'

Akbar Khan was aware that his brother would look to him for guidance. Other people's lives were no easy matter, and leadership was more a burden than a pleasure. He decided not to comment further – he hadn't decided what to think about Henry's casual attitude, and he didn't want to make Bazigh hot-headed. Bazigh had that tendency and was prone to speak or act without thinking things through properly.

Instead, Akbar leaned forward to study the blue paper. It was a detailed map of a shop floor, straight lines sketched with precision. 'How did you get this?'

Henry just smiled, and then he tapped the plans. 'This is the front door that unlocks when customers have been screened by a security guard. There is a buzzer on the outside of the door.'

'They won't let us in,' said Bazigh, his voice defeated.

'If they think you have oil money, they will.' And Henry winked as he pushed two luxury watch cases towards each of them. 'Consider these a down payment,' he said, raising his glass in a toast.

Weeks later, Akbar and his brother were being driven in a red Maserati Quattroporte on the way to the jeweller's.

CHAPTER 33

1974

The brothers sat in silence. If this went wrong, they would face prison. Or worse.

The uniformed driver parked outside the Knightsbridge jeweller's, revving the engine just enough to announce their arrival.

Akbar Khan and Bazigh got out and quickly adjusted their robes and headdresses. They'd been told to flash their new watches and keep their expensive sunglasses on until they were directly at the door, and they weren't to look back at the Maserati. The driver would wander off in two minutes, as if going for a cigarette, and the car would be left where it was. It had been stolen to order that morning from an underground garage and belonged to an acquaintance of Henry who was currently in Antigua, so it was unlikely the police were looking for it yet. The driver and the brothers had worn gloves in the car to avoid fingerprints, and Akbar had been told to make sure fabric from the cuff of the robe was between his finger and the doorbell. They weren't to touch anything once they were inside.

They had been schooled in the appropriate accent by Henry, who had an ear for this, and in how to have the swagger of oil-rig heirs capable of purchasing every diamond for sale in London.

A taxi would be waiting on the nearby corner for their escape, driven by one of Henry's cronies.

Even though he had been told otherwise, Akbar had expected window displays boasting millions of pounds worth of gemstones.

But from the outside it was all very discreet, with not much on show. This was stealth wealth: only those privileged enough knew what was behind the doors of this establishment. Inside, the jewellery was displayed in gleaming glass cabinets against the walls and in glass topped cases on the counter. In one of these, resting on a purple velvet cushion and embedded in the centre of a necklace between twelve other stones, was the diamond they were there for. Henry's contacts had cased the place and their information was accurate, down to the colour of the mosaic tiles that paved the floor. The brothers had been told to expect five employees – and saw three of them when they entered the building. The others were presumably in rooms on the upper floors of the shop.

Akbar glanced up at a mezzanine level that ran around the sides of the room, steps leading up to it opposite them. A woman in a fur coat was sitting in a chair up there, being served by a member of staff. For a moment Akbar Khan thought it was Elizabeth Taylor. Henry had said she bought and borrowed gems from here. Through an open doorway behind the counter another staircase led to the upper floors. The wood-panelled walls were polished to such a high sheen that Akbar thought he would be able to see his face in it if he was close enough.

The brothers crossed the tiled Victorian floor towards a suited man smiling at them. Akbar had spent enough time with Henry to be able to distinguish between a quality tailor-made suit and an imitation. Polyester never cut or hung like wool, and the man was clearly in an off-the-peg suit. As he got closer, he noticed the man's pupils widen at the thought of the commission about to come his way, thanks to the fat-cat Arabs who'd entered the shop.

Bazigh held back a little, walking a step behind his brother, as they had practised countless times. Walking like the privileged took work. So did pulling a weapon. But the Khan brothers were quick learners and committed to whatever task life put before them.

Akbar Khan looked at his brother, and then let the gun he'd been concealing in his sleeve slip into the palm of his hand. He wrapped his fingers around the pearl handle. In one swift motion he swung his arm around, pointing the gun towards the salesman's temple, his eyes cold and clear, adrenaline clearing his mind and placing him exactly where the universe had decreed. And as he looked around the room with his finger on his lips to tell everyone to be quiet, Akbar Khan felt power flood through him for the first time since he'd arrived in England. He felt the weapon in his hand, the way it sat, hugging the curve of his palm as if it belonged there. He thought of the times he'd picked up a rifle in Pakistan, the way that Kalashnikovs were everywhere, strung across men's backs or held across their chests as they guarded the houses of the wealthy.

Akbar realised he finally felt at home, and it was the gun that did it.

As everyone remained frozen, Bazigh pointed at another shop assistant who was standing close by. He pulled a concealed bag from his robe and threw it towards her, gesturing to the diamond necklace in the case. She moved quickly, unlocking the case and removing the necklace, then opening more cases and drawers and scooping jewellery into the bag, spurred on by the pistol he'd pulled out.

Akbar saw the suited salesman's hand tremble and move. He whacked him in the temple with the gun he was holding, not so hard as to knock him out but enough to wound, enough to make sure that everyone in the room knew he was serious.

'No noise. No panic buttons,' he said in a much calmer voice than he was feeling, and even impressing himself with his Middle Eastern accent. Fearing further repercussions, the injured salesman stifled his pain.

It was over in less than a minute.

Not a shot was fired.

They had been so swift, so smooth, that staff and customers on the upper floors hadn't even been aware of what was happening.

The Khans left as quickly as they'd arrived, ducking into the black cab. The taxi made a sharp left turn, followed by a right into a maze of backstreets, as Akbar and Bazigh took off their robes and put them in a bag left in the back of the cab for them, along with their sunglasses and weapons. Then the cab rejoined the London traffic. They had worn their ordinary clothes under their disguises.

Akbar gazed out of the window at the grey streets lined with mustard-coloured Datsuns and chocolate-brown Ford Cortinas, all angles and straight lines. Bazigh wriggled beside him in an adrenaline surge, his forehead dripping sweat.

The lit-up advertisement for Cinzano on the curve of the building ahead signalled their arrival at Piccadilly Circus. Next to it were the red and white lights that made up the Coca-Cola sign, and Akbar felt parched. They were about to meet Henry for a secret rendezvous.

But Akbar hadn't decided how much of the truth he was willing to tell.

CHAPTER 34

1974

When Akbar Khan had left the jeweller's, he'd fully intended to hold up his end of the bargain.

But then something changed.

He realised that now he'd broken the law, he was going to lose Mary. He had just done precisely the thing that meant she was going to break his heart.

Mary liked Henry, but she had always made it clear to Akbar that she didn't appreciate the way Henry lived his life. But in the excitement of preparing for the raid, Akbar had chosen not to pay attention to this. Now, in the back of the taxi, he understood he had taken everything Mary felt for him and slain it in one fell swoop. More than that, he had chosen his brother over her.

He gazed out of the window, staring at nondescript shop front after shop front. The world began to blur, the cognitive dissonance between where he was and where he wanted to be, growing ever wider.

His brother sat silently beside him, his mind processing what they had just done, what that meant, and what was to come. Sitting in the backseat of a black cab, the two men who had crossed an ocean for a better life, knew they had been dragged from the path they'd planned, back when they were in Peshawar.

Reality snapped them back to London, as without warning, the driver slammed on the brakes, narrowly missing a pedestrian who had stepped out in front of them.

'Bloody pisshead!' he shouted at the man, who'd clearly been enjoying a heavy couple of hours of merrymaking.

The man's suit had probably looked better when he'd put it on this morning. He was so unsteady on his feet, that Akbar Khan wondered if he'd make the other side.

The man paused briefly in front of the bonnet, straightening his blazer, his head bobbing in a way that made it seem as if it was too heavy for his neck. Then, he looked up, pointing his finger at the windshield as if taking aim, his eyes cold, and the tension in the taxi rose a notch. Akbar Khan sensed his brother straighten up beside him, as if in recognition. The man began laughing. He dropped his arm, and stumbled across the road, making his way to the other side of the pavement.

Akbar watched, as he lurched towards the alleyway, his hands flailing for something to keep him upright.

'I'm so glad we don't drink,' he said turning towards his brother, but Bazigh Khan wasn't there. He was on the other side of the road, standing in the alley, having slipped silently out of the car door.

Winding down the window, Akbar shouted after him, but Bazigh didn't turn. He just stood there.

'Oi! Where's 'e going?' said the cabbie to Akbar Khan, his cockney accent dropping the h, in a way that had confused the Khan brothers the first time they'd heard it. 'I can't 'ang around 'ere!'

Akbar Khan stayed silent, trying to understand what was happening. His brain reaching for a fragment of information, adding to it everything he knew about Bazigh Khan, all the while, his eyes on his brother, who was towering over the man that up until a minute ago had been going about his business.

The air seemed to crackle with electricity, as something snapped inside Bazigh Khan and awoke a need for vengeance, a hunger for revenge that he had been nursing since the day he was arrested.

What followed was a volley of punches, the younger Khan brother releasing the full force of his wrath, making contact with the inebriated man's head and torso, over and over again.

By the time Bazigh Khan felt his brother's calming hand on his shoulder, the man was bloodied and bruised. That didn't stop his mouth.

'You motherfucking Pakis,' the man cried defiantly. Akbar Khan stood calmly beside his brother, considering how easy it would be to shoot the man between the eyes with the gun he'd been holding so recently.

'We must go,' said Akbar to Bazigh in Urdu, pulling Bazigh after him so that they were well away from the alley. 'We haven't yet finished what we started. Who was that?'

Bazigh didn't answer, but Akbar could guess.

'It was the policeman who arrested you, wasn't it?'

Bazigh nodded.

And the brothers stood and looked at each other for a long time. 'Motherfucker,' Akbar eventually said in a low voice.

And then the brothers just turned away, the bag with the jewels they had stolen slung over Akbar's shoulder.

Out of their London lives they walked. Out of their arrangement with Henry. Out of everything they knew.

Years later, when Akbar Khan looked back, his only regret was that he hadn't handled things better with Mary. It still hurt him that they had never said goodbye. Not a single one of those diamonds, not even the special one that Henry had so coveted, could make up for that.

CHAPTER 35

1974 onwards

There was something about the way Mary smiled that had seemed to make the world better. With her gone, Akbar's world felt colder. The wintry weather in the north of England didn't help.

The streets were wider, the hills steep, and nights seemed to draw in earlier.

But there was a bigger group of people here like him. Some had brought their wives over.

Every evening, he and Bazigh would hang out at the Taj Mahal restaurant. It was wonderful to eat authentic, familiar food, speak their own language and laugh without judgement.

Akbar felt braver in the north of England. Maybe it was the place, maybe it was what he had done, or possibly it was because he had lost something he cared about deeply, but it had changed him profoundly.

'You should get married,' his brother said to him one day. They were sitting in the Taj, sharing a meal with new friends. One of the men they'd got to know in the last six months had got married, and they were celebrating his walima.

Akbar Khan looked at his brother. They'd been living in each other's pockets since they arrived. And while he loved Bazigh, he longed for female companionship. He missed the gentleness that Mary had brought to his life.

'She isn't coming back, Brother,' said Bazigh, as if reading his mind.

Akbar nodded.

'You need to move on. I wrote to Khala Nafisa last month. She has arranged everything.'

'What do you mean, she's arranged everything?' Akbar Khan looked at his brother with raised eyebrows, surprised at plans being made behind his back.

'Sanam is quite beautiful, and of marriageable age. Look, I never told you this, but Khala confided in me before we left Peshawar. She said our mother always hoped you and Sanam would marry.'

Akbar Khan stayed silent. His mother's dreams for his marriage left him heavy-hearted. But if she were here with him now, would she feel the same? Would she accept a dark-skinned African woman as her daughter-in-law? He knew she wouldn't.

'If I get married, who will look after you?' Akbar said to his brother.

'Sanam has a younger sister, Gulerana, remember? If they came together, they wouldn't miss home so much and would keep each other company while we were at work.'

***

When Sanam stepped off the flight, eyes lowered, Akbar Khan was shocked that she was as beautiful as promised. Her vulnerability endeared her to him immediately, and he knew he must take care of her. Mary had never needed him, and he'd often wished that she had. But Sanam Khan was an old-fashioned Pukhtun woman. She expected him to make the decisions.

He didn't want to begin his marriage with deceit though, and so he told her about Mary. Sanam cried silent tears, her eyes becoming as red as the dupatta that covered her head, and his heart wrenched at causing her distress. But she had nowhere to go and so she said they needn't talk of it again.

The brothers opened a small shop that sold newspapers, fruit and vegetables, and began importing the things that the Pakistani women arriving in the city wanted. Sanam soon tired of the tasteless food in her adopted country, and so they began importing deep-yellow turmeric, chilli powder the colour of burnt sienna and coriander, both as seeds and ground up. Each spice brought with it a tiny bit of home.

'We plan and Allah plans, and surely he is the best of planners,' Akbar said to his wife several years later as they looked at their children gathered on the rug in front of the fire. They had just bought Pukhtun House, a wreck of a building, but whose bones were strong.

'Let me teach you about Surah Fatihah,' Akbar Khan said to his children, taking down his copy of the Quran from the high place he kept it in. It was wrapped in silk, the way his mother had taught him. 'That way, whatever happens, I have put your hands in the hands of our Creator.'

'What is Fatihah, Baba?'

'It is the whole of the Holy Book in just seven verses. We will read it today, but you will spend your entire life finding beauty and nuance in it.'

***

As Akbar Khan's business interests grew, so did his generosity.

He helped the poorer families with food, inviting them to his house for large gatherings, protecting them from embarrassment. He offered them loans when the bank said no. He always did both diplomatically. He spoke words of kindness and encouragement, never judging poor decisions, instead writing them off as bad luck, nudging his people up the hill of achievement.

People began to ask advice and Akbar consolidated his power by helping poor British-Pakistani young men and women through university into careers in law, medicine and politics. He did exactly the same in his homeland, paying school fees, covering the costs of books, pens and uniforms for children who would otherwise have sold cheap plastic combs on the streets of Peshawar to support their siblings. When the time came, he encouraged them to apply for international study programmes, as he did with his own children. They headed to the United Kingdom, to Oxford and Cambridge, to MIT, Harvard and Yale in the US, to Russia, to Nigeria, to Singapore, China and Bombay. His reach began to grow and swell from a river to an ocean.

He was a fixer, an influencer, and he was a kingmaker, but few knew his name. He operated in the highest echelons of society but nearly everything he did was untraceable to him.

Although Akbar Khan strived for diplomacy in all his dealings, there were times when a hammer was the only tool that would do. Early on, as he was starting his business empire, there were families that took his kindness as a sign of weakness. In West London, the Urdu-speaking gangs of Delhi tried to encroach on his territory once they saw how lucrative his drug trade was, intercepting deliveries at Heathrow. The payback was swift and brutal and so extreme that Akbar Khan never had to worry about somebody trying to snatch his territory again.

Akbar Khan saw Henry Paxton shortly before he died, when Jia had arranged to take him out for afternoon tea in London. He was in the hotel restaurant, waiting for her to arrive, when he heard a voice behind him.

'Akbar Khan.'

He turned to find a silver-haired man in a three-piece suit.

'Henry Paxton,' said Akbar Khan.

'Lord Paxton,' corrected Henry. 'But I expect you know that.'

Akbar nodded in acknowledgement.

'What you took from me served you well, I see,' said Lord Paxton as he took in Akbar's expensive clothing.

'I like to think so,' said Akbar Khan. 'My daughter will be here in a moment, so I won't ask you to join me.'

Later that evening, Jia wondered at her father's distraction during their tea. Normally she had his full attention, but on that occasion he had felt remote, his mind somewhere else. She had asked him why, but he hadn't wanted to talk about it.

CHAPTER 36

By the time Jia Khan came to, every part of her body hurt. She'd lost a lot of blood and was unsure of what was happening.

The shadow looming over her knelt down beside her. 'Try not to move,' he said. His voice was concerned, gentle and familiar, but she couldn't figure out where she knew it from. 'Paramedics are on their way.'

Her eyes found focus. It was Idris. The look on his face told her it was bad. 'Hey there, boss,' he said, putting his hand on her shoulder. His voice was softer than she'd ever heard it, full of relief and gratitude that she was alive and conscious. She winced in pain, and he took his hand away. Endless emotions and a sea of questions surrounded her. She felt like she would drown in them.

'Elyas? Lirian?' Jia said. She had no way of knowing if the attack had been meant just for her or for her family too.

'They're safe. I checked on them. I've called in reserves from across the Pennines. I'll call Benyamin again when we get you to hospital.'

'Call Sakina,' she said.

Idris nodded. He didn't know why Jia wanted him to do this, but he knew better than to argue.

A sudden pain shot through her left side and she screamed. She saw the blood on her hands, soaking through from her abdomen to her T-shirt. The adrenaline that had been coursing through her was dissipating, and every cell in her body was waking to what had happened.

Idris eased her out of the gym bag strapped awkwardly across her body. He unzipped it, taking out a pair of boxing gloves.

'Looks like you got lucky,' Idris told her. He held them up so she could see. They were bullet-ridden, the stuffing coming out of them.

Jia felt sorry. These gloves had been faithful servants and were older than some of her relationships, more trusted than many of her friends. They'd been brilliant white when new, with red and black lines running around the wrist strap.

She watched Idris put them back in the bag. She'd been calm until then but something about seeing her gloves unsettled her, and she felt close to unravelling.

'Jia, Ahad is missing,' said Idris gently. He'd been weighing up whether to tell her or not. But he knew if he didn't, he wouldn't be playing fair with her.

'My son...' Jia wailed. She was devastated. She'd made a mistake, an awful, hideous set of catastrophic mistakes, and now Ahad was going to pay.

'Jia, you must go to hospital and get strong for all of us,' Idris urged. 'And I will find Ahad, I promise.'

When the paramedics arrived, Idris hurried off, knowing Maria was minutes away. Jia's sister held her hand as they stretchered her into the back of the ambulance.

'It was Meera Shah,' Jia whispered to her. She didn't know how she was so certain of this when she wasn't a person without enemies, but the moment she said it to Maria, she knew it was the truth. 'Tell Idris. It has to be. And, Maria, take care of my sons. Meera Shah, remember. For me. And Ahad.'

The machines in the ambulance started beeping. And Maria saw the monitor flatlining.

CHAPTER 37

Across the city, oblivious to the attack, Benyamin was describing the Tesla Roadster he had on order to his mates. 'Zero to sixty in 1.9 seconds, and a top speed of 250 miles per hour.'

The crew had grown through the years. Benyamin and Emrose had been at school together. Emrose had arrived as a scholarship student, and the two of them had hit if off immediately. The rest of the crew had been adopted through the passing years since. Their monthly meetups were legendary, but now Emrose was getting married, something Benyamin thought he'd never see. Indeed, the wedding was the next day, meaning they were soon to be in starched shervanis, dancing to the tune of responsibility.

But for now they were in limited-edition trainers and no-logo T-shirts. They were third and fourth generation, with less bling and more self-certainty. These days it was more about thriving than surviving.

'Yeah, that's great, Ben, but can I get my wife and future kids in the back?' said Emrose.

The guys laughed as they sipped chai and ate milk cake in a roadside restaurant.

It had been a journey, but Benyamin understood now what Jia's loyalty was worth. He was proud of his sister and what she had achieved. Others allied themselves to what was easy, he could see, but there were consequences that came with this, and Benyamin understood that a good life should be built on solid foundations. He listened to her, took her counsel and followed through on her requests. He also loved being an uncle, and he didn't want his nephews to have to handle the things he had had to.

Jia's presence in his life and Pukhtun House, and his status in the Jirga that his connection to Jia afforded him, had lessened the cultural pressure Benyamin once felt to behave in a certain way. The idea that manliness meant domination, and aggression was the way to succeed, no longer sat right with him. Not all of his friends had reached this point though.

'You know, only men are chosen for prophethood,' said Emrose, as the conversation moved from cars to faith.

'So?' said Benyamin.

'They're obviously better equipped.'

'Maybe that's not the best thought just before marriage. Maybe it's the world that can't take a woman as a prophet. Remember, Moses was raised in the house of Pharaoh by Asiya. Jesus was raised by his mother.'

'What about the Prophet? His mother died when he was a child and then he was raised by his uncle and his grandfather.'

'He was. But the time from his youth to middle age was spent with Hazrat Khadija. Bibi Khadija was there during his most diffi-cult time.'

'Man, are you comparing your sister to women from Islamic history? Because I've got to tell you, that's some dangerous shit,' Emrose said with a smile.

Benyamin laughed. 'No, but it sounds like you are! When did I mention Jia? What I'm saying is, you're getting married tomorrow, so have some respect for your wife or she is going to kick you into next week. The old days of making you roti and rubbing your feet are long gone, my friend. I'll say this about my sister – she is going to change the world, you watch. And I'm going to be right alongside with her.'

Just as Benyamin's words were out, what felt like every single phone in the dhaba where they were sitting started buzzing.

The collective rings and beeps seemed to spell the end of the world. Benyamin rummaged in his pockets for his own phone. He must have left it in the car.

'Bro, I'm so sorry,' said one of the guys, turning his phone round so Benyamin could read the news he'd received.

Nazar was a nasty thing, and Benyamin regretted what he'd said about Jia just now, but it was out in the ether and had done its work. It didn't matter how educated one was, or how secular, at some time or another, every man and woman who was raised in a Muslim household had wondered if the evil eye was real and if it was upon them.

The men looked at each other, swiping furiously for information.

'Brother,' said Emrose to Benyamin. 'Let's go. I'll drive you.'

The colour had drained from Benyamin's face, and he looked like he was about to vomit. A cascade of thoughts ran through his head, from his mother to sister, to Jia's children. He wasn't ready to be Khan himself, but some would see him as the obvious choice if she were to die. He had thought previously that it would be him one day, but now he knew that could never be.

Jia must live, Benyamin told himself, and he would will her back to life if he had to.

Emrose bundled him into the car, while other friends promised their help if he needed it, offering to drop his wheels back to Pukhtun House. Emrose's green Audi sped out of the car park and down the street, the engine surging.

'It seems Jia Khan is dead, bro,' said one of the crew as the sounds faded away.

'Don't say that out loud, man. The city will fall in on itself.'

'I got another message, but I didn't want to tell Benyamin. Someone's heard his nephew's been taken.'

'Shit.'

CHAPTER 38

They left Ahad with his bag and his phone on the road.

The van pulled up on a one-way street, speeding away after Ahad had been pushed out.

Ahad was confused as to precisely what was going on or what had happened, but once that woman who wanted his fingers cut off had left, he did know the other women were afraid of what they'd done. They'd taken the Khan's son. This would unleash a hell hitherto unvisited upon them.

Ahad lay on the tarmac, bewildered, blinking in the sun. He wrapped his arms around himself. His ribs ached from where that woman had kicked him over and over in the back of the van.

He was found in the foetal position, unconscious.

'Hey, mate, let's get you to a hospital,' said a voice that roused him, trying to help Ahad to stand up. But Ahad pushed him away, disorientated and afraid of what was coming next. 'It's OK, man. Your uncle sent me. We've been looking for you.'

'I've found him,' the man said into his phone. 'Yeah, he's OK, I think.'

Idris had sent out an order to find Ahad. And so a multitude of men had been scouring the streets, as well as guarding Pukhtun House. War had come to their door.

'Put him on the line,' said Idris.

The foot soldier handed Ahad the phone. 'It's your uncle.'

Ahad placed the phone to his ear. 'Idris? My mum?' He didn't even feel embarrassed that his voice shook and he was obviously close to tears.

'She's in surgery, Ahad. She's going to be fine, inshallah. Did you get a look at the guys who took you?'

'I don't know who they were. I was blindfolded.' He felt too tired to say much, and he didn't want to be the cause of any revenge attacks being visited upon a group of women who had made an error of judgement.

He was as much his father's son as he was his mother's. He needed time to think about what to tell Idris. Right now, Jia's life hung in the balance, and the last thing the Khan family needed was to have more oil poured on the fire.

Ahad passed the telephone back to the man, and then vomited on the side of the road.

'I'm bringing him in,' the foot soldier told Idris.

***

They sat in the hospital, waiting for the consultant. The chairs were soft, the sofa hard, and a box of tissues told Maria that this was the room where bad news was delivered.

Maria stared sightlessly at the painting of a daffodil hanging opposite her. It was the colour of sunshine, something that felt dim and distant today. Benyamin was sitting nearby, scrolling on his phone. They'd been here for hours, waiting for news of Jia and her operation. Maria turned her attention to Benyamin, watching his thumb flicking up and down endlessly, knowing he was in pain.

She reached over and touched his hand. 'It's going to be fine,' she tried to reassure him.

He stopped scrolling. 'You don't know that.'

She hugged her little brother and added, 'I know that whatever the news, we'll deal with it together.' Maria was the affectionate sister, the one who wore her heart on her sleeve. Benyamin felt like he would break in her arms, and although she was feeling the same, she made herself strong. This was not the time nor the place. Jia was fighting for her life. Her family had closed their eyes and let Jia carry the burden of everything alone, and now look at what had happened.

'Who picks this shit artwork?' said Benyamin, moving away from Maria, before going back to scrolling. Vulnerability didn't come easy to either of the Khan siblings.

Elyas walked back into the room, tucking his phone into his back pocket before sitting down next to Ahad, who was now out of A & E with strong painkillers and some cuts dressed. Elyas put his arm around him, and the boy rested his bandaged head on his father's shoulder, a faraway look in his eyes. 'Sanam Khan said to keep her updated,' Elyas said to Maria, and Maria nodded, knowing her mother was at home taking care of Lirian.

Idris came in carrying a cardboard tray of coffees and a brown paper bag that he placed on the table in front of them.

He leaned down in front of Ahad, his hand gently holding the back of the boy's head, looking him in the eye. 'I'm going to fix this,' Idris said. 'I'm going to get who did it.' He turned to his cousins. 'There are croissants and Danish pastries in there. I'm afraid they didn't have any protein shakes, Ben, and the coffee's not great.'

Benyamin looked up from his phone. He was googling 'survival rates for gunshot victims'.

They sat together for what felt like hours. Elyas found a box of backgammon and set it up in front of his son. His mind was swimming, and he was going through the motions.

The doctors who'd seen Ahad had said he'd only suffered minor injuries, but the look in his son's eyes worried Elyas. He wondered what had possessed him to come back to this family with Ahad.

He cursed himself for not staying away. There was a small part of him that wished Jia would die on the operating table, leaving him free to take both boys and get the hell out of this place. If she died, they could start again, without secrets and lies. He wondered what kind of man had thoughts like that and was gripped by shame. The air felt heavy, the walls seemed to be tightening around them.

When the surgeon arrived, the oxygen returned to the room. 'Ms Khan is very lucky,' he said. 'The bullet missed her vital organs and exited the other side. She can have a visitor but only briefly – she needs to rest. They're making her comfortable now. Which one of you is Idris? She's asking for Idris.'

'Are you sure it was Idris she said?' Elyas asked in a quiet voice as he felt Ahad tremble beside him in disappointment that it hadn't been him Jia wanted to see. Elyas almost groaned. This served him right for what he had just been thinking.

'Don't take it personally,' said Idris, placing his hand on his shoulder. 'She just wants to keep you safe. And Ahad too.'

He followed the surgeon to where the Khan was waiting, two police officers posted outside her room. Chief Constable Mark Briscoe had been quick to make this call. He didn't want a riot on his watch, and in any case, he had become fond of Jia Khan.

Idris stepped tentatively into the room. He was fine with guns and conflict, but the weaponry of soft emotions wounded him in ways that felt unfathomable.

Jia looked tiny surrounded by various machines and monitors. The wires and tubes coming out of her horrified Idris. It was a combination of bad memories from childhood and the unknown of what was to come.

What had happened was his fault, ultimately. While Jia Khan might forgive him, he knew he never would forgive himself.

She gestured to him to lean in. Idris hesitated at first, then came closer, placing his face close to Jia's. 'We fucked up,' she said in a hoarse whisper.

'Maria told me you think Meera Shah is behind this terrible day,' he replied in a trembling voice.

Jia kissed Idris on the cheek, the way a mother kisses her prodigal son. Fear flooded through him; he couldn't lose more family. He thought of the last time he'd seen his mother, the smell of burning, the hospital, the tears.

'Jia, we've got Ahad back. He's fine apart from some cuts and bruises and is waiting for you outside. He's reluctant to talk about it, but he did say he thought the people involved might have something to do with the Kismet Killings too – there was more than one of them. He says they heard that you'd been hurt and let him go because they became scared when they found out who he is.'

Jia closed her eyes. They'd pumped her full of painkillers but the news about Ahad brought with it a different kind of hurt, one that she could barely stand.

She wished she'd trusted her gut about Meera Shah, but women were always talked out of their instincts. Trust was an evolutionary need. Without it, the human line would not have continued. But her personal experiences had taught her survival, and she should have concentrated on that. She'd known something was coming, she just didn't know it would be *this*. Poor Ahad.

Exhaustion overwhelmed her and Jia fell asleep. But when she woke, she could see the shooter in her mind's eye, as clear as day. It was the security man at Hujra, the one who had taken the elderly couple outside when she'd been there with Elyas.

Jia was livid Meera Shah considered herself above the law of the city. But the fact she was stupid enough to underestimate the justice that would be dispensed by the Jirga didn't make sense.

Someone else must have supported her, Jia saw. Someone powerful.

And the brazenness of the attack spelled trouble for the future that Jia Khan was building for her people. Unchecked, it would destroy everything that she had created.

The question was, what were they going to do about it? Meera was responsible for livelihoods. Taking her out would disrupt the lives of ordinary folk. Removing Nowak had left a vacuum in the lives of those he'd taken under his wing, one she still hadn't been able to rectify fully.

She couldn't let that happen again. She had to be smarter this time. But she was already on the back foot, as Idris had always been the person she'd relied upon in moments of crisis, and now he had proven her wrong by having encouraged her to meet with Meera Shah.

Things were falling apart, and Jia Khan had no one to turn to for help. And for the first time ever, she was starting to doubt her ability to run the Jirga and hang on to the empire she had fought so hard for over recent years.

She closed her eyes and felt the pain ravaging her body. But she refused to give herself another pump of the morphine-rich painkiller on her drip.

Jia Khan needed a clear head if she was to win.

CHAPTER 39

Jia was kept in hospital for a fortnight, even though she was desperate to go home, to sleep in high-thread-count sheets that didn't smell of sterilisation and eat food that didn't taste like it had been boiled to death.

Elyas was by her side a lot of the time, bringing her chocolate and taking her iPad away, trying to get her to rest. He had grown increasingly protective after the shooting and was reluctant to have her discuss business just yet. He had encouraged Ahad to return quickly to university, convinced it was safer for him there.

Jia didn't agree with this, thinking Elyas naive, but she had held her tongue, not wanting to frighten either her husband or son further. She had been cautious, too, when questioning Ahad about what had happened to him. She could see the wounds were deeper than the cuts and bruises left on his skin. What little he told her backed up many of her suspicions without her having to push him on the details. It made her blood boil, but it also made her even more determined to handle things carefully and patiently.

'It's too early for her to go home,' Elyas said when Idris arrived one morning.

'It's where I need to be. But for now I will sit outside the hospital for an hour to see how I get on,' said Jia, climbing into the wheelchair Idris had pushed into the room. She didn't need it, but it was hospital policy that she had to sit in it until she had been discharged.

Elyas tried to protest, saying she was safer with the police outside her room. But Jia insisted.

'There are five of my own burly men outside the hospital who are being paid to keep me safe. Nothing is going to happen to me.'

Her husband didn't look convinced and told her he would wait in the hospital's café until she came back.

Idris pushed her out of the hospital building and across the grounds, towards a patch of hospital garden that was flower-filled in spring. He put the brake on the wheelchair and helped her to a bench. The guards stood nearby.

The sun was warming up now. Jia ran her hands along the dry-stone walls to the side of her, looking out on to the spectacular view. She knew this area well, with its winding roads that hugged the hills as the inclines became steeper, the city nestled in the valley below.

Jia made a promise to herself to walk the streets again as soon as she was able.

'We used to pass these buildings on the way to school,' she said. 'Remember the snicket?'

Idris was glad to hear her speak. She'd been quieter since the shooting, leaving space for his mind to wander to dark places.

'How is the support of the Jirga holding?' she asked.

'They have not forgotten that you've more than quadrupled their earnings. The accounts firm, the investment arm, it's all more than they could have imagined. They no longer have to hide their wealth, and they have more of it than they ever dreamed possible,' Idris tried to reassure her.

'The wealthy have no allegiances to anyone other than themselves,' Jia murmured thoughtfully.

The rich lived in a land without borders. It stretched across the globe, existed beneath all the nation states, money flowing like an underground river with its water carving a path until it was every-where, or nowhere, because that's the way they wanted it to be. The rich enjoyed the privileges of money without the obligations that came with it. And this made them dangerous, and the Jirga was joining their ranks, of this Jia Khan was convinced.

'Paxton did this to me,' she said. 'It may have been Meera Shah who carried it out on the day, but he was behind her every step of the way, I'm sure. We humiliated him over that share trading and look how he has responded.'

Having delved extensively into Henry Paxton's life and business dealings, she knew he was more than capable. And how typical that he had used a pawn to do his dirty work. She'd been piecing together what she knew. 'How else could Meera Shah have got her hands on weaponry? No arms come in or out of Yorkshire without us knowing about it. He met with her earlier this year – you said he was up here on the hunt for business opportunities. He provided her with the investment she wanted and which she'd failed to get from me. It was him. The guns and Shah's confidence shouts it.'

A wave of pain hit in her abdomen as the pills wore off, and Jia clenched her teeth and held her breath till it passed. She let out a sigh. 'How did we get here, Idris?'

'What do you mean?'

'I mean, you let me down. You were one of the main reasons I stayed after Baba's death. I thought together we would clean up and quit. But now... Well, what the fuck am I doing in this city? I had a nice, quiet life. Yes, I was alone, but no one tried to kill me, or take my son, or get to me through him. How the hell are we living this life? This is not normal. This is not how ordinary people live. You do know that?' These thoughts had been going round in her head for days, and she was upset. She needed to get out of the hospital; staring at the same four walls was making her uptight.

Idris looked sadly at Jia Khan, the cousin he'd talked into staying and doing what needed to be done. Sometimes she looked so powerful and strong, and other times she seemed small, like the little girl he'd grown up with. He hadn't had any choice but to convince her to stay. When Akbar Khan died, they'd had few options.

He didn't know if he believed in predestination or not, but he knew they were all playing their parts, and these roles were not going to let them go, even if she and he did try walking away from their responsibilities.

'We are not normal people, Jia,' he said. 'You know this. You can't quit now.'

She looked him dead in the eye, her vision crystal clear. 'Then you take it. It's yours. You run the family empire. Benyamin is too soft and stupid, and Maria too kind – everyone would take advantage.'

'I don't want it,' he said. 'I am not up to it. I know that. You are our Khan, and we all love and believe in you.'

Jia looked away, thinking about all the times they'd been at this hospital. All the losses they'd incurred. How many more would there be?

'He hates me,' she said.

'Who, Paxton?'

'Ahad. He hates me. I can tell by the way he looks at me, and he went back to London the moment he could.'

'Elyas insisted he go to keep him out of this.'

'That's not why Ahad went. Ahad never does anything he doesn't want to do.'

'It'll be fine, inshallah.'

'And what if Allah doesn't will it, Idris? I messed up. It's not like it was when we were kids. Those clear lines our parents taught us don't exist. When we did things they didn't want us to do, they told us to stop acting like white folk. We can't do that anymore – we are more like white people now than we care to admit. It is a terrible admission, but it is true. There is no divide. We've bled into the middle, and I don't know how to bring it back.'

They sat in silence for a while. They had both seen too much of life and its outcomes to disrespect each other with false hope. The birds could be heard singing in the trees to the side of them, and occasionally a car would drive past, causing the guards to straighten up, their gaze never leaving the entrance and exit.

'You're right, I let you down, but not by convincing you to stay. I fucked up over Meera. If you want me to go, I wouldn't blame you for freezing me out,' he said.

Jia shook her head. 'Not unless you want to go, and if you do, it's with my blessing. There's part of me that hopes you save yourself, Idris. However, it's a strategic decision on my part to keep you with me if you stay. And if you do, it will be on new terms.

'I know that you don't want this any more than I do, you just said so. So I'll give you a different kind of out. A good, clean out. Our parents' world is slipping away from us, the circles we move in are changing. You must feel that? We are diluting the Pakistani ways we were raised in. We're not like our forebears, and despite what I said just now, we're not really like the white British either. But our business extends into those communities ever more, and I need someone who understands both sides and their pasts and presents. And you are the best at that there is.'

Idris understood the subtleties of Jia Khan's words. He hadn't admitted it to himself, but even though he and his cousins had made a break from the old order, he didn't quite speak the language of some of the younger men. The various threads of the North's immigrant generations had dropped from his hands when he had moved away, gone to university and left the city. With Akbar Khan gone, the separation between generations was growing, and Idris wanted to find a way to these younger men, men whose own fathers no longer understood them.

'But there are things that are going to be challenging,' said Jia. 'I'll need you to take a rest for a while. Plan a holiday, not just yet, for next year, when things slow down. I don't doubt your loyalty to me, Idris. If you stay at my side, I won't hold Meera Shah against you. Well, not all the time. You're not out and I've listened to your advice. Now I need you to listen to mine. You helped make me the

Khan, but I will make the call. And the call is I want us to work together in a different way.'

Idris felt crushed, but he knew he would accept his fate even though it seemed Jia was sidelining him. Yes, he'd thought he wanted a normal life, but now he was faced with it, the fire in his belly that was growing from a smouldering ember shouted to him that he wasn't ready to quit.

'We will still work together, cousin,' said Jia. 'I want you to focus solely on our legitimate business interests. Sakina will gradually take on the other responsibilities. She understands the way things are as she's not steeped in privilege – at least not like you and I are. We need a clear divide between what we do above board and below. Idris, this empire of crime and violence, I don't know what will happen after I'm gone, but I don't want my boys to be part of it. You will have the responsibility for them on your shoulders. It is the biggest responsibility you can have, and it is a sign of my trust in you.'

The sun was setting in the distance, the sky turning red and streetlights starting to glow. There was a chill in the air.

'And Meera Shah? What do you want to do about her? We can't leave her to get away with this,' said Idris.

'I have a plan for Meera Shah.' Idris shivered at the harsh, cold tone in Jia's voice. And then she added, 'But for now, Henry Paxton is the priority.'

'Our business is the size of a fly in comparison to his.'

'You know what they say about flies,' said Jia. 'We just need to find the right bull, climb into its ear and let it destroy the china shop.'

CHAPTER 40

Maria walked around the classroom, clearing up the children's work-books. It had been a long morning, the kind where she wondered what she was doing still teaching in the inner city when she could easily land a position in a leafy-lane primary, the kind of place where helicopter-parenting pushed kids to achieve. But this was exactly why she stayed, as who else would advocate for her pupils? They needed to see a woman like her at the front of the classroom.

Most of the pupils were of Pakistani heritage, but all the teachers and teaching assistants, except for two, were white. They drove in from the outskirts of the city, the kind of suburbs with farmers' markets at weekends selling twenty-five varieties of cheese to be served with artisanal sourdough bread, and ostrich burgers for the few that were not vegan.

Maria and her husband had visited one of these areas over the weekend. The brown traders had nodded at them knowingly, like they were strangers in a foreign land exploring the souks and bazaars.

'I don't feel safe here,' Maria had said to her husband after a while, and they'd bundled up their baby and driven the sixteen miles back to Pukhtun House, where they'd been offered English Breakfast tea with the scones they'd purchased. 'Will you make me some pakorai?' Maria had asked Hamsa, the young woman who was helping out in the kitchen. 'Do you mind if I watch you make them?' Hamsa had nodded, a little surprised, because the younger mistress who lived in the house usually turned her nose up at fried food, preferring olives, sundried tomatoes and humous, with torn pieces of flatbread.

Maria stood in the kitchen, watching as Hamsa peeled and chopped potatoes, onions and cauliflower ahead of preparing the batter. Hamsa took the yellow and red bag of gram flour from the pantry and measured it by eye into a large bowl, adding salt, garam masala, fragrant cumin seeds and crushed red chilli flakes, before adding water and mixing with her hands. 'You don't measure anything, Hamsa?'

She showed her fingers, moving her thumb along the lines on her index finger to show how she measured different spices.

Maria watched Hamsa dip the vegetables in the creamy batter and drop them deftly into the hot oil. They sizzled and fizzed to the surface, where she lifted them out with a slotted spoon and placed them on a paper towel. She took a jar of green chutney from the fridge and placed it in front of Maria, along with ketchup and a plate.

'I love pakorai with ketchup,' said Maria. Hamsa went back to frying another batch as Maria took the tray of hot, crispy goodness into the living room, where her husband was chatting with Sanam Khan.

Maria thought about the children she taught, the way their culture was evolving. They, like her, ordered chips with their salaan when they ate out, dipping them into the sauce of the tomatoey curries, and they ate ketchup with samosai and pakorai, often under the eye of white friends who could not help but comment and judge, as if it was the English cultural heritage they were bastardising, not Pakistan's.

Then Maria thought back to Friday at school, how she'd wearily pushed the door to the staffroom open to be greeted by a sea of white faces. She'd taken her place to listen to the head's words and opened her lunch box ready to eat her humous sandwich and fruit salad.

'We'll keep it short as we're tight on time,' the headteacher had said. 'We want all children in our school to succeed in an ambitious career and make a positive difference in the world.'

One of the year-5 teachers was sitting with her arms folded across her argyle cardigan. She was the kind of woman who believed her life was a result of 'good choices'.

'I agree,' Maria had said, glancing across at her. 'We should encourage the children to aim high, to be barristers, scientists, CEOs, whatever they can dream of.'

'But what if they want to be cleaners? And if they're happy with that, we should support them,' the year-5 teacher had said.

'Why would we do that?' Maria demanded.

'Well, otherwise we're defining what makes an "ambitious" and "successful" career from the standpoint of our own privilege and not understanding the lives our children live, aren't we?'

Maria had wanted to pick up her fruit-salad fork and stab the teacher in the face.

'What did you do?' said Jia later that evening, eating her pakorai as Maria told her about it. She was sitting up on the sofa and was now well on the road to recovery.

'I said that if the students at Eton are being told they're destined to be world leaders, then ours bloody well will be too. They just stared at me, their mouths open like fish. I wanted to pop a gulab jamun in them, but it would have been a waste of a good sweetmeat.' Maria helped herself to some of Jia's pakorai.

'They're teaching our children but they have no faith in them,' said Jia. 'That hurts everybody.'

'She had a problem with the word "commit" too. Said we shouldn't encourage the children to commit to a goal. Sometimes I think some white people have been eating so much halwa they don't know how to commit to shit.'

Jia almost choked on her water. Maria was usually so measured and good-natured.

'What's wrong with "commit"?'

'Apparently it implies a restriction of freedom, and the kids should have more choice rather than dedicate themselves to something they believe in and work towards that.'

'Not everyone has choices though,' Jia acknowledged.

Maria could only blink crossly at her sister.

She was disillusioned these days. Children with empty lunch boxes, fellow teachers who didn't understand or give brown kids options or allow them to dream. All Maria felt she saw was capped potential, bias and white saviours. This was not what she had signed up for, and it just wasn't enough.

As she lay in bed that night, unable to sleep, Maria decided she could no longer deny the rage that had been simmering inside her; it was getting hotter. It was only a matter of time before it boiled over and scalded someone.

CHAPTER 41

The sun was streaming in and sprinkling light on to the swings in the park. Jia stood next to Costel and looked out across the valley as the children played. It felt good to be on her feet. The view stretched endlessly into the distance, a sea of green hills cut into curved squares by the grey of roads. The cloudless sky reached down to kiss the land. The past few weeks had been intense and she was glad to be out in the open.

She looked back at the grand Victorian neo-gothic museum looming behind her. So much had changed since the days of her childhood, when Akbar Khan and Sanam would bring Jia and her siblings here with a thermos of tea and a picnic blanket. Now she was the one bringing her son here. Lirian was playing in the sandpit with the other children, being watched over by Elyas and Costel's wife.

Idris emerged from the long glass conservatory that ran down one side of the building, a tray of drinks in his hand. The café served cream teas, sandwiches and the best quiche for miles.

His shoulders were open and he smiled easily at Jia as he approached, and she thought he looked as if he was adjusting to his new role and Jia's plan that they should do a slow handover to ease him wholly into the legitimate side of the business.

'Thank you both for meeting me here,' she said to the men.

'It works for me,' Idris replied.

'Childcare is a luxury,' added Costel.

He was the man who'd once been part of Nowak's organisation and to whom Nadeem had taken her to meet last November in that cold, dank house. Jia had asked Nadeem to find him some decent work within the tech side of their operations.

They watched as the children toddled around the sandpit. Jia wondered what Elyas and Costel's wife were talking about, what the rules were for them.

'How is it going, Costel?'

'Good. It helps that, where I work, you have given us access to state-of-the art kit and the freedom to develop new ideas, like the short-selling scheme.'

'I want to make things as easy for you all as possible.' Jia considered her next words carefully. 'Did you manage to give any thought to the problem that I think Idris has spoken to you about?'

'I did. I've been trying to come up with something strategic that we can control from a distance and manage timewise.'

She listened as he sketched out plans, his mind moving in and out of ideas swiftly but with simple explanations. Jia respected ideas, research and academic capital. She'd given Costel the freedom to work on whatever he wanted, and it seemed her faith in the spark of intelligence she had seen in his eyes had been sensible. 'Tell me more about the logic bomb,' she said with a smile.

'A bomb of this type is a set of instructions secretly encoded into a program, and when a particular condition is satisfied, the instructions are carried out. It is a good bet. We get the team to insert logic bombs that freeze a target's assets, and then we hold them hostage until they meet our demands.'

'What kind of conditions could we set for the logic bomb to be activated?'

'Anything really. We can set it to the number of transactions that have been processed, a specific date – this is also called a time bomb. We can even set the malware to contain logic bombs that behave in one way at first, and then change tactics on another date and time.'

'This sounds like what we need,' Jia said to Idris as they walked around the museum afterwards. Elyas had taken Lirian to the toilet.

They entered a room that looked as if it might once have been a ballroom. It was filled with glass cabinets housing stuffed and mounted birds.

'This place hasn't changed since we were kids,' said Jia. She stopped in front of a case containing lots of different birds. There were buttons at the bottom that, when pressed, lit up lights behind each bird and played its call.

'Was it always this creepy?' said Idris.

'Probably. We just didn't know any different.' Jia studied a pair of swans surrounded by their tiny grey signets, thinking that humans were predisposed to have a fascination with the macabre. 'This sort of taxidermy wouldn't be legal now. These days it's mostly performed on creatures that are already dead.'

Idris tapped gently on a display case. 'I'm sure this family of tawny owls is relieved to know they didn't die in vain.'

'Someone always pays a price for change,' said Jia. 'I just wish it didn't have to be us any longer. The pace of change is so much slower than I'd hoped when I became Khan. I worry it will destroy us before long.'

'I know. But what choice do we have?'

'You're right. I'm just feeling a little fragile today. I'm not sure if the Khan is allowed to admit that.'

'If Tony Soprano can go to therapy, I think you can admit to this. We are a trauma-informed criminal organisation,' said Idris. 'We don't run from our past, we weaponise it, remember. Besides, you may be fragile, but you're fragile like a logic bomb.'

Jia laughed. She needed a day like today, a few low-key hours filled with sunshine and honesty.

Running the family business was taking its toll on her. As a barrister she had worked endless hours with no one to come home to, days had run into weekends, and she had lost herself in her profession.

It had loved her back and rewarded her with money, accolades and success.

Life with a family and the responsibilities that came with being the Khan had firmly put an end to that. Jia thought her body was starting to rebel against the pressure she was putting it under.

Her mind flicked back to work. 'Get Costel the team he needs and let's start this process. It's time Lord Paxton was taught a lesson. No more falling upwards for this mediocre white man.'

'And Meera Shah?'

'I'll handle her.'

CHAPTER 42

A couple of weeks later, things were taking shape.

The mill looked like any other start-up incubator. The security man stood aside as Idris approached the glass-fronted double doors, the young woman at the reception desk having conveniently taken a comfort break at this exact moment. Bribes still went a long way to helping gather intel, smooth over transactions and gain access to buildings. Like this one.

Idris reached inside his jacket pocket. The grey card had been created by one of the trainees at the Opium Den, one of Jia's companies which, despite its name, was more to do with cyber analysis and digital money laundering than any drugs. Hacking the front end of just about any organisation was pretty much foundation-level antics for the men and women at the Opium Den.

The security turnstiles opened without resistance, allowing Idris, Jia and some fifty men to step through.

The receptionist arrived after they'd gone through into the offices, the door swinging shut behind them. She took her seat as if nothing had happened and began to file her nails.

Light the colour of honey filtered across the warehouse floor. This room was normally a hive of activity with workers taking calls and tapping away on their keyboards, but today something was wrong. An outage had stalled activity. The workers were sitting quietly at their desks, but a deeper hush descended, confused glances were exchanged, as the room filled with Jia's men.

Idris walked ahead of the group of men, who were ready to do whatever it took for Jia Khan. She came in last. She had not consulted the Jirga over her requirements and instead had demanded firmly what she needed.

The Jirga had responded swiftly, eager to help. The money their family businesses were bringing in due to Jia's leadership was enough to keep them in line. For now.

Meera Shah's main man, short and red-faced, ran out of his office. 'How did you get in here?' he shouted. 'Security. Security!'

He was in charge of running the operation, the sweat patches on his shirt indicating the stressful morning he'd been having and his fury at the unexpected glitches.

But Idris already knew this. Indeed, he was the one who had suggested it to Jia. 'We send in some small virus, one that demands a ransom. While they're busy sorting that, we'll hack into the back end and take it all down.'

'We're the cavalry,' he said now to the office manager. 'You seem to be having a little trouble, no?'

The office manager's eyes widened. Shit! So they'd been hacked. And Meera would blame him, his worst nightmare. He looked around for the security guard, but there was nobody there and full realisation dawned that an already grave situation was much worse than he'd thought.

'We know everything worth knowing,' said Jia, stepping forward as her men went to stand beside every desk like sentinels.

The warehouse was about a hundred metres end to end, with windows running right the way around. Thick horizontal girders held the walls up, and equally strong, grey columns stood like soldiers down the length of the former textile mill.

The invaders were silent, and the fact that they were so confident without weapons on display made them more imposing.

Jia peered casually at a screen over the shoulder of a young woman seated at a desk, picked up some paperwork, perused it. Dressed in a geek-chic unzipped hoodie and a T-shirt declaring 'Gabbar is my homeboy', the young woman stared nervously at her keyboard.

Jia smiled at the reference. 'I always wanted to be more Jai than Gabbar,' she said to Idris as if they were just having a chat.

'Well, look how that turned out,' he replied.

Jia turned her attention back to the screen and carefully studied the call centre script the woman had been following. '*Sharia-sanctioned halal investment opportunity,*' Jia read out loud, and then went on, '*YourCoin – British Crypto Coins for British People. The world's best cryptocurrency, guaranteed to make you rich while helping end poverty.*'

Below there was information on e-commerce and e-currency, simplistic ways of explaining blockchain. The con was impressive, targeting every corner of the market, from far right to liberal left, and touching religious bases in between.

Quickly, she copied the material into another document and AirDropped it to her phone.

'One mustn't believe everything one hears, should one?' she said to the office manager, who looked at the point of passing out. She held his eye in a lengthy silence, in which one really could have heard a pin drop.

'Let's talk in there,' Jia Khan said to Idris in a voice that cut the tense atmosphere, and everyone relaxed a little as she gestured to a large glass-walled room to the side of the mill floor.

Jia stopped at the doorway to the break-out space and turned to face the room. 'One last thing,' she said. 'I am Jia Khan. And I am *the* Khan.' Abruptly she turned and went inside, closing the door behind her.

The sentinels remained at their stations, their stoicism a sharp contrast to the emotional upheavals being felt by the start-up's employees, and the office manager made a hasty exit in the direction of the toilets.

The workers looked at each other with no idea of what to say or do, or what was to come. Were they about to be fired? Or worse?

They all knew who Jia Khan was the moment she had walked in. There were few in the city who didn't. Many of them had applied to work at her organisation and not made the cut. Meera Shah had offered the only alternative in town.

One thing they did all know for certain was that they had just witnessed Jia Khan throwing down a very public gauntlet, and none of them wanted to be around for Meera Shah's response.

'You were right to suggest we come here,' Jia said to Idris. He nodded. 'We have frightened them, but now we need their loyalty.'

'Did you hear that?' Idris said, moving towards the filing cabinet.

'No,' said Jia. 'I can't hear anything.'

'Listen…' he said. They fell silent.

Then a tiny sound. A squeaking. It was coming from a corner of the room, like a nail on a chalkboard.

Jia shrugged. 'Get Gabbar in here,' she said.

Idris went out and came back with the girl in the *Sholay* T-shirt.

Jia smiled at the young woman, who stood with her arms folded defensively across her chest, her shoulders hunched.

'What's your name?' said Jia, moving round to make sure that the woman was standing with her back to the glass wall, in case there were any lip-readers on the other side. She stepped up close so that her face couldn't be seen either.

'Mishal.'

'Do you know what happened here today, Mishal?' asked Jia. 'Before I walked in.'

'A hack with a ransom. A wormhole. Probably with a logic bomb.'

'Do you know who I am?'

'Everyone knows who you are. And anyway, you have just told us.'

'Good. Then we are halfway to where we need to be. Firstly, it's important you understand that I'm on your side, Mishal, and secondly, that Meera Shah has been taking money from people who can't afford it. I want to know if any of you were aware of this?'

The girl looked uncomfortable. 'Our job is to sell coin packages to a list of people we're given to call. There's a small bonus if we can add to that list, so, as it seemed like people were making a big profit, I persuaded my friends and family that it was a good thing and they couldn't lose. But recently I overheard gossip that there is no crypto, no blockchain, that it's all a hoax. I didn't know what to think – maybe someone was just stirring up trouble. So I contacted your brother, Ben. I know him a little through my big brother from back in the day.'

Jia nodded. It was what she'd expected, and she was relieved to hear Mishal's account tallied with what Benyamin had said.

Mishal hadn't been the only one worried. Jia's network was picking up other rumbles of discontent, whisperings that were filling the void left by a currently inactive Kismet Killer. But the fact that Benyamin had history with this source convinced Jia the fruit was ripe for picking.

Jia leaned forward so that her face was close to Mishal's. 'I can fix this, but I will need you and your team on board. This is a choice, and you must make up your own mind. But if you decide not to help me, then those friends and family you mentioned will lose all of their money. That is how it is.'

The girl nodded.

'I'm going to need you to keep an eye on your colleagues and make sure they all understand who's in charge now. But don't be obvious – if they ask you what we've been talking about, tell them I was making you go through the script you used to sell the coin packages. Now, can you send them in?'

Soon, every member of staff was standing before Jia in silence, the sentinels against the wall, staring them down.

Jia heard the squeaking sound again. It seemed to be coming from behind one of the filing cupboards.

'What's that noise?' she asked the office manager.

'A mouse. It has its tail caught in the trap. We're waiting for it to die so I can dispose of it.'

Jia looked at Idris in disbelief.

'Do you not have pest control or humane traps in this place?' Idris asked.

'Meera expects us to sort these things out ourselves,' the manager said.

'Move the cabinet,' ordered Jia.

Sure enough, the mouse's tail was caught in a red-and-white trap. Jia reached down, released the mouse, holding its tail, and picked it up. She dropped the wriggling body into a half-filled glass of water somebody had left on the table, and then she pressed a finger on it until it had drowned.

When it was over, she handed the glass to the office manager.

'You let your fear make you cruel,' she said. And then Jia turned to Idris and added, 'He who doesn't show mercy does not deserve mercy. Have one of our men escort this man off the premises. And make sure he doesn't work in this city again.'

CHAPTER 43

Investment was the next part of the plan, and for this they needed contacts in new businesses and industries that were more halal than their usual line of work. And they needed someone who had nothing to do with the Jirga or the family businesses, someone Jia Khan could trust.

Dressed in jeans, a blazer and black trainers, Jia looked like everyone else in Silicon Roundabout. Her face hidden behind dark glasses, hair tied up and tucked under a baseball cap, she walked down Old Street towards the tube station.

Adam Diaz had come through for her. 'I always wanted to work with you,' he'd said.

They set up a small office in Tech City. It wasn't really needed, but it gave them the respectability of a postal address in the right area of London, people being narrow-minded when it came to companies based in northern towns. All kinds of fraud went on in London and no one judged the city, but such forgiveness was not held for places north of the Watford Gap.

This was a legitimate business interest, as Jia wanted no excuse for it to fail. She headed to the hotel where she was meeting a client whose business had suddenly become highly lucrative.

'Once your name is taken off the asset, it's disappeared,' she explained to him. 'We know several banks that can help with this process. It's perfectly above board. We set up a series of shell corporations here in the UK. Register them with Companies House, open a bank account in the Bahamas or the British Virgin Islands, Jersey, Switzerland, it's up to you.'

'Why British companies? Surely this is a red flag to HMRC. I mean, our justice system is pretty robust.'

'British companies look legitimate, but it takes twenty minutes to set one up online. There are four million of them registered. We can create a chain of shell corporations long and complicated enough so that no one will come after you.'

'How can you be sure?'

'Because the authorities don't have the manpower or funds for thousands of investigative hours, and in any case, they're not interested.'

'What's to stop me doing this myself, or getting one of my people to do it?'

'Nothing. You can do it. You can use multiple companies to own multiple bank accounts in multiple jurisdictions. But you still won't sleep at night because you'll know where the bodies are buried. And, frankly, you'd be right to be worried, as without the expertise, you might make mistakes. But we have that expertise and we are meticulous. Let me handle this for you, and you can have a restful night's sleep on the Egyptian cotton sheets I'm sure you love so much. Every night.'

The entrepreneur had already made his decision before the meeting. Jia Khan came highly recommended, and Adam Diaz's seal of approval also meant he was more likely to help with the next round of fundraising. Jia's services were highly sought after, and rumour had it that she was about to close her client list. But he was dithering over the technicalities of compliance to keep it above board.

'I will make it simple for you,' Jia told him, and he believed her.

They shook hands on the deal, and Jia called Idris to confirm the start of a new business chapter from a café nearby.

It might not have been possible were it not for Paxton's arrogance all those months earlier at dinner, and Jia's gently leading questions about his business as she'd looked at him with doe eyes. He hadn't been able to resist boasting, oblivious to the thoroughness with which Jia Khan was picking his brains.

The best part of it was that none of it was illegal, and they could clean their own cash alongside too. They were merely exploiting loopholes that had been created decades earlier to keep city bankers rich and London flourishing.

The café was busy, and Jia could hear discussions on latest leadership trends, the power of regret, the monetisation of digital media. 'How self-important we all are,' she thought.

She watched a couple sitting with their son; he was on his iPad as the man and woman talked. The woman was slim and preppy, the man equally so. She wondered what it would be like to be ordinary like this, to be carefree, to believe oneself to be the sun around which the world orbited.

On her way back from the restroom, Jia saw that their chairs were blocking her path back to her table. She waited for them to move, but neither of them looked up. Years earlier, when she had started out in adult life, she would have apologetically asked the couple to make space for her, but she didn't do that anymore.

Instead, she found herself intrigued by the games. She no longer felt the need to appease, and so she simply took up room.

She watched the man sigh and then make way.

People like this had no idea of the approaching tsunami, one that would wash away their comfortable lifestyles. Power had shifted to China and India, while African nations were taking back what had once been taken from them. One only had to look at the heads of the world's biggest tech companies, the holders of our personal data, to see that.

No amount of tennis, piano or tutoring would give the children of a couple like this access to a world they had long ignored and looked down upon. They had no idea that the British would become butlers to the people they had once ruled over, and Jia Khan couldn't help but smile.

CHAPTER 44

The attempt on Jia's life had rattled Elyas.

He'd stayed out of his wife's business for the last few years, partly because journalism was the only thing he felt he knew how to do and partly because of timing. After Akbar Khan's death, Jia had quickly fallen pregnant thanks to their resuscitated relationship, and Elyas hadn't wanted to do anything that would make her bolt. And then, when the baby came, they'd become so busy in the day-to-day of it all that there hadn't seemed time to discuss anything other than practical matters.

If he was honest with himself, though, Elyas had known more about what went on than he wanted to admit. He had been too good a journalist not to; although these days he deliberately avoided covering any stories that seemed too close to home. He wanted to shut out the parts of Jia's life that scared him and throw away the key.

He didn't like conflict in his personal life, and Jia Khan had already left him once before.

But now everything was coming to a head, and he needed to keep his sons safe, he had started once more to be the investigative journalist that he'd been when he first qualified.

'Jia, I never ask you about your work,' he said one evening. Lirian was asleep and they were getting ready for bed. 'I know where the line is,' he added, pulling on his T-shirt. 'I know what you do, and I made peace with it. Or I had.'

Jia stuck her head out of the en suite and looked at him with an unreadable expression.

'But you nearly died, and Ahad could have too,' Elyas went on, determined to have his say. 'And it seems this woman from the restaurant where we took our small son that night, this Meera Shah, tried to have you killed. You've not said that to me, but this is what Benyamin tells me.'

Jia decided she must have words with her brother; she thought he knew not to say anything about the family's business to Elyas, even though he was her husband.

Elyas clearly knew his wife well as he spoke the first word of his next sentence very loudly to steer Jia's mind away from thinking about Benyamin and concentrate on what he was saying. 'Anyway... Anyway, I've been looking into Meera Shah's background and I've found several sources who have told me that if someone owes her money and doesn't pay, she has them killed. If she owes money, she kills the person she owes. If she doesn't like the way someone looks at her, she has them killed. I expect you see where I am going with this.'

Elyas's face was sombre, his eyes afraid, as his voice quietened. 'And, Jia, I'm willing to put money on the fact that Meera Shah is behind the Kismet Killings.'

Jia put down her water flosser. 'This is what you've been doing instead of working on your book?'

Elyas gazed at her. With her face washed clean, her hair tied back, a slight glow on her cheeks, normally these moments were when he felt Jia Khan belonged only to him, as if she were still the girl he'd first married. But not that night. She wasn't that girl. She was someone else: a woman who now had a price on her head.

She walked over to the bed, put her hand on his arm and kissed him on the cheek. 'Try not to worry,' she said. She took off her robe and climbed into bed, resting her head against the upholstered grey of the headboard.

'She used to be a people smuggler too,' Elyas said, to show that the kiss hadn't mollified him.

'You've really done your research on this,' said Jia. 'I know, I know – you are a journalist, and this is what you do.'

Jia was tired and she wanted Elyas to stop talking. She understood her husband's concerns, but she didn't want to be worrying about him on top of everything else right at this moment.

'I think I should take Lirian to London,' Elyas said.

'For how long?'

Elyas didn't answer.

'For how long?' Jia pressed.

'I don't know,' said Elyas. 'For as long as it takes to…'

'Finish the sentence,' she said. 'What are you really saying?'

'I'm not saying anything other than that.'

'If you're leaving me, be brave enough to say it.'

'Jia, I want to leave this city. I know you have things to do here. I'll not stand in your way.'

'No.'

'What do you mean, no?'

'You're not taking my son,' she said. 'I won't let you. You already took one of them and that didn't turn out well – you remember the trouble he used to get into.'

'And you hold me responsible for that? Can you hear what you're saying?' Elyas asked.

'And you're not thinking it through, that you make me seem vulnerable if you are seen to be taking Lirian away.'

'It's not always only about you, Jia!'

Jia had to try very hard not to shout as she said, 'Isn't it, Elyas? It really is all about me in so many ways and you know it.'

Elyas looked at Jia as if he didn't recognise her anymore.

He'd been so afraid of losing her that he had turned a blind eye to what she had become. And what a mistake this was turning out to be.

His feelings for her paled in comparison to the love he had for his sons. Elyas had far more to lose by staying silent and doing what she wanted. 'Don't think that because I love you, Jia, I will stand by and watch you destroy our children's lives,' he said.

'You don't know what I'm capable of, Elyas,' she said, turning away from him. 'Don't make me show you.'

CHAPTER 45

Idris stared into the fridge. It had been a long day and he needed to eat. He was tired of take-aways and too weary to cook.

But the fridge, like so much of his life, was empty, except for a box of olives, a few cold cuts and a carton of orange juice that had been there for a long time. He pulled out the juice, taking a glass from one of the overhead cabinets and setting it on the cold granite worktop. He poured a little into the glass and took a sip. Then he poured the rest of the bottle down the sink.

He'd have to settle for tea and toast. He opened the double doors to a pantry that concealed the small appliances normally found on countertops. Pouring water into the kettle, and dropping two slices of bread into the toaster, he waited, thinking through the day's events.

His relationship with Jia was straightforward, clear cut, and he liked it that way. He knew what was concealed and what was revealed; that was his job. Her asking him to take a step back had hurt. He was family in a way that Sakina was not, although she was Jia's closest woman confidante and Girl Friday, and so who knew what the two of them talked about when they were alone. She was younger than him and she was Punjabi. His people had little respect for hers, regarding them as uncouth farmers who drank too much and ate even more. Idris had always considered himself accepting and open-minded, so this thought took him by surprise, and he flushed with shame, an emotion he was uncomfortably familiar with these days.

He'd been wrong about Meera Shah, and because of this he knew that he did need to have a bit of air between him and Jia so that he could look at things with fresh eyes.

He considered what his father, Bazigh, had told him about Jia and her mindset, about the things that had transpired between her and Ahad when he was a baby. He didn't see it the way Bazigh Khan did – that Jia Khan was willing to do whatever needed to be done to save her family. Bazigh Khan believed Jia Khan to be ruthless.

Instead, Idris saw a complex woman with many facets, who was loyal to her cause. Jia loved her family and would live, die and kill for them. She had clearly been unwell when Ahad was born, and this was no sign of weakness.

Idris heard the doorbell. He checked the video monitor on the wall and pushed the buzzer, before walking to the front door to let her in. She slipped off her shoes in the hallway, placing the red trainers next to Idris's in the cloakroom.

'I'm making toast – would you like some?' he said.

She nodded, following him into the kitchen. She took a seat at the island, watching him add more bread to the curved green KitchenAid toaster.

'How's Jia?' she asked.

'Better now, well on the way to a full recovery. Smashed avocado?' he said, pulling the ripe fruit from the bowl.

She smiled and watched him add lime juice, a couple of red and orange flakes of dried chilli and a grind of salt and pepper to the mashed avocado, before arranging it on to two of the slices of toast. He wiped a smidge of green from the plate with a paper towel and placed the dish in front of her, alongside a knife, fork and napkin.

They ate in silence. And when they'd finished, Idris cleaned the plates away swiftly, and then he said he'd make more tea.

He opened a cupboard door to expose row upon row of teal and golden tins, all labelled. 'What kind of chai do you like?' he asked.

'You decide,' she said.

She liked being looked after, not having to make the decisions. As the eldest daughter of a widowed mother, it was not something she'd ever experienced. She moved to the sofa and watched as he carried over a tray with two small cups and a black teapot on it and placed it in front of her.

'Shall we get to business, Sakina?' he said, smiling.

She nodded and swung her legs on to the sofa, tucking her feet underneath.

He saw how much she liked being here, and Idris realised he felt the same.

CHAPTER 46

Jia Khan checked her watch. She drummed her fingers on the desk and then, after what seemed an age, checked it again. Only a minute had passed. She waited for the receptionist to finish her call. She checked her watch a third time, then realised what she was doing.

The knots in the back of her neck ran like rocks either side of her spine as she fought not to look at the watch again. She took a deep breath, removed her Tag Heuer and slipped it into her pocket. Her father had given it to her as a gift when she started university and she'd worn it almost every day since then.

But she had no need for timekeeping this weekend. She was learning to unwind. Supposedly.

She'd just arrived in Edinburgh, away from everyone who knew her and far from the responsibilities and demands placed upon her by work.

She put her phone in sleep mode. She stared at the blank screen, tempted to turn it back on and check one last WhatsApp, but resisted. She would put it in the safe once she got to her room, as she had promised her husband. It was part of the tacit deal between them, with the unvoiced accusation that she was burnt out.

'I can't be completely absent,' she'd said to Elyas.

He'd booked her the trip after their argument. They'd not spoken about it again but were still circling each other.

'I know,' he said. 'That's why I've got you this.' He handed her something small, gold and black.

'What is this?' she said, flipping it open. 'Can I call the *Enterprise* on this?'

He smiled at the reference. 'It's a dumb phone, for people like you. You can make calls from it but nothing else. It means we can call you if we need to. But it's not a smart phone, and you're not to take a laptop or iPad.'

Jia smiled at him, not having the heart to point out that she could easily buy a burner phone to reconnect herself to the digital ether. She was bone tired, and so she'd sat in silence, her hand in his. Maybe, just this once, she should do what her husband told her to.

Elyas made her visit the GP, booking the appointment for her and scheduling it with Idris. He'd even driven her to the doctor's, waiting in the car as she went in.

'Your blood tests show that you are vitamin-D deficient, but that's pretty standard in South Asians,' the doctor said. She shared Jia Khan's heritage and was probably a decade or so older.

'I'm just a little tired,' said Jia. 'I have a toddler, and so I don't know if it's parenthood or perimenopause,' she'd said, making light of the situation.

The GP checked her date of birth. 'It's probably a little of both.'

It felt like only yesterday when she'd first started her periods, and here she was almost at the end of that journey.

'*A lot of women get divorced around this age, as some women feel extreme annoyance with their partner.*' Jia had read this in a women's magazine in the waiting room, and she suspected it to be true.

'How are you feeling about it?' Elyas asked her as they waited for the HRT prescription to be filled.

'Mixed feelings. So much of who I am has been defined by my youth, my looks, even my ability to have a baby. This feels like a formal notice of the end of all that. But I don't want it to be the end of Jia *Khan*.'

She'd thought about it all on the train journey to Edinburgh. Once she was settled in her room, she sat by the window, looking out at the square, an empty page of hotel notepaper in her hand – the failed attempt at writing a letter to Ahad – an ancient oak tree framed in the oval window by beautiful teal walls and mustard-coloured velvet drapes, Billie Holiday crooning from the radio about bad men, love and heartbreak.

She headed to the spa, hoping that a dip might help. The water was warm as she eased herself in, the perfect temperature, and she had the place to herself. She began to swim, feeling the tension in her neck depart with each length. She turned over and floated on her back, looking up at the spotless white ceiling. She had always been fascinated by the dead man's float, that when one stopped fighting to survive, the water held you up.

Slipping on a towelling dressing-gown and sitting by the low-lit swimming pool, she finally understood whom she needed to call for help, although she was still reluctant. She was supposed to be independent and without need for anyone else's help, wasn't she?

She returned to her hotel room, looked through her overnight case for her book. Her hands fell on the white jar of body cream her sister had given her when she was leaving.

Maria knew cosmetics better than anyone else she'd ever met. The scent of sweet almond oil and rose felt luxurious as Jia rubbed the rich cream on to her arms and her legs. She thought of her sister, of all the ways they were the same and all the ways they were different, of how much that difference enriched her life, and the similarities that made her feel safe. She picked up her phone and dialled.

'How come you're not video calling?' said Maria.

'Because Elyas made me swear to turn off my phone,' she said. 'He gave me this device that looks like it's straight out of *Star Trek*.'

Maria laughed. 'And are you relaxing?'

'Not really.'

'Why don't we ever talk about your work?'

Maria's question took Jia by surprise. She had always felt there was an unwritten rule between them not to discuss the family business. She thought about her reply carefully before deciding to go with honesty.

'I worry that once I tell you, I can never take it back.'

'I'm not a child anymore,' said Maria. 'I was, and even as an adult, I was glad that you protected me. But things are different now, and you need me.'

'You don't know what you're asking.'

'I do, Jia. Just because I've not been looking doesn't mean I can't see. Half the kids at my school know who we are. Do you seriously think I don't? And now I want in on the family business.'

Maria knew more about the city than Jia. She had been born and raised there and had chosen to stay. She worked in schools that were full of kids with abilities but whose potential was being squandered because of a whole range of things.

'Last week we went to Whitby on a school trip.' Maria filled the silence when Jia didn't reply. 'The kids were so excited to walk on the beach, eat fish and chips, go somewhere new. You know what happened? Overt racism. People stared at them as they walked along the streets, and they were called names, and the white teachers stepped in, but that made it more complicated rather than better. We teach these children about the Romans and Saxons and the British Empire, and we leave out the rest of the world. The white kids are raised up and the global majority kids are sucked down by the vacuum that's left. The woke white generation is the worst, the one that's telling its kids to save us. Our kids do not need saving. They need opportunities. They need the same opportunities as their white friends, and they need access to the same confidence-building beliefs. I have been planting the seeds and watering their self-esteem for years, telling them they are good and clever and worthy, and I see the disappointment in their tiny faces when they go out into the world and find that the world doesn't value them. I know you are changing that. Let me help you, Jia.'

'I'm not sure,' said Jia. 'People like me, we live outside of the law, we break the rules, we rebel, we can live on our own terms. We pay a price for this, though, and it is a high price. But I guess there is always a price. The trick is to know which problem you're willing to have.'

CHAPTER 47

Sakina watched Jia as she asked the cashier for a lipstick shade at Chanel.

Sakina looked through the colours, trying them on the back of her hand. She usually wore reds, but something about the subtler tones was appealing today. She admired a tawny pink but put it back when she realised the price.

'We'll take the lipstick my friend was just looking at too,' said Jia, handing her card to the cashier. 'In a bag please for her.'

'Of course, madam.'

Jia took her own lipstick and handed Sakina the black bag, knowing that Sakina would enjoy having something with a prestigious logo.

'A luxury handbag has become shorthand for status. And these days it's the same for the packaging our make-up and clothes come in,' Jia told the younger woman. 'When I was at school, the carrier bags for PE kit were important. I used to keep a nice one from a department store just for my kit. A Netto bag spelt social death.'

Sakina listened carefully, the way she did with everything Jia Khan said.

'I grew up a Bourjois girl. When I was a teenager, the rumour was that Bourjois make-up was made by the same people who made Chanel,' Jia told her. 'I used to buy all the little pots of eyeshadow in purples and pinks, and the different shades of blush. They smelt so delicious, as if they were candies. And now it's hard to buy in the stores.'

Sakina knew this wasn't true. There was a world of difference between her and Jia Khan, a chasm that was created by class, education and money. She wasn't naive enough to think that she could ever close the gap, but she did know that the opportunities the Khan was offering her would mean, one day, her children would have less distance to jump, and their children might not even need to make the leap. She was no longer selling her body to feed her family, but she wasn't living within the law, and it was unlikely that she ever would.

'How is Ahad?' she said to Jia.

'He's getting better. I'm sure he'll need therapy, but how do I find him someone he can be honest with about all this?'

Under different circumstances, Sakina would have been able to recommend the perfect therapist, someone she knew personally. But that was impossible now. The thought of that friend made her nervous. She would have to tell Jia sometime, but it would lead to a complicated conversation, a conversation that would implicate others, endanger their lives even.

But maybe it was time.

Ahad's abduction hadn't been her friend's fault, or those other women's. But they had been there. And while they weren't guilty of hurting Ahad, there was blood on their hands.

Sakina had been carrying their secret around with her for long enough, since that panicked phone call the day after the attack. She had been waiting for the right moment. Maybe this was it, although it could damage her growing friendship with Jia Khan.

CHAPTER 48

'It's good you've made the decision to have it removed, because it's dangerous,' said the tree surgeon. 'In this state it could fall at any time. Removing it today means you take back control of your garden and keep your family safe.'

He worked steadily through the day, pollarding and pruning, until the tree was bare. Jia was working from home and watched from the kitchen as he cut a wedge out of the trunk, ready for it to be felled.

'The end of an era,' Benyamin said.

'Yes, it is,' she replied. She had put off this day for a long time. 'We played a lot under that tree, do you remember?'

He nodded, recalling the summers of hide and seek, tag and ball games. 'My earliest memories are of you reading under that tree. I miss those days.'

'Me too,' she replied. 'I'd do anything to give them back to all of us.'

He put his hand on his sister's shoulder and kissed her head. They were far from the time when she towered over him. For a long while they hadn't been close, but they had found their way back to each other in the last few years, only because they had both wanted to. Sakina had been instrumental in this process, and Benyamin was grateful to her, feeling that sometimes strangers had the clearest insight into what was wrong. The trick was being able to hear and handle the truth once it was presented.

'It's not your job always to keep fixing things, sis.'

She smiled. 'You're right, I know that. But old habits are hard to break.'

They watched in silence as the tree hit the ground, ready to be woodchipped and carted away.

'Are you seeing Sakina later?' asked Jia.

'Not today, she's been busy recently. I think she's seeing someone.'

'Really? Are you OK with that?'

'Makes no difference to me.'

'I thought you might be interested in her.'

'If I was, would it have been all right with you?'

'Because of her past as a street girl you mean? I don't know. Maybe I'd worry about how you would handle it the closer you got and the more you thought about it.' Jia wondered if women were ever forgiven for the things they had had to do to survive.

There was pretty much nothing that a rich or handsome man could do that could not be forgiven. And in some families, societies and cultures, it was not necessary to be rich or handsome to be forgiven. You just had to be male.

For women, the line was wafer thin, and once crossed, it solidified into something so hard that it could never be removed. One had to learn to live with it, like a blot on the landscape.

Jia knew she had a lot of blots on her landscape.

CHAPTER 49

The hotel had that smell of money. Sakina wondered if it was a fragrance they pumped through the building to make it this way. The effect seemed to be that people stood a little taller, their backs straighter, their eyes colder.

She glanced at a couple of young children dodging around the orange marble pillars that ran, two by two, down the length of the foyer. The black, white and grey of the marble floor shone to a sheen but without being slippery.

'Rich people look different, don't they?' Sakina remarked. 'It's the way their skin glows, as if gold is coming out of their pores.'

'It's the small things,' said Idris.

Sakina nodded. These women could afford to have manicures, to have their hair coloured regularly. They bought new shoes because they could, not because the heel had worn down until it could no longer be repaired. It was the tiny things. Sakina thought of the girls she'd worked with, who were worried about bills and how they would feed their kids some breakfast, and the way they couldn't get real jobs because the high cost of decent childcare was prohibitive to them, no matter how many punters they serviced. 'Every problem is solvable for the rich,' she said.

'Not quite every problem,' said Idris.

'Almost everything.'

Sakina inspected her hands. Her nails were clipped, but she hadn't had time to file them, and the tips of her thumbs felt dry. She caught a glimpse of herself in the mirror across the room. Her mascara had smudged slightly, and her foundation had gone a little patchy. She felt shabby here. She worked hard not to feel like this, but somehow she never quite got the knack that other women seemed to have instinctively. She wondered if she would ever feel adequate.

A tall, tanned man in a navy coat walked past, arranging the scarf of his girlfriend lovingly around her neck. The two children were now running around the pianist, their mother calling out to them from her sofa. A nanny was quick to shepherd them towards her and she gathered them up into a hug.

Sakina couldn't help wondering what her life would have been like if she'd had the connections of the wealthy. The ease with which they picked up the phone to call someone when they needed something doing. Everyone knew everyone else. That was how the work was done.

Idris read her expression. 'You can't let your mind go there. It will kill you. I feel the same way. I wonder if people like us get to live normal lives and do the things others do without having to watch our backs.'

She didn't know how he did it, but he seemed to answer her questions even before they formed on her lips.

Sakina shrugged. There were good days and bad. Some days her mind went to dark places, triggered by certain smells and sounds. Revving engines and the smell of frying onions were two that always set her off. But the pangs that came with witnessing other women's joy or receiving of love always took her by surprise. She didn't want to be that kind of woman, the kind who wanted less for her sisters. But that's what time seemed to have done to her.

'I sometimes ask myself if I made bad choices.'

'You didn't have choices, Sakina, remember that. Your choice was survival. Your choice was family. People who talk about making better choices have options at their disposal already.'

He was right, and she knew that. She tried to raise a smile but failed.

The waiter arrived and placed cups, plates and a three-tiered stand of traditional British afternoon dainties in front of them.

Idris poured the tea. He had brought Sakina here so that she would feel spoiled and appreciated for an hour or two.

She watched him navigate the whole affair without spilling a drop on to the saucers. He added milk and passed her the cup. She took it and thanked him, reaching for the sugar pot.

'That drug will kill you. Try the scones though. I ordered the ones without raisins so you don't have to pick them out.' Her smile spread and filled her face – that he had remembered this one small thing about her. Being seen and still respected warmed her right through. But Sakina wasn't used to someone treating her like this, and it made her uneasy at the same time, as deep down she suspected she wasn't worthy of this sort of good intention. She put the sugar pot back without taking anything from it.

'I didn't mean to tell you what to do,' said Idris quickly. 'I'm sorry.'

'I know,' she said. 'That's why I listened.'

They looked at their teacups for a few seconds, and then Idris began to prepare a plate of food for her.

'Idris…' Sakina paused, and then took the plunge. 'I seem to be doing a lot of the work that used to be yours.'

'You are, and of course it's at Jia's request. Things are changing, Sakina, and I am fine with being moved to a different role in our organisation – I want you to know that. I didn't think I would be at first, but now I've got used to the idea it is obvious that Jia is right. It's time for something new. And you and I have different skills. The Jirga needs both. So I'm glad we get to work together. And there is another thing.' Idris paused, and he felt his heart beating very quickly. 'I like you.'

Sakina wasn't sure what to say, and then she asked cautiously, just to make certain, 'What are we talking about?'

'You already know, I hope. I think that you've been feeling it for weeks, just as I have. The question is, what do we do about it?'

She looked into his deep-brown eyes, his face serious with concern, and then she said, 'Idris, I need to tell you something.'

CHAPTER 50

Leeds Road bled red Ferraris on Chaand Raat. And the night had brought out the black Beamers too, and the white Mercs, all shined so much the moon was reflected in them. These cars were packed with men and women dressed to the nines.

The moon had been sighted and Eid was confirmed. The month of Ramadan was over. These people had fasted, prayed and held their tongues. They had broken bread together and given even more to those in need than usual. Women had risen early to make the dough for parathas, cooked eggs, made chai, and families had eaten together. Men had filled the mosques in the evening, standing shoulder to shoulder, offering Taraveeh prayers kept for the holy month. They prayed in sets of two rakats each, offering between eight to twenty depending on which imam they prayed behind, the mosque they attended and which sect they belonged to.

At the end of the holy month, the women poured into the salons to get hands hennaed and eyebrows threaded. Girls bought brightly coloured bangles and checked on the tailor for their latest outfit as the boys picked out trainers, shirts, suits. The newness of Eid clothes never got old. It was the time when life started afresh. For the lucky ones whose Ramadan was accepted by Allah, they left the month with a soul as unblemished as a newborn baby's.

But with the protective bubble of Ramadan gone, the devil could escape his chains.

The neon signs of Akbar's, Mughals and Icestone Gelato stood proudly on both sides of the street.

As Jia's car drove down the road, orange streetlights filled the horizon ahead of her like a million fireflies. The downward dips made the landscape of her hometown beloved to her. It was one of the things she'd missed when living in London.

Even though the air was filled with the scent of charcoal cooking the meats of mixed grills, it always felt cleaner here.

A little like the work that her men did.

The politicians of Westminster, the bankers and accountants of the City, were as crooked as they came. They covered their crookedness in the gnarled language of the law, with all its crevices and shadows. Legalese was how they soothed themselves and the lies that what they were doing was much better than what the Jirga and Jia's men did.

But to Jia, people who hid from themselves were weak. Once the impending news of Lord Henry Paxton and his unfortunate demise spread, they would fear her and her Jirga.

Maybe it was a Yorkshire thing, the ability to handle cold, hard truths, to look at oneself in the light of day and still get out of bed in the morning. Maybe the colder climate had toughened them, or maybe it was the years of being lied to, starved of investment and opportunities, side-lined and avoided.

As she stared at the lights they passed and heard the sound of the engines of the Ferraris, Beamers and Mercs, Jia allowed herself a rare minute to gloat.

Today, Henry Paxton would have discovered just how far he had come down in the world, how his comfortable life was about to be shattered into a million miniscule fragments.

CHAPTER 51

'What do you mean we can't get into it?' said Henry Paxton, his voice rising in temper. 'Sort it, now. I don't pay you the money I do for you to waste my time. I want those securities bought now, so use another account and do the damn trade and stop pratting around.'

He was in the back of his car being driven to a meeting at the Ministry of Defence. 'I'll call you back,' he said as the phone vibrated. He pressed the button and accepted the second call. It was his wife. 'Your card's been declined?' he snapped. 'Rubbish. Try another... You have?'

Mrs Paxton had been having lunch with friends and was mortified. 'Elizabeth had to cover me, and I have never felt so foolish,' she said. 'Henry —'

'I've got to go,' he said, cutting her off, and even though he knew the days of his wife being impressed by him hobnobbing with government ministers were long gone, he added grandly, 'I'm on my way to the MOD.'

Henry Paxton sat back and felt the first glimmer of unease.

He opened the app to the account his wife used. Sure enough, a large sum had been withdrawn. He checked another personal account, and another. It was the same story.

His personal identity must have been hacked, and he immediately reported it to the company to whom he paid a monthly premium to sort out things like this.

Henry had only just finished that call when the phone rang again.

It was his chief financial officer calling to say that one of the business accounts had been frozen by the bank and another was missing substantial sums. He was just about to check their financial situation across the board, but he didn't like what he'd seen so far.

Neither did Henry.

He clicked into the real-time app that kept track of what he owned, how much all of it was worth in trading terms, and how much in turn this meant he was worth personally. His graph showed a net value that was tumbling.

Panic rose in Henry, but then he told himself to get a grip and get to the MOD meeting, which had taken weeks to set up and having all the people there he liked to schmooze with. He knew he could wing it there for an hour.

But things dipped further when he arrived at the anonymous-looking building where he always had his meetings with the Ministry of Defence.

'I'm afraid your clearance has been denied, sir,' said the security man, putting out an arm to encourage Henry to step aside.

'Everyone in this building knows who I am. You know me, goddammit! Call Morgan now and tell him I'm here. I insist.'

Henry had to sit on a sofa for what felt a long time. He didn't dare check his phone again, much as he wanted to; security measures would be in place to scan digital activity, and he didn't want a record left anywhere of that, and particularly not here. He turned his telephone off completely.

A civil servant in an off-the-peg suit came through the glass doors of security and walked towards him. Henry felt the room tilt and he was suddenly short of breath. If he was being handled by low-level staff now, something that had never happened in his life before, this could only mean one thing.

Lord Henry Paxton had a very big problem indeed.

The man in the suit told him, without a word of explanation, that the meeting was off and asked security to escort him off the premises.

Trying to convince himself he could still turn things around, as he hadn't held on to his powerbase for this long by throwing in the towel too easily, he returned to his car and asked the driver to drive around. He didn't mind where they went, and he would say when he was ready to go back to the office.

Henry Paxton thought carefully. He had enemies, sure, but he hadn't put anyone's nose spectacularly out of joint lately. No, try as he might, Henry couldn't imagine any of them doing this to him.

And then he remembered the Khans. And he knew in his gut that this was Jia Khan's doing.

Most of all, Henry felt affronted. He'd helped Akbar get his first job in the country, and then Akbar had disappeared with the jewellery – *his* jewellery – from the heist Henry had planned, Akbar presumably using it to set up his own empire. Henry had employed the best private detectives to find Akbar and Bazigh, but their community had closed around them, and by the time they surfaced, they were too powerful, their criminal network too dangerous, to make it worth the risk to take them on. Henry had had to live with what had happened, and this had stuck in his craw for many years. Akbar had got away with it and was able to give Jia a place in society he could once only have dreamed of – *by using what rightfully belonged to Lord Henry Paxton!*

And the fact that Jia wasn't content with this really stung. Why was she doing this to him? It made no sense.

Devious and slippery as Akbar Khan had been, it now seemed nothing to how Jia Khan was behaving. And whatever Akbar had allowed his daughter to think about Henry seemed to have ignited something inside her that made Henry Paxton truly afraid.

He needed to know what he was dealing with. And so Henry Paxton got all his fixers to put urgent feelers out to assess the full extent of how much she had damaged him.

And by the evening he knew it was more or less game over, as apart from his London mansion and a holiday home in the Caribbean, it seemed control of his assets had been wrenched from his ownership.

Over the afternoon it had become clear that, for a long time, Jia Khan had been slowly picking off his friends and colleagues, putting them in situations that made them distance themselves from him. And as Henry's good standing relied on reputation, the discovery that cruel and untrue rumours had been planted at every angle, just waiting to be released, made him understand he was being blackmailed into submission.

Henry knew he should never have listened to Meera Shah. He'd been caught up in her plan to teach the Khan family a lesson, and he felt pitiful now for the way his delight at the thought of belated payback for Akbar's audacity over the diamond had made him careless. The result of a life of ease was weakness, and he had become complacent. He understood that now.

The streets of London were paved with gold, but only if you knew where to look. The Paxton dynasty had always known exactly where that was. His grandfather had owned textile mills, inherited from his grandfather before him, before they went into the defence sector.

Their money had been built on the backs of men like Jia Khan's people, at first through their labour, and then through arming them against the Russians, years later calling them terrorists and supplying guns to destroy them. These truths had been well hidden under layers of philanthropy, charitable giving and social enterprises, but blood money was at the root of it all.

He might never get his money back or keep his reputation intact. But what was certain, Lord Henry vowed, was that these two brown women – Jia Khan and Meera Shah – would have to pay. Jia most of all, then Meera, and then every single person who had helped them in one way or another. They would all pay big time.

For a moment, Henry felt better.

CHAPTER 52

Two hundred miles north, Jia Khan was easing herself back against the soft cushions of her linen armchair, enjoying a soft, sweet Medjoul date left over from the last iftar of Ramadan.

Fasting brought back the taste of everything, or maybe it was patience that did it. 'With every hardship there is ease,' the imam had said at Jummah-tul-Vida, the final Friday sermon of the holy month of Ramadan.

The city was poised for the celebration of Eid.

The shooting had hurt her physically, but it had brought with it an unexpected clarity too, and enabled Jia to sift through the unwanted voices in her mind, the fear of what was to come. It had grounded her in the simple reality of 'what will be will be'.

She was the Khan, Ahad and Lirian her sons, and she would defend her family vehemently – and violently if need be.

What had happened to Ahad would be repaid, a pound for a pound, an eye for an eye. And the reparations would continue until she decided otherwise.

The first of her plans was nearly complete. The second message would be delivered by hand.

Eight weeks earlier, she had convened a private meeting in the Opium Den. Her revenge would be slow and clever, respecting both her people and their religious requirements.

As she recovered from being shot, Jia knew she must send a message to anyone who came after her: that those who crossed Jia

Khan could expect a public shaming, and then total annihilation of their lives.

On the wall at the meeting, Jia pinned up a detailed schematic of all of Henry Paxton's investments and business interests, and those of his friends and family.

They were going to blast it all in one go with worms, logic bombs and Trojan horses, and during the meeting they plotted carefully how to do this.

It started gently enough, with warnings to Henry's friends and colleagues, small digital viruses that hid until predetermined dates and then flashed a message on to the screens, outlining snippets of personal information, followed by demands that the recipient distance themselves from Paxton. The threats were intensified by assertions that those who did not comply would have this personal information made public and their financial dealings revealed to HMRC.

The last logic bomb was saved for Chaand Raat, so that Eid could begin with a real spectacle.

And now, as she sat in her comfy chair on the eve of Eid, Jia Khan waited patiently for Lord Henry Paxton to call her.

CHAPTER 53

The video call came in exactly as predicted. Jia was just finishing off a second date and was about to drink her chai. She was dressed in a soft pink chiffon and the henna on her hands had dried enough for her to pick up the bone-china teacup without smudging.

Idris had emailed Henry Paxton a link an hour earlier.

He was sitting in his office.

The old Jia Khan might have felt the tiniest bit sorry for him. The new Jia felt nothing.

'I don't have much time, Henry. It's Eid tomorrow and we have a lot of things to do. I'm sure you understand.' She straightened her chador around her shoulders. It was embroidered with flowers. 'Here's the thing: you live in a house of cards. I've been taking them away, one by one, and now it's all about to topple, taking you down too.'

'Look, Ms Khan, I'm not sure why you're doing this, but you've had your fun and now it needs to stop.'

Jia looked calmly at him. 'No.'

'I think you've forgotten who I am. What I stand for.'

'Not at all. You are the top tier, the one per cent. You own more than anyone can ever know. Or you did. But now I know everything about you. You believed that money made you powerful. And it's true that money does give power. But then I learnt about something that is even more powerful. Information. And that is something I have and you do not.'

'But why me?'

Jia thought that Henry's voice had come close to a bleat.

She made sure to answer with just an enigmatic smile, as if to suggest he was very stupid if he didn't understand.

'All right, Ms Khan, I see how powerful you are. But you and I should make a deal. I could open doors for you across society and the government.'

Jia looked at the henna pattern on her hands as Henry Paxton grovelled, telling her what he could give her, make her, show her. The henna had hardened and was flaking, just as it should, to reveal the deep orange colour beneath.

'Let me tell you a story about another Chaand Raat, Henry,' she interrupted. 'When I was about eight or nine, my father built a house in Peshawar, this great sprawling thing with marble floors that gleamed in the sun and high sky-blue gates to keep anything we didn't want out. The lawn was perfectly clipped, and the gardener used to visit every day to water the pots that ran all the way around the grounds. But when we visited, the place was crawling with cockroaches. The cleaners had not been doing their work properly. My father didn't fire them. He said they were people, just like we were, and they needed the work. But the cockroaches, they were another story. I watched him take off a shoe and crush one after another. Then he called in the exterminators and gassed the rest of them.'

Henry stared at her, clearly confused. 'Bloody infuriating Paki,' he hissed under his breath.

Jia didn't flinch. Her rage was measured; she knew where it came from, and she knew it was valid. Her rage was steeped in grief, for the invisibility of her father, for the squandered potential of her people, for every time a white Yorkshireman used the P-word, and for every time a young kid picked it up, internalised it and hurled it at his kinfolk.

'Maybe so, Henry. A Paki is all I ever want to be.' Jia could see from Henry's shocked face that he thought he'd uttered this too quietly for her to hear. 'That's OK. I knew what you thought of me from the moment we met. I recognise a grudge when I see it. I've held a few of those myself.'

'So you know about the Grosvenor diamond? You know how your father double-crossed me, built this empire of yours off the back of what was rightfully mine?'

Jia laughed in surprise when she heard this. 'You accuse *us* of building empires off *your* back? That is priceless, Henry. It's not the loss of some diamond that upset you, is it? It's that a brown man took advantage of you. You couldn't handle it. So much so, you made allegiances with Meera Shah, and the result of that was an attack on my life, an attack in which I should have died. Giving the time of day to Meera Shah was the most stupid thing you ever did.'

Jia looked at the man on the screen, who almost seemed to be shrinking before her very eyes.

Akbar Khan had come to Britain to march with giants. But what he found were little men standing on fat wallets. Henry Paxton was one of those men. In Paxton's world, men like Akbar Khan knew their place. The bottom rung of the hierarchy.

Akbar Khan had played the long game. And the long game was Jia Khan.

Henry's phone rang, and he picked it up to see who was calling, although he didn't answer. 'I apologise,' he said.

'Always so polite,' said Jia. 'Especially while you are trying to cut off our kneecaps.'

'What makes you think you will succeed when others have failed?'

'Because I'm a woman. Because I see the world in ways you never will. Because I'm – in your words – a Paki.'

His phone began buzzing again.

'Your PA must be out of town. Elena, isn't it?'

Henry stared at Jia, and slowly his face reddened as the phone vibrated once more.

'You know what that sound is, Henry? It's the sound of rats leaving a sinking ship. It is the sound of you realising that I will never let you go. That I am destroying you right now in every way you can imagine. Take your call. It's time. It's the end of the road,' said Jia. 'Believe me when I say I will see it through until you are nothing.'

Various emotions passed over his face as he listened to his handset. It seemed he did believe everything Jia had just told him.

And Jia knew what was being said right then.

Idris had updated her before the meeting.

And then a man came into the room where Henry was sitting and placed something on the table that made a heavy sound as it was put down. It was a handgun.

Henry seemed to freeze as he stared at it.

'Let me know when it's done,' Jia announced, and then she turned off her computer screen.

She was straightening her dupatta in the mirror and checking the gold jhumkas in her ears that her father had bought her for her wedding, when a message arrived.

Lord Henry Paxton was dead. He'd just shot himself, apparently.

It was time for Jia to join the rest of the family to celebrate the night of the new moon. She popped another date into her mouth and went to find them.

CHAPTER 54

The air was fresh, the sky clear and the sun was shining as they climbed into cars for Eid namaaz the next day.

Elyas was in the driving seat, Jia seated beside him, their sons in the back. Benyamin was bringing Sanam Khan in another car. They could almost pass for a normal family.

As they drove through the familiar streets, making a journey Jia had made countless times, she couldn't help but think back to her childhood when the mornings of the celebrations were always furiously busy. Arguing over bathroom time with her brother Zan, ironing the new kurta pyjama she'd designed and selected fabric for, then endured countless fittings with the tailor to make sure it was perfect. She could still taste the vermicelli her mother would have made the night before that had been lightly fried in butter and cooked in gallons of milk and spoonfuls of sugar. This had been her father's favourite dish.

The family were always tired from a Chaand Raat spent on Westminster Road, picking out chappals or khusa shoes. The leather of the flat, domed slippers would cut into her feet – they were rarely as comfortable as they appeared – but beauty, like everything else in life, required sacrifice. With the years, these early memories gave way to high-street heels purchased in the shopping malls of Leeds, and then to Jimmy Choos and Christian Louboutin shoes bought during weekend visits to London. The boys would shine their black brogues, buy Pathani chappals, and Idris would pick whatever trainer

259

was most fashionable at the time, Jordans or Yeezys or some such brand.

They would arrive at the mosque, tumbling out of the car, and Jia would cover her head with an organza, dupioni or silk chiffon dupatta before adding her bejewelled footwear to the rows and rows of shoes already outside the prayer room, and then running to join her friends, her mother telling her to slow down as Akbar and Bazigh Khan adjusted their pakols. Zan, Idris, Malik and Nadeem opted for a mix of skull caps and baseball caps worn back to front.

Then came the sound of all the clinking gold, silver and glass chooriyan, the scent of henna and expensive perfumes, as the women embraced each other, saying 'Eid Mubarak'.

Old arguments and animosities were supposed to be left behind, but Jia knew this didn't happen. It was a veiling of the past, the way the see-through chiffon veiled Auntie Fazilat's heaving bosom, pointless and instead drawing attention to something that needed to be left alone.

As the car pulled up outside the mosque the morning after Henry Paxton died – its Yorkshire flagstones scrubbed to within an inch of their lives, because cleanliness was next to godliness, its countless minarets, paid for by the Jirga, gleaming in the sunshine, its lavish Arabic lettering announcing it as a house of Allah – Jia wondered what deals had been done by her father, what decisions really made, on this auspicious day.

For her children, this was a day of family, gifts and feasting. It was a day when Pukhtun House was filled with loved ones, laughter and joy.

But for Jia Khan, today was also a day of reckoning, when a debt would start to be repaid. Jia's organisation was now extremely wealthy. She had left a tidy sum for Henry Paxton's wife to continue her lifestyle, but with the rest she could begin to improve the lives of many of the poorest people in the city, including those who had fallen victim to Meera Shah.

With Henry Paxton gone, Meera was left dangerously exposed. Jia had enjoyed the thought of the sleepless nights her son's attacker must have had since the failed assassination attempt on Jia, and Paxton's death would only make her sweat more. But not for too much longer. Another day of reckoning was on its way.

CHAPTER 55

The women's prayer room was filled with perfume and attar as well as the sound of bangles clinking every time their owners raised their hands to their ears and that of small children gurgling as they sat on the floor in front of their mothers. The women turned their hearts to God as they watched their babies, multitasking even in prayer. The Eid namaaz was different to the daily prayers, '*Allahu Akbar!*' declared numerous times in repetition.

'A reminder that God is the greatest of all time,' Benyamin had told Ahad over breakfast, as he'd asked for a refresher on how many times he'd have to place his hands to his ears before folding them.

Jia Khan stood holding Lirian. Her mother had drilled her in Arabic as a child, and Akbar Khan had helped her understand what the words meant. He'd taught her the Fatihah, the greatest surah in the Quran, and a cure for many ills. 'Even if you lose everything else, you will still have this. It is the only true jewel – the Koh-i-Noor, bigger than the Grosvenor diamond.'

Jia marvelled at how Akbar Khan had never wavered from his faith, even in a faithless world.

At the mosque, rows of women stretched behind her, soldiers in the army of Allah standing shoulder to shoulder, each with their head covered as they prayed. It was a rare time that they united.

The circus of life continued outside these doors, with arguments over what was best for women, drawing them into discussions about the place of women within society, whether the headscarf oppressed them or emancipated them. Inside here, the veil between them and their Creator did not exist.

Motherhood was opening Jia's mind and eyes to another world, one that previously only existed in her peripheral vision. In this world she found a maternal mafia that looked after its own. And she felt herself being absorbed into it, knowing that while it contained factions, it was here that she now belonged.

The imam called the salaam, signalling the women's return to their worldly duties.

Jia thought back to last year, at the same ceremony.

She had picked up Lirian, who had started fussing, and stood up to find herself facing a young woman. The woman smiled and moved to hug Jia as was the custom. They had embraced three times, right, left and then right, as a symbol of love, respect and friendship.

'You're Jia Khan, aren't you?' she'd said. 'My mother and I talk about you a lot. She would like to meet you if you have a moment. My name is Fozia.'

Jia nodded, and Fozia went to fetch her mother.

The woman wasn't much older than Jia, but her hunched shoulders made her appear as if she was carrying the weight of the world on her back.

'I wanted to thank you for inspiring my daughter, and all the women here. We didn't have that growing up, did we? Our lives might have been different if we had.'

The words were meant in kindness, but Jia knew that for the Khan to be a role model was a dangerous thing. She believed that if the world ever saw what she had done, knew what she was capable of, it would push her off the pedestal it had placed her on and bludgeon her with it. Leadership, and setting an example, wasn't part of why she did what she did. She needed it to not be true, but still she thanked the woman, who seemed eager to talk a little more.

'It was a different world when I was growing up. We got married young and then did what our husbands allowed. I'm married to a good man. But like most of the men, he wasn't taught to value the work women do in the home. He has tried, but when he supports me, he's judged by his family, even by his mother and sister.'

Women made their way around the room, hugging and wishing each other well, making plans for Eid chai and gatherings, moving closer to Jia Khan. It occurred to her that it had always been men who came to see her father with bulging boxes of mithai and Eidi for the children – and armed with requests for help. Even after his death, the tradition continued unchanged, and she knew there would be people gathering at Pukhtun House, eager for a meeting with her.

'I studied business management at college,' added Fozia's mother. 'I was top of my class. That's why my husband married me. Then, when I had children, I stayed home to look after them. They teach us that mothers are respected in Islam, but it's only when I dropped the last one at school that I had time to realise the truth. In giving up my financial freedom, I had lost the respect of everyone around me, but by then I had taught my daughter Dimple to do the same. We called her that because whenever she smiled, she had perfect dimples. She doesn't smile so much now and she doesn't like to go out.'

'She's not here?'

'She finds it too difficult to come to the mosque, what with the divorce. Her father-in-law, Mubashar Mahroof, is in the men's section pretending to be the most pious man who ever lived when he's nothing more than a slaver, and his son is a weak coward. They're spreading lies about my Fozia now, but what can we do?'

Jia made a throwaway remark that some men deserved all they got, and Fozia's mother nodded, and then she said, 'My name is Bano, and I am pleased to meet you.'

The crowd around them began to pool and swell. It was if the women had been waiting for a place to speak. There were professionals, homemakers and women who straddled both. They were young and old, rich and poor. They all had stories to tell and hoped that Jia would listen. The erosion of their rights and freedoms had been incremental, like the wearing down of the great white cliffs that hold back the sea. The younger women were eager for things to be different for them.

'There is no place for us,' said one fresh-faced woman. 'The imam tells us purdah emancipates us. Western feminism tells us the hijab oppresses us. Women who cover, and women who don't, we fight among ourselves. Does any of it really matter?'

And then there had been darker tales, of women who'd been abused, held against their will, deprived of their freedoms and, in many cases, blackmailed.

As her car had pulled away from the masjid, Jia Khan pondered the problems these women faced and what she could do to help.

A year on, at this very Eid prayer, she looked for Fozia and Bano, but they were nowhere to be seen.

CHAPTER 56

'You'll love it,' said Maria. 'It's an old-fashioned wedding.'

'No Bollywood dance routines for me. You'll find me dancing at Shai Guy's Bollywood club night, not a family mehndi,' answered Jia.

They'd left their children home and were here to help an old friend mark the last night of her single life. Jia hadn't been to a mehndi since her sister's wedding.

Scores of tealights flickered throughout the venue. Women and girls in green and yellow ghagras, saris and ghararas swished around, catching up on family news, work advice and each other's love lives.

The dance floor was markedly absent, replaced by a group of women singing in the centre of the room.

Jia sat beside them, clapping to the beat of the dholak. A young woman played the ghara, the rings on her fingers hitting high and low notes as they made contact with the clay pot. The thrum and *thrap* of the drum was powerful, taking older women back to their childhoods and the young girls they had once been.

Everyone knew the rhythmic sound and at least one verse of the traditional tappay tales, even if they didn't know what it meant. The women split into two camps, one group calling out a verse and the other responding. It was a conversation between a woman and her lover, sometimes teasing, sometimes romantic, always the man at the receiving end. It was one of the few places they got to be this honest about their lives without fear of repercussions.

Jia had reasons other than celebrating the wedding for attending. Sakina had brought a message a few days earlier from the people she'd told Jia about, the women who had saved her son's life. They wanted to speak, and Sakina brokered the meet.

She was proving to be the asset Jia had known she would be, bringing fresh vision to the table. Her way of doing business, her advice, her insight, were different to the men of the Jirga. There was something holistic about Sakina's method, and it came with foresight.

As the division between legitimate and illegal interests was widening, Jia wanted more and more distance between the two. Sakina was getting to be very good with the shadier side of the empire, and Jia was beginning to trust her judgement greatly and rely on her to tell her like it was.

Servings of pulpy mango juice, iced lime and red pomegranate crush filled the drinks table where Sakina was waiting for Jia. She offered Jia a glass before leading her through a large, carved wooden door and into a low-lit room where a group of women was waiting.

They were gathered around a circular table, lit candles at its centre and in the alcoves all around.

Jia recognised them.

They were women she'd seen in places of business, in homes, those of friends and in her own. The face that surprised her the most was Hamsa's, the young woman who worked in the kitchen at Pukhtun House.

'Salaam, Jia Khan,' Hamsa said, holding out her hands and taking Jia's in them.

'My mother said you don't speak,' said Jia.

'In a world where I'm not heard, I choose to stay silent.' She kissed the Khan on both cheeks, before introducing her to the other women in the room. 'There are more of us – we change with time and days. You have already met Bano and Fozia, although not for a while. This is Mahboobeh – she's a medical examiner – and here is Iram, a psychotherapist and friend of Sakina's.'

Iram nodded her head. 'I reached out to Sakina after what happened with your son, as we were keen to find the most respectful way to connect with you. We should have sought her advice much earlier, before your son was taken, but we didn't want to implicate either of you in what we were doing.'

Jia glanced at Sakina, who'd remained silent during these introductions. She had come far since the days of walking the streets, and Jia could see that she was stepping into her power and owning it.

Since Ishtiaq's murder, Jia had been convinced that women were behind the Kismet Killings. But she had kept those thoughts private while she decided what, if anything, to do about it, until Sakina came to her with the same idea. Jia had been impressed by her instincts and that Sakina had been open with her. It was one of the reasons Jia had given her the position she had.

For the Khan to have been oblivious to the workings of her city would have been embarrassing. Sakina provided her with information that her men were not privy to, and this changed everything.

Hamsa offered Jia a seat at the table, pouring her some Kashmiri tea from a floral teapot.

Jia watched the steam rise from the cup as a pale-grey pot of sliced pistachios, and another of sugar cubes, was placed before her.

'You're probably wondering what I've been doing in your home,' said Hamsa very quietly to Jia. 'I've been watching you and learning from you, the things you say and do, the things that no one else sees.' She leaned in closer and dropped her voice again. 'I want to assure you, Jia Khan, that you have nothing to fear from us.'

'You women saved my son's life,' said Jia. 'I am in your debt.'

'There is no ledger between us here,' said Hamsa, gesturing to those around her. 'The men turn on us to get better standing. We choose to be better than them.'

'The men don't like themselves,' said Iram. 'It's internalised so deeply that they won't even admit it to themselves, but we see it. We see it in the way they treat us, the lack of value they place on women who share their heritage. But you, they treat better. We want that for us too.'

'We can't keep carrying the faith,' Mahboobeh said, 'feeding the children and massaging their egos. We want to be seen.'

The sounds of singing outside the room formed a constant backdrop to this most private of conversations. Men were markedly absent by design today. This wasn't segregation but the exercising of free will.

As the women spoke, the dholak got louder, along with the clapping, and the laughter began rising. Jia knew the women would be on their feet now, encircling each other as they danced together, the way women had done for centuries: the attan dance of the Pashtun and the Baloch, the bhangra and luddi of the Punjabis, the Sindhi dhamal and juhmro. The lines drawn by men to divide were being crossed right now, crossed by women as they connected via the common ground of sisterhood.

Bonds and friendships formed or renewed, a regeneration of the earlier ones that had outlasted time and travel, been carried overseas and passed on to women born on foreign soil, and at their core the same message: the value of togetherness, tenderness, resilience and solidarity of womanhood.

Jia understood what it was all about, what Iram, Hamsa and the other women were trying to tell her.

'You killed those men,' said Jia. 'The victims of the Kismet Killer that the police and the newspapers are hunting.'

'We did,' said Hamsa. 'We didn't take the decisions lightly, but they were bad men and they deserved to die.' Her voice was clear, and Jia was impressed that she wasn't trying to shirk away from the responsibility of what they had done.

Jia looked carefully at each face. There were no regrets in this room. She knew how this felt. These were her sisters in spirit.

'They were holding our lives hostage on purpose. And so we sent a signal to those who would harm us,' said Hamsa. 'We have women working in every part of this city. We come together at mehndis, mother-and-baby groups, the women's gym, and everyone assumes we are here to gossip. We decided to put our time to better use. They didn't see us coming. They assumed that only men were capable of doing the things we did. And we had help to cover evidence and throw people off the scent.' Hamsa nodded at Mahboobeh, who inclined her head to indicate a truth had been said.

'What about the white man my son told me about?' Jia pointed out.

'We decided to hire a professional from outside. He only did what we told him to do. He was our tool, our weapon. But not the day your son was taken, of course – as Sakina has told you. He wasn't working on our orders then.'

'When we spoke on Eid last year, Jia Khan,' said Bano, 'and I told you about my daughter Dimple, the thing you said in passing about some men deserving all they get, I know you were teasing but the thought stayed with me. As I spoke with my friends and sisters, I realised nothing would change unless we changed it ourselves. And I thought that man who ruined my lovely Dimple deserved nothing short of death.'

'And so you began teaching these men a lesson,' Jia said.

'We did. A very strong lesson. And once we agreed what we should do, things fell into place. It was as if a veil had been lifted from our eyes. We saw we didn't have to live in servitude, earn less, give more. There were enough of us to kill every last man in their beds if we wanted to. They have enslaved entire countries of women, so why shouldn't we do the same?' Bano replied.

'Why didn't you?' asked Jia, curious, as she had never thought about these things in quite this way before.

'Because then what would be the difference between them and us? We are women. We give birth to men. They are a part of us before they can breathe alone.'

Jia understood. As a mother of sons, she felt the responsibility towards women and men in equal measure. There was no divide. There was only humanity.

'Why have you come to me now?' she asked the women around the table. 'I told Sakina to make it clear that I hold no grudge against you for what happened to my son. I know exactly who was responsible. So what do you want from me?'

The rooms of men were filled with ego and hidden agendas. This room felt different. Cards were not being played here; instead, hands were being shown openly.

These women did not want bloodshed, they wanted peace, but experience had taught them that swords could never be put away; they must always be sheathed in readiness for battle.

'We want your friendship, given freely and openly as we will give ours to you,' said Mahboobeh. 'It doesn't matter how strong we are individually, patriarchy snaps us like phalanges. Together we can form a fist and become part of one body.'

'But you are powerful without me,' Jia replied.

Bano added, 'But we need strong leadership too. Leadership we can respect. What that evil woman tried to do to your boy in our name must not happen again. It was a grave mistake. And abhorrent to every single one of us. And we are very, very sorry.'

This open acceptance and clear apology was a rarity in the world Jia Khan inhabited, one that she valued greatly.

With these women in her armoury, there was no end to what she could achieve, Jia thought. And as she looked from one hopeful face to the next, Jia Khan knew exactly what she would do.

CHAPTER 57

'It's now,' said Jia. 'We need to move swiftly.'

Just over two months had passed since Paxton's death, and a new Eid was approaching, the second in the year, this time the one of sacrifice.

The women were gathered in the penthouse of a hotel for this celebration, and the space was filled with laughter and their perfume. They were in a corner suite on the top floor, looking out over the darkness as the crystal moon watched over them. The orange glow of the city surrounded the women in the dimly lit room. And they were ready for what was to come.

Jia Khan had arranged the celebration to bring her most trusted and closest together, as she wanted to consolidate their plans and make sure everyone knew what they were doing. For they were about to be put into action.

Dressed in their finest silks, brocades and chiffons, practicality became as important as style.

'We need pockets,' said Fozia.

'Why?' asked one of the other women.

'Where else am I going to hide my gun?'

The women had laughed at her words. They didn't need guns. They were lethal without them. Jia Khan had made sure of that. They were skilled in martial arts, able to fight with sticks, knives and whatever came to hand. But their greatest strength was one another.

They straddled cultures, generations and class, all things they would use to their advantage. It was said the devil's greatest trick was convincing the world it didn't exist. These women hadn't needed to trick the world; they simply took advantage of its blind eye. They were hiding in plain sight, these women who had rescued themselves.

Now, under the guidance of Jia Khan, they were about to take it to the next level.

Their Khan stood before them, the brocade of her gharara shown to its best effect as she moved gracefully over the polished wood floor to take her seat at the table. Her silver bracelets clinked gently as she adjusted her chiffon dupatta across her shoulders. These bracelets had belonged to her grandmother, and whenever she wore them, Jia felt a connection to all the women who had come before her. Tiny pearls daintily hung from the edges of the long scarf.

There were three stages to Jia's plan. Dealing with Meera, then the Jirga, and, finally, handling the fallout from Paxton's death.

Adding women to the Jirga would be the easiest of the three. The final part was risky, a moonshot. But if they pulled it off, it would leave no doubt as to the reach and ambition of Jia Khan.

'Is the clean-up team in place?' she asked Sakina.

'By sunrise, it will be done. I will take you to Meera Shah, and the rest of the women will come after.'

'And the final piece of business we have to attend to?'

'Every piece is in play. Tomorrow will bring good news, I promise.'

In the car on the way home, Jia looked at the paisley design embroidered into her gharara, tracing her finger over it, and thought of Akbar Khan and all the things he had taught her.

'It reminds me of my homeland,' he told her when she was a child and had asked him why he wore the pattern so often. It was in his ties, waistcoats and, of course, his shawls.

He'd looked up from his newspaper to give his daughter his full attention. 'It comes from the Parsi symbol of the cypress tree and means life. The Parsis were like sugar in milk, sweetening our country the way you sweeten England. Kashmiri princes gave these shawls as gifts to European officers a long time ago, made from rare goats' wool. In our culture, we share the best of what we have with others. Always remember who you come from, Jia Khan. Our history is important, and it helps us move forward in life. If your roots are strong, you may bend with the wind, but it means you will always find your balance again. But if your roots are in shallow ground, then just one strong gust will break you and you will never recover.'

'How did you get so clever?' she'd asked.

'I have lived long enough to see time come full circle,' was the answer.

CHAPTER 58

Meera Shah walked restlessly around the kitchen, stroking the cold, clean steel with fidgety fingers as she surveyed her empire.

With Henry Paxton dead, she had lost the investment that kept her food business afloat, while the failure of her crypto business had further decimated her reserves of cash, and now the bank was threatening to shut her down. The final letter had arrived today.

She had been trying to bat away some rumours around the quality of her food, but they were proving remarkably persistent, while a deduction in her hygiene rating had meant customers had stayed away all Ramadan. Iftars would normally be her most lucrative times, but even the free dates and chaat she'd laid on hadn't been enough to lure her customers back.

Meera Shah frowned as her thoughts turned to Jia Khan.

At the time, Meera had been delighted with herself that she'd been so bold as to snatch Ahad, and in broad daylight to boot, as it had shown to everyone that the Khans were not invincible. And for the first few hours it had calmed her fury a little, Ahad's bruises a balm to hers, her desire to cause discomfort to Jia Khan so potent that it made her mouth water. But as the weeks had passed since then, she couldn't look back on what she had done with the same glee.

For while Meera's taking and beating of Ahad should have been a clear signal to all of Jia Khan's loss of control of the Jirga and the community, instead it had turned out to be a rapidly diluting message, and furthermore one that few people seemed to notice or care about one way or another.

The groundswell of rising opinion and support for Jia Khan in the wake of her own life-threatening gunshot wounds had proved sobering; Meera had underestimated the regard and affection in which Jia was held. And just as bad was that, in the slipstream of the assassination attempt, Meera Shah found herself unable to crow about her role in Ahad's abduction without implicating herself in the crime precisely at the time when the Khan's star was very obviously rising. Meera Shah might be many things, but she wasn't so senseless as to risk that.

And Jia Khan's subsequent lack of retaliation was confusing too, unless she genuinely didn't know that what had happened to her and her son was a direct result of an idea Meera Shah had had. Once Jia was out of hospital, Meera had been banking on the sort of showdown that would leave her clearly the victor. But Jia wasn't upholding her end of the bargain in this. She had attacked Meera's business interests while ignoring Meera herself, which hurt as much as if Jia had physically slapped her face with all her weight behind her hand.

The police had kept their focus on the non-existent Kismet Killer as the likely abductor of Ahad, even though Meera knew he had heard her voice and those of the other women. But now that the spree of Kismet Killings had stopped, the interest of the general public had moved on to other, juicier crimes, and Meera was furious that the brutal deaths of a series of brown-skinned men who had had religious words cut into their foreheads no longer held the community in thrall.

She had no choice but to wait now. She would bide her time, build up her enterprise and then return, forcing back into her employ the women she had been happy to exploit previously. This city of women was hers and hers alone, Meera Shah was convinced. She controlled everything about it, and that's where true power lay. Jia

Khan did not understand this, for the stupid woman had built her Jirga with men.

***

Jia Khan stood in the unlit alley outside, the glass in the top half of the door giving her a clear view inside. She watched Meera in her kitchen, pacing, staring around in frustration and licking her wounds as she made ineffectual plans.

She had offered this woman leniency too often, believing that, despite their differences, Meera Shah was part of the sisterhood; their ancestors came from the same nation and their struggles were alike.

As always, her father's words echoed in Jia's head: 'He who does not show mercy does not deserve mercy.' Previously, she had thought this meant that she should show clemency in all matters. But after Ahad was beaten, something inside her snapped, and now the words meant something completely different.

Meera Shah had not shown herself worthy of mercy. She had caused Ahad pain, a young man who was just figuring out his place in life, who had hope and dreams, and whom she had never been able to be close to because she was afraid. In order words, Meera had brought Jia's worst fears to life, and there would be a high price to pay for that.

Jia had looked into her son's eyes and he had been the baby she had given birth to, the boy she had carried within her, just him and her, alone with her grief. She had loved him completely, wholly, and without prejudice. In his bruised face she had seen Zan coming home broken from the police station after a grilling by officers about Akbar Khan and his business dealings. She had seen Benyamin, his eyelids purple and swollen from where Nowak had hit him over and over again.

Their collective hurt had pooled like liquid, surrounding Jia from all sides, and now their hurt had seeped into her. Her heart and lungs had cracked open, the sins of her father pouring out of her, and now it was her sins that joined with those. What kind of God would allow this? Was this His justice, to hurt the ones sinners loved?

Jia Khan stood in the doorway to Meera Shah's kitchen, letting her wrath work its way through every cell in her body. She could feel it spread like molten lava throughout her torso, her legs, her arms, and on and up to her brain, and there it stopped. There was a metallic taste in her mouth as the adrenaline sparked.

And then Jia Khan was filled with a sense of clear and calm purpose. None of what was about to happen would be a gut reaction. Instead, it would be ice-cold and calculated.

'You hurt my son,' she said behind Meera, stepping from the dark doorway and into the bright lights of the kitchen. Jia's gharara swept the floor, making a low swooshing sound, as she walked slowly towards the older woman, each heel a delicate click on the tiles that sounded like the hammer of a gun being cocked.

'What are you doing?' Meera looked around to see if anyone else was here, but the place was empty. It was just the two of them.

'Somebody left the door unlocked. And I just walked right in.'

Meera swallowed nervously as she realised somebody who worked for her must have left the door like that for Jia.

Chairs had been stacked on tables and the floors had been cleaned. Everyone had gone home.

Meera moved to the other side of the steel-topped preparation island, trying to keep some distance between her and the Khan. But Jia kept putting one foot in front of the other, never taking her eyes off her prey.

'You just couldn't let it go,' said Jia. 'I tried to warn you, but you kept pushing, and now here we are.'

Jia took off her dupatta. Her bangles clinked as she twisted it tightly, turning it into a rope, moving towards Meera, the tiny pearls coming together in a cascade of lethal prettiness.

The first strike was so fast, it took Meera by surprise, the pearls making contact with her face, slicing into the top of her eyebrow.

Blood began to ooze out of the cut, but Meera knew Jia wouldn't stop there.

Jia thought of Ahad, the bruises on his face and body, the black, blue and green map on his skin that this woman had inflicted. Each bruise transferred to her, Jia, the woman who had given birth to him. Meera had made Jia's worst nightmare come true, and now that Jia had faced and consumed that monster, there was nothing more for her to fear. There was only revenge to extract, so that this mother would never feel this way again.

An example would be made of Meera, a loud and clear message to anyone who considered even looking at the Khan family with greed or hurt in their eyes.

Jia watched as Meera reached for a paper towel, dabbing the blood now slowly dripping towards her eye. Her hand shook, her fear evident. She was a coward, clearly, and Jia thought this was why Meera had done what she had.

Now that Meera was backed up against a wall, against an industrial oven, Jia unleashed a volley of punches, and they came fast and furious, her movements small but powerful, each time hitting Meera in the chest, over and over, like a drumbeat. Meera tried to move out of the way, and then she tried to wrap her arms around herself in protection.

Jia knew the rhythm of the fight. It was in her hands, it coursed through her body alongside her blood, her eyes steely cold. Punch after punch after punch.

Meera hadn't expected it to come to this. She had suffered and struggled and been hardened by heat and experience, whereas this woman had lived a life of privilege, worshipped by her father, adored by her husband. That she was about to lose to her made Meera feel sick to her stomach.

She could not let it end this way. She felt her back hit the wall again and again, and when Jia Khan took a step back, Meera seized the opportunity and snatched something with a curved handle from a container beneath the steel work-surface. She swept her arm up and out, brandishing her weapon close to Jia Khan's face, kitchen lights glinting off the sharp blade of the knife.

'You think you're so much better than everyone else, don't you, Jia Khan? Coming back here and taking over. Well, this is my home, it is my city, and I stayed here while you were going soft down south. I'm going to cut you into tiny pieces and feed you to the dogs,' Meera spat through gasps of pain.

Jia moved back a few more steps. She had planned to teach Meera a brutal lesson, one that she would not forget, but spare her life as a sign of goodwill to all other women.

But as Meera lunged towards her, Jia understood the error of this plan. In death as in life, men and women should be treated equally. And had it been a man who had harmed Ahad so, Jia would have killed him without compunction.

She sidestepped the blow of the knife, too fast for Meera, her intuition too sharp, and swiftly knotted the scarf around Meera's arm, pushing her hand back and her body down, until she screamed in pain and the knife clattered to the floor.

Jia wrapped the other end of the scarf around Meera's neck, pulling it tighter and tighter, so that the life began to leave the woman's body. But still Meera Shah fought to live, gasping, 'Mercy!'

Jia let go, watching the other woman drop to the floor, broken and weeping.

She picked up her phone and made a call, then turned on a tap, running her bloodied and hennaed hands under cold water. Then she turned it off and dried herself, took two glasses from the sink and filled them with water from the fridge.

She walked over to Meera, who eyed her warily, her eyes filled with shame, and Jia handed her a glass. The woman drank deeply before returning the empty glass to the countertop.

Jia unfolded a chair from the side of the room and sat down. She was tired as it had been a long day and Lirian still wasn't sleeping well.

'You have children, right?'

Meera nodded. And Jia nodded back, and for a moment it was almost as if they were friends about to talk about their sons.

But then Jia Khan said, 'You and I are very different. We might appear the same but we're nothing like each other. I wish you'd left me alone. I really do. Because now you've left me no choice.'

The team came in through the back door. They'd changed out of their finery and were dressed in black, awaiting their Khan's instructions. Meera recognised many of them as workers from her samosa plant.

'They don't work for you anymore,' said Jia wearily. 'You should have been kind, Meera. Kind to the people who were good to you.'

She turned to the women who were awaiting instructions.

'Kill Meera Shah,' Jia Khan said. 'And, Sakina, make sure they do to her the worst thing Meera Shah has done to somebody else. You might as well have a choice of heinous acts.'

She went out and climbed into the backseat of her waiting car. And it was then that she saw she was still carrying her glass of undrunk water.

CHAPTER 59

'You killed her,' said Ahad.

Jia didn't answer. It wasn't Meera's death that troubled her, it was her son's distress, the danger she had put him in, and the explanation she now needed to give.

She had been afraid that she would lose him. And now she had killed for him. As she turned towards him, she wondered how she would bear the loss she was about to face.

His face bloodied and bruised had etched itself into the gallery of her mind, alongside images of Benyamin after he'd been beaten up, and of Zan's body, of the men she loved and how they had suffered as a result of their connection to the Khan.

Mother and son sat in silence, looking out across the car park.

They watched Sakina lead the clean-up crew into the kitchens. Things moved pretty fast after that and it wasn't long before a bundle that was Meera Shah was taken out of the building. They'd wrapped her in a roll of hessian over the top of plastic sheeting and deposited her in a van that quickly drove away. Then an army of cleaners descended like locusts. It took fifteen minutes for them to be in and out.

Jia stared intently from her car. Something about the situation compelled her to stay.

'Shouldn't we get out of here?' said Ahad.

'Probably,' she said. 'I want you to understand how much I love you. And for you to see that you need never fear this woman again.'

'You didn't tell the police?' he said.

'Well, did you when it happened?'

Ahad didn't answer.

'In my world,' Jia said, and then paused before starting again 'In our world, calling the police is a sign of weakness. We sort out our problems and then we clean up our own mess. The police are not on our side.'

Ahad didn't know what to say. The slow realisation of exactly who his mother was and what she could do in the name of vengeance, and the shock he kept reliving of being taken and beaten and being so scared, was washing over him.

The retaliation she had wreaked, a lot of this in his name, was something Ahad knew he'd have to find a way to live with, and he wasn't sure he could do that. In his naivety, when he'd told Jia about being queer, he thought his confession to her was the most difficult thing he'd ever have to do. How wrong that assumption had proved to be. Now the real challenge in his life was finding the energy to wake up in the morning and just keep going throughout the day.

'We're not like everyone else, Ahad,' said Jia. 'I don't just mean that in terms of what we do, but in terms of who we are. I know you feel bad at the moment and that is perfectly understandable – I would feel like that too. But one day you'll have made peace with it all in your mind and see that what Meera Shah did to you – and to me too – was unacceptable, and that to put the balance back into our community she had to die. She was a weak, vain and greedy person who only ever cared about herself.

'When I left here all those years ago, I lived a kind of white life. I stayed silent about many things, things that were wrong, miscar-riages of justice. I was tired and I wanted to disappear. The truth is, I was a coward. I wanted to go skiing and eat scones and take walks in the countryside without having people look at me like I didn't belong, without people commenting on how good my English was.

But no matter what I did, I was still brown, Muslim, female. There was nothing I could do. No amount of success or hard work could erase the ideas that others had of me.'

She looked at her son, scarred by the legacy of their family. She had tried to save him from it so many times. She wasn't going to do that anymore.

'Ahad, I may have done things that society considers immoral, illegal and unacceptable, and people might look at me and see a cold-hearted bitch, and maybe I am, I don't know. The only thing I do know for sure is that every day since my father died, I have been taking in the darkness that came for you and my siblings, my mother and her people, and I have been taking it in like a sin-eater. And I don't regret any of it.

'I wanted to keep Maria and Ben out of this, just like my father tried to save me and your uncle Zan, but Akbar Khan failed, and I've failed. I have tried to protect you, but I don't know how to do this anymore. And I hope you know that I am not talking about your sexuality when I say this – for me, that is just part of you, and in a perfect world I long to keep every bit of you safe and protected.

'But our reality is that we have to keep moving forward out of this swamp, or it will swallow us whole. And I love you too much to let that happen. I want for you and Lirian to feel a sense of belonging until the end of your lives. To feel psychological safety, to not be judged for the colour of your skin or for not knowing which fork to use in a fancy restaurant.'

Ahad was staring out of the car's window and Jia couldn't see his face.

'I am sorry that I have handled this badly, so badly,' she said, desperate to make him feel better. 'But my only regret is what I did to you.'

Jia kept her gaze on her son, the once tiny baby that had been hers alone but who was now a grown man with stubble and a life completely apart from hers. 'I want you to know there is nothing wrong with you. In no way did you invite this on yourself.'

He shrugged. 'I know there's nothing wrong with me.'

'No, baby boy, there really is nothing wrong with you.'

'Right.' His voice was skirting anger, as if she were placing a finger on something he didn't want to discuss, the thing he'd been hiding from himself, the part of him that had wondered if he *was* something sinful and wrong, if his feelings *were* an abomination, because it wasn't the mad mullahs that had got to him, it was the middle-ground ones, the ones who appeared to be rational and kind.

She repeated her words. 'You are a good man. There is nothing wrong with what you feel.'

His mother's voice was so gentle, so filled with affection, that Ahad couldn't look at her.

She watched him rubbing his hands together as if trying to warm them up, a nervous response that he shared with his father. Through that invisible umbilical cord, she felt the heat of hurt he had been carrying deep within him. It was in his eyes that he had cried endless tears because of her, and in the ears that had burned with the bigotry of other people, the worry he'd carried within his chest.

She took his face in her hands. 'I didn't want you to feel what I have felt every day of my life for as long as I can remember.' Then Jia placed her forehead against her son's. 'But, fuck! Fuck anyone who tries to hurt you. I will not let them come for you.'

She'd broken him now and he wrapped his arms around her and wept.

The pain poured out of him like a wolf cry, harrowing and deep and ancient. And when he stopped, he felt lighter, as if the darkness he'd been carrying in his heart was gone. Jia Khan had stopped his pain from festering. She had set him free.

She started the car and drove them home, the silence gentle and tired on her side, unnamed on his.

'I need you to be happy,' she said as he climbed out of the car. 'Go on camping trips. Whatever.'

He looked at her, the woman whom he'd ached to know as a child, whom he'd watched over the last few years, this smart woman who commanded an army, who had just killed for him, and it was as if he was seeing her for the first time. She was a woman simply trying to do the best by her family.

'Why would I want to go camping in a forest without central heating and flushing toilets?' he said.

She laughed, the tension leaving her shoulders. She'd been carrying this worry about Ahad on her person for so long, it had felt insurmountable, as if she had lost her son and she would never get him back.

He took her hand in his and squeezed. 'I get it,' he said. 'We'll figure it out.'

And with this, Jia too had a new understanding. The baby her post-natal psychosis had made her fear had turned out to be the one person she was able to be totally honest with. She hoped Allah would guide her from here.

CHAPTER 60

It had been a long time since Jia and Elyas had made love. The exhaustion of parenthood left little room for sexual urges, and they'd been walking a tightrope since Ahad's conversation with Jia. The switch from Khan to mother to lover was not an easy one.

As they lay on the floor of the study not long after Jia had got home, their energies spent, she felt she had reclaimed a part of herself. Somehow what had gone on between her and Ahad in the car had helped husband and wife find their way back to each other. Elyas recognised Jia and Ahad's new-found closeness the moment they walked back into Pukhtun House.

Elyas loved her, that was clear, and the fact that in that moment she'd wanted him too had been a reminder of why he stayed.

He traced his fingers over the surgeon's scar on her abdomen. The bullet was gone, the danger averted, but he wondered what other scars she hid deep within herself, all the things she didn't tell him.

'You don't have to hide from me,' he said.

She reached down and pulled the blanket from her feet up over herself. Her husband was a bright and brilliant man, and his misfortune had been to fall in love with her.

'I know, Elyas,' she said. 'I'm sorry that you are caught up with me.'

'I'm not caught up. I choose to stay.' He traced his fingers from her forehead, down her neck, her chest and over her belly. Her body was a map of their time together. It had carried their children, growing and changing and never quite returning to its original form.

It bore the scars of her existence, showed the parts of her that were parched, those that were full to the brim. There was so much life left in her still to be lived, and he wanted to stay to see what lines and markings it would bring.

He started to say so, but she shook her head, her eyes like unlocked tomes speaking volumes. He could see the sadness in them, the secrets she kept hidden.

'It's never me I'm protecting,' she said. 'It's you and our children. If you ever want to go, I won't stop you. I'm in too deep now. I'm trying to break us free, but I don't know if I'll make it.'

They stayed beside each other, the music playing, the candlelight dancing, afraid to move in case the spell they'd accidentally cast broke.

They'd managed to travel back in time, but who knew how long they had before their responsibilities resumed.

CHAPTER 61

Dawn brought Eid-ul-Adha, the larger of the two festivals, and news of change.

Jia's phone buzzed constantly with messages, mostly from Adam Diaz.

She glanced at them quickly before heading to the mosque for prayers, with Elyas beside her and Ahad and Lirian sat in the back, having an unlikely chat.

Her work was done and she'd deal with any fallout and explanations later. The women had carried out exactly what had been asked of them, and the sun had risen on a brave new world.

'Elyas, take the longer route home,' said Jia on the way back from prayers. 'It was a favourite tradition of my dad's, the different route on the way back from Eid namaaz. He said it was something to do with change.'

Their cook, Chilli Chacha, was back at long last from Peshawar, and with him had returned the davaat. A marquee was in the garden as the weather was unusually mild, the cousins were en route and the dining table bulging with every kind of meat imaginable. There were tender pieces of boti tikka, seekh kebab and fish that had been coated in fennel-fragrant masala and deep fried until golden. There was Kabuli pilau with orange threads of carrot laced through it and dotted with sultanas. Flat breads the size of a toddler were stood up against a naan tree to the side of the table.

'Chacha, looks like the only vegetable is the sweetcorn in the pasta salad,' Benyamin said, teasing the old man, who handed him a plate of breaded, shallow-fried aloo tikkis.

'Benyamin jaan, I have made a vegetable karahi for Ahad jaan.'

Benyamin turned to his nephew. 'What's going on?'

'Nothing, just trying out being vegetarian.'

'You're so much like your mother. You think you'll make it longer eating that than she did? She didn't even eat eggs or milk. And then she came home and it was all downhill.'

The Khan family piled their plates and milled around the house and garden, Lirian playing in the new swing chair. Every room was filled with aunts, uncles and cousins chatting and catching up on the last few months. Children ran around the house and back out into the garden, where a pergola had been set up for the barbecue.

Bazigh Khan was there, giving instructions. Jia was glad to see him and walked over to offer him Eid wishes. He took her in a big bear hug and lifted her off the ground, before kissing the top of her head and letting her go. His physical strength always impressed her.

'Ghee is good,' he said. 'I never ate any of that other rubbish. Even when the NHS decided it was bad for us. And look, I was right. Now they call it a superfood. I saw Idris buying a small jar for £24.99 the other day.'

Jia smiled. It was good to have her uncle home.

'Did you get everything sorted out there?' she asked.

'I did. Come to my house tomorrow and I'll tell you all about it.' Bazigh took a purple bank note from his pocket and put it in her hand, closing her fingers over it into a fist.

She looked up at him the way she had when she was a child. He knew everything there was to know about her. Well, almost everything. He knew much of what she'd done, and what she was capable of, and yet he still loved her. She felt herself welling up and bit her lip hard. The softer emotions, those exhibited more readily by women, were not respected in the world of the Jirga, but they would be. Jia needed that to change for the men under her care, as much as for herself.

Seeing her trying to control her emotions, Bazigh Khan came to the rescue. 'Would you like my help with the Eidi today?'

'I would like that very much,' she said. 'The company men will be gathering soon. They are the old guard and respect you more than me. And I have some news to deliver.'

'You might find that isn't as true as you think. They do respect you. You have built quite an empire, Jia Khan. Your father would be proud of you.'

Jia Khan wondered whether her uncle would feel that way if he knew that she had been the one responsible for his brother's death.

Bazigh Khan seemed to understand something of her silence. 'My brother and I were different in many ways, but he knew what was coming, Jia Khan, and he knew how you would go about things.' He locked eyes with his niece to make her understand. 'Akbar Khan had made peace with it, and he told me so. It is time for you to make peace with that too. Now, I have other Eidi for you, so come and sit with me in your office, as we need to be private.'

Jia Khan settled down beside her uncle as she had done countless times before. That her father had known the way many of her plans would pan out did not surprise her. Akbar Khan had always been astute and strategic, with a deep understanding of people in a way that she had not appreciated fully until she became Khan. That he had spoken with Bazigh of her, and Bazigh had had no judgement or question, surprised Jia. She had so far to go to fill her father's shoes.

'Listen to me, Jia. Trying to make sense of all of life will bring you no joy. Life is for living. What's gone is done with. Now we look to what comes next. You did not come this far to only come this far.'

He handed her a parcel wrapped in brown paper and shiny brown tape. It was covered in old stamps. Jia looked at it, and then at her uncle incredulously. The parcel's postmark was 1974.

Bazigh Khan handed her a pair of scissors, nudging her to open it. Jia cut the brown tape, and inside the wrapping she found a small box covered in pristine blue velvet. She realised she was holding her breath, and she inhaled deeply. 'Baba...I don't understand.'

'Idris mentioned the diary you found while I was in Peshawar. When I heard, I travelled to Chilli's village with him. This,' Bazigh Khan said, pointing to the box, 'is why we have looked after Chilli's family so well, and why, in return, he has looked after us.'

Jia opened the box slowly. Inside was a diamond practically the size of Lirian's fist. She turned to her uncle with a wrinkled brow.

'Akbar Khan would have wanted you to have this,' Bazigh told her. 'It is why we are here, why we became what we did, and why you are Khan today. These men, white and brown, they think they are clever. That is their downfall. I am waiting to see what you do next, my bacha. Akbar and I, we are strong because of our own father, although it was our mother who made us as we became. You are mother to these men. Their paradise is at your feet. Remind them of that, even when they are blind to it. Allah loves his people ninety-nine times more than a mother. No man can understand what that feels like. It is why we don't understand the ways of women. Until they learn respect, fear will have to do.'

'This is the Grosvenor diamond, isn't it? How have we got it?' Jia asked, although she suspected she already knew the answer.

'When we came to London, things didn't go well with me and Akbar for a long time. Nobody wanted us. And then Akbar did a smart thing to help a man called Henry Paxton and —'

'Let me guess,' Jia gently interrupted. 'You were supposed to steal this diamond for him, but you never gave it to him. This diamond is why Lord Paxton loathed me and my father.'

Bazigh nodded.

She didn't know the precise details of what had gone on between the posh white man and the two poor brown brothers, but she didn't need to. For now that the pieces had fallen into place, she could make sense of what she had detected in Paxton's expression a year ago in London when she had orchestrated their first meeting, the quiet but violent hatred lurking behind his eyes. She had wondered occasionally since then what it was about that self-satisfied man that had made her want to annihilate him, and that too was making more sense to her.

For she realised now that Henry Paxton's disdain had detonated her own uncompromising response and determination to wound him badly, and ultimately to cause the end of his life. She hadn't known it initially but her instincts about him had been correct – if she didn't get to him first, he would get to her. For Henry Paxton hated Akbar Khan for denying him this glittering trophy – and years later, by mere association, Henry had hated her too with an equal passion.

Jia and Bazigh could hear the bustle and chatter coming from the other side of the carved wooden door of the study. Her Jirga was gathering outside.

'Come,' said Bazigh Khan. 'It is time you told us your plans.'

CHAPTER 62

As the Jirga entered her office, Jia looked out of the window at the lush grass of the lawn at Pukhtun House. Thanks to the steady hand of the gardener, the garden was back to its former glory after the mess and the trampled plants that the forensic team had left behind following Ishtiaq's murder.

She turned to look at the men, and Jia was reminded of the photographs her father had hung in this very room, of Eids gone past, when the Jirga first formed and Pukhtun House became its home.

The men had worries and concerns, Jia knew. Some of these were personal, others business-related, and every man here was agitated about the bodies of the men they had once known, the men who had died with religious words carved on their bodies.

'My sons don't even call me,' said Janaan Khan. 'I raised them with love and gave them everything I did not get. That it has come to this...' He paused and shrugged his shoulders, turning his hands outwards to show his empty palms. 'I have three sons. When they were born, everyone was so happy. We had male children – we thought we were blessed. I look at the parents of daughters and I see now that they are the ones who are truly God's chosen ones. Someone comes to see how they are, asks them if they want chai, if they have eaten. My wife and I sit alone in our house. It has become like a prison for us.'

His eyes hadn't left his aging hands. The lines were pronounced, the veins bulging as they worked hard to keep the blood flowing through his fingertips. Jia would have felt sorry for him had he not once been her harshest critic. He had told her she was not his Khan, because she was a woman. He had taken her silence back then for fear. 'She will lead us into destruction,' he'd said, and the words had echoed in her head, over and over. He had tried his best to turn the Jirga against her.

How quickly life turned. These men who thought that male children brought honour and female offspring brought trials understood the error of their ways only when their sons put them aside. The kindness of women was seen as weakness, until it was taken away from them. Jia didn't comment on the words Janaan had said, but after a while she saw that he had finally understood the message: her silence was strength.

Idris, Nadeem and Malik had taken their seats, drinking chai steeped in cardamom, as they waited to hear their Khan's words. Everyone in the room knew that what Jia had to say was as important to them as the imam's Eid sermon.

News of various events had been filtering through – about Meera Shah, about Lord Paxton's legacy now being their future, about the lack of leads in the Kismet Killings, as well as larger events that had happened overseas.

Her men hoped Jia Khan would shed light.

Change was coming, and quietly Jia had been preparing everyone for this news. She knew the difference in how men and women were perceived. Men were implicitly trusted without evidence, as it was just assumed they'd be good at what was asked of them. Women had to prove their worth and get their way by other means.

The women Jia Khan was bringing into the Jirga had already demonstrated what they were capable of. It was just a question of showing this to the men in a way that wouldn't lead to thoughts of retaliation or give anyone firm information that might be used against them should the police pursue lines of enquiry more aggressively than their chief Mark Briscoe had allowed or funded up to this point.

'From today there will be women sitting beside you in the Jirga,' Jia Khan began, and then paused.

A murmur ran through the group exactly as she had expected.

Jia raised her hand, and the men stopped. 'Before any of you tell me women are weak and not hardy or clever enough to take a seat at this table, know this: know that these are the women who have gone about their lives this past year, refusing to be cowed by the Kismet Killer or anybody else. They went out when *your* foot soldiers were too afraid to, causing those of you who rely on late-night custom to lose money as a result. You can take my word that these women have stood firm and are every bit as worthy to be members of the Jirga as each one of you here. They will not waver over hard decisions or whether violence must be used.'

The door opened and Sakina entered, followed by Hamsa, Bano, Fozia, Mahboobeh and Iram. They came to stand to the side of Jia's desk, in clear view of everyone.

'Where are they going to do wudu? Where are they going to pray? With us?'

'That's your biggest concern?' said Sakina. 'Where us women are going to take a piss?'

'Some of you haven't even covered your heads.'

'Avert your eyes if that is too much for you,' Sakina challenged. She could feel Idris's eyes on her from the other side of the room, and she thought she saw a minute smile.

Sakina spread images of the Kismet Killer's victims out on the table in front of them. 'Those of you who dined with Meera Shah and tried the shami kebab, the shami kebab we cooked, might have cause to wonder.'

Afzal Khan turned pale at the thought of what Sakina was implying. Or was she? He couldn't quite tell. But the confidence with which she had spoken had stunned the men into silence. Jia Khan pointedly looked at her expensive watch, and then the Jirga remembered just how much money she had sent their way, and they suddenly felt as one very strongly that they didn't want to lose their income.

Jia Khan was smart, and she was cold, and she did what was necessary. She was loyal to the cause and not to them, they knew, and so they stayed silent.

Casting flinty eyes into those of each man in the room, one by one, Jia said, 'What Sakina is saying so clearly is that these women joining the Jirga started in the kitchen, and it is where we women learnt to wield knives and learnt to nourish ourselves and our children. We taught ourselves to work together, build a community, raise boys to be men and girls to be women, precisely because we were in the kitchen. Somewhere along the line, you men forgot our power when you decided to forego the respect our religion gives us. When you decided that maleness was the source of power, and that "women's work" was lesser work.

'But our grandmothers were wise women. We were not relegated to the kitchen, we chose to be there, at the heart of the home, because that is where we grew to our full potential. The problem isn't why *we* were there; the real question is, why weren't *you?*'

Jia paused but she kept everybody rapt with a fierce look.

'You think that if we win, you lose. But there are things that nature teaches women that men do not learn. When your mothers fed you at their breasts, the more you fed, the more milk they had. Women shared their knowledge, and even their milk, with other women to make brothers out of you. We have been lighting candles from each other's flames, raising each other up – and your offspring – while you played at being men. And now you cannot survive without us. Without us, you have no connection to your past. We are the future, because we hold our history in our hearts. We are the keepers of the faith, the holders of morality, and, well, we are here to dispense justice accordingly,' said Jia.

'You are my Jirga,' she continued, 'and I have made good on my promises to you. You know this, and so you will do what I ask. If you choose to leave, you are free to do so. But you leave without my contacts and as my enemy. And I think you know what happens to my enemies.'

Jia knew that even twelve months earlier these men would have put up a fight and argued against her decision.

Bazigh Khan went to stand beside Jia, a sign of the old order accepting the new.

He asked each of the men to step forward to receive their Eidi from their Khan.

The men were unusually silent, and Jia knew they would discuss what she had said among themselves later. They were a wolf pack, and wolves had teeth. But whatever they did or said, it would get back to her, and she knew they knew this. Her eyes and ears were everywhere.

'Democracy doesn't work for everyone,' her father had once told Jia, commenting on the state of his homeland. 'Young nations need a dictator to shape and form them before they are ready to be left to their own devices.'

Jia Khan's Jirga needed the same, and until such a time as things changed, she would govern them with fear, and the extent of their fear had a direct correlation to how much they respected her.

The men left, having kissed Jia's ring, each clutching silken bags stuffed with bank notes in their hand. It was small potatoes but nevertheless a potent sign of the future prosperity Jia Khan promised. And the fact that money bought silence and loyalty swirled in the air around them all.

Idris hung back, waiting to catch his cousin. 'Let's eat,' she said to him. 'I saw rasmalai out there.'

Idris stayed where he was.

'If this is about Sakina, I already know,' she said.

'It's not about that.'

'What is it, then?' She sat down on the desk, her gharara draped across the front.

'Jia, you wanted me to take a step back and work on legitimate interests, and I have done that. I have shared with Sakina everything I know. But I feel there's more to this than you're telling me.'

Idris was right, but Jia had hoped to leave the matter till tomorrow, wanting the day for her family and her cousins to be about joy, family and the inevitable food coma.

Jia sighed, her face sombre. 'War is on the horizon, Idris. We upset powerful people when we destroyed Henry Paxton. The hedge-fund short selling was the first domino, and we have come to the attention of those whose reach is far greater and who have pockets much deeper than ours. We live above and behind the law, but we follow a code of honour. These people, on the other hand, have no regard for life, as they are the kind of men who traffic women and children and use them to move money, drugs, contraband. They worship money and live in plain sight without any intention of utilising their money to do good. I am preparing for what is to come.'

Idris was downcast. 'I can help, Jia. Don't shut me out.'

'You're not hard enough, Idris. None of you are. Nadeem is still dealing with what we did to Nowak, and I manage him because I love him, but I can't look after you guys like babies.'

'Sakina, she's just a young woman,' he started to protest.

Jia stopped him. 'Don't do that. Don't make your ego pop by trying to protect her. Sakina has seen sides of life that you and I could not imagine. She knows hunger and hardship. She is Akbar and Bazigh in a way that you and I are not. She is tougher than steel and we need her. I know you think you love her, Idris. But men rarely see women as they are. You see us as you want us to be.'

Jia Khan placed her hand on her cousin's shoulder. 'It's done, Idris. Don't let it eat you up as you are more dear to me than you will ever know. Now, let's get some food.'

She left the room, heading towards Elyas and Ahad, sweeping Lirian up in her arms.

Idris watched, and for a moment they looked like any other happy family.

Sakina found him, taking his hand and leading him to where everyone was waiting.

CHAPTER 63

Yanick Kaplan's wife had been asleep in the other room when she'd heard his shouts. His doctor had told him to lose weight or he'd be dead in ten years. He'd taken the doctor's words to heart, and these days he went running with his dogs in the family compound every morning.

But on this particular morning, he'd been woken by something other than his 5.00AM alarm. His bed was warm and sticky, and he felt something like treacle running down his legs. He was a big man and on hot nights his bed was often soaked with sweat, even in winter, but this was different. Something wasn't right.

He could smell old coins: that's when he began to worry. He knew what the smell of iron meant. He reached his hand out to the side and recoiled instantly, jumping out of bed. He flicked the light, shouted for his staff and security. Everyone came running, along with his wife, Sarauniya.

It was blood. It was everywhere, soaking into the sheets, dripping on to the marble floor and pooling at the bottom of the bed.

Yanick Kaplan didn't scare easily; he was the kind of man that nightmares were fearful of. But the thought that someone had come into his house in the dead of night rattled him.

He pointed at the bed, shouting to the security men. They slowly pulled back the covers, the maids covering their mouths and eyes.

Then the calls began, coming from Tokyo, Lagos, Mumbai, Lahore and LA, from those men Yanick Kaplan called friends, the ones who ran syndicates, the ones he had a truce with.

***

On the other side of the world. Jia Khan was talking to Adam Diaz. It was nearly midnight by the time she was free to take his call.

'They're the heads of the world's most powerful crime families, Jia. Yanick Kaplan is more powerful than your father ever was. Whatever were you thinking? You've started a war.'

Jia knew exactly what she'd done. She'd planned it this way. There was no option.

She wasn't going to wait for them to attack her. Instead, she would bring the fight to them.

They would either take her bloody message as a sign of strength and invite her into their fold. Or they would read it as a declaration of war. Whatever. A woman had to do whatever she could to get a man's attention.

'You said the families were going to come for me. What did you think I was going to do? Sit by the wall and wait to be asked to dance?'

Adam Diaz knew Jia was right. She was too far in to pull out now. It was belt and braces all the way. And he had picked his side the moment he met her.

'You worry too much, Adam. Just wait.'

Jia knew she had made her point, that she could get to anyone, wherever they were.

'Jia, we were going to get out,' said Adam.

'No one gets out alive,' she said, and Jia Khan turned to look at her sleeping husband.

CHAPTER 64

The new tree was looking strong thought Jia from her office chair. Its roots had settled and were running deep into the rich soil of Akbar Khan's garden. Jia had had it planted where it could grow tall without damaging the foundations of Pukhtun House, and where the family could still benefit easily from its fruit, shade and beauty.

A calm had descended, and Jia was enjoying this, even planning to pay Ahad a visit in London. She was lost in thoughts about the future when Sakina interrupted her.

'You believe in God?'

'Some days,' said Jia. 'It's getting harder but also more necessary.'

'I don't know if I do anymore. I say "inshallah", "mashallah", "alhamdolillah", like people say "bless you" and "excuse me", but it feels hollow. I stand for Fajr and feel nothing. It makes me think sometimes.'

Jia liked Sakina. She was building trust; she was sharp, quick-witted and her humour was dark, and sometimes that was all life had to offer.

'Sakina, is this about the past? I don't think God, if God exists, cares about you having sex for money. Men have been manipulating the Quran and hadith for years, conveniently dropping hadith they don't like. And Idris doesn't seem to care either.'

Sakina hoped Jia's words were true. Being around Jia left her feeling as though the things she had done hadn't tarnished her but instead had rubbed her to a shine. And that they had shown her the beautiful, awful truth of the world and taught her to be human in a way that unblemished things never could.

'We take every brick and stone that has been thrown at us and build something new. My loyalty to the loyal is unwavering,' Jia said. 'The gratitude that comes from my heart towards my people is more powerful than prayer. When I place my trust in someone, I expect the same. If that trust is betrayed, there are consequences. I'm sure you understand. I am telling you, Sakina, not to doubt yourself or think that I have any doubts in you.'

Sakina could see that the line Jia was drawing was clear.

'We want our leaders to be better than we are, and so we pretend they don't have flaws, that they don't weep, or break, or even make mistakes. I don't do the things that I do to be celebrated. I do them for my family and for those in need. Our organisation and everything in it needs to have a purpose far beyond me. I had been planning on speaking to you anyway, as I'm going to ask you to do things that you won't understand, and you can't ask why. Some people are going to get hurt. And once you say yes, there is no going back. Do you hear me, Sakina?' asked Jia.

Sakina nodded.

'I need to hear you say the words,' said Jia. 'For you to say yes, if that is what you want.'

'Yes,' Sakina said as she looked dead into Jia's eye. 'What do we do first?'

EPILOGUE

Jia glanced around the attic, at the piles of boxes that filled the space. There were large circular windows on both sides of the room. The loft spanned the length and breadth of Pukhtun House, and lit from all sides, it was warm and welcoming.

Her heart was set on making this space a sanctuary. The architect had offered some interesting ideas that were in keeping with the style of the house and incorporated the original features.

But first the loft needed to be emptied.

Jia understood that her parents' refusal to part with anything was a side effect of being an immigrant. They had already left everything behind in another land once before. The objects and artifacts they collected through their life afterwards were important. They gave them a feeling of control, and with age they were receptacles for memories that were fading, holding the laughter of a son who had passed and a daughter who had left home.

There were stacks of wooden crates, the old-fashioned kind that used to hold imported tea and huge black trunks with padlocks. They were the witnesses of a life lived, sometimes several lives.

Alongside these were cardboard boxes, each one taped up with masking tape and labelled with a year. Organisation was one of the ways Sanam Khan maintained her sanity in the chaos of life. She'd roped Zan in one summer to help her sort things out downstairs. He'd raided WH Smith for markers and labelling machines and thick brown tape.

Slowly, Jia traced her fingertips over the penmanship, the Berol pens and calligraphy class he'd taken evident on the boxes. A couple had Jia's scrawl on them, the date markedly absent.

Jia used her fingers to spell out Zan Khan. She'd spent the months she was pregnant with Ahad sorting and packing away her brother's things. Akbar Khan had asked her not to, but she'd been adamant, as if possessed by some kind of otherworldly force. She knew now that this had been the start of her psychological illness.

At last she found the box she was looking for, right at the back of the attic – '1974' was written in red ink across it, this time in her father's handwriting. This one wouldn't be sealed. Jia knew this because she and Zan had sometimes crept up here to take out the contents, look through them and whisper stories about their father.

Akbar Khan had found them once, sitting on the floor, pulling out the vinyl LPs from their sleeves.

He'd taken the box down that day, and they'd sat around the living room, the fire lit, the November sun having set around 4.00PM, handling each record like precious cargo. They'd listened as Akbar Khan played them each one of his precious records, his face tinged with loss and acceptance of years past.

Jia's mother was resting in her room, Elyas had taken Lirian for a walk, and a rare silence filled the rafters of Pukhtun House. She carried the box downstairs to the living room, sitting beside the hearth that had been the focal point of evenings during her childhood, warming the hearts and bodies of everyone who came to visit. Jia had loved to hear about her parents' homeland.

She placed the needle on one of Akbar's old records, and suddenly she was back there, sitting by Akbar Khan. She could almost smell the candles her mother used to burn on an evening to clear the house of the smell of the fried onions, garlic and spices that had gone into dinner, tastes they loved but didn't want to carry out into school, the supermarket or town.

Jia was still making her way through the box when Elyas returned home. 'May I have a look?' he said.

She pushed the box towards him. He leafed through the albums. 'They're all from a very specific time. Look,' he said, laying them down next to each other. 'It's all early 70s and very British bands. He must have bought them when he first arrived.'

She reached over, placing her hand on the records, and she saw Elyas was right. How had she missed this?

'I suppose everyone has a favourite era,' said Elyas. 'I never had your dad down as a rock man.'

'There were always cassettes in his car, and we were the first people I knew to have a CD player. But it was always songs from Mohammed Rafi and Noor Jehan that he played us,' Jia said.

'Did he ever talk about what it was like when he first came here?'

'Not really. To be fair, I didn't ask. I should have. But I didn't.' Jia fell silent, watching as Elyas lifted the albums out and put them on the table.

'There's something in the bottom of this box,' he said, holding it up to show her. Lodged under one of the flaps was some flimsy blue paper. Jia put the box on the table and tried to pull the sheet free, but it was stuck, maybe due to the tape, and Jia didn't dare give the paper a tug in case it ripped. She turned the box over and tore the masking tape off the back. The overlapping cardboard separated easily.

Jia Khan looked at the pale-blue paper, a broken red and dark-blue line running around it. The stamp was bright pink, a picture of an elegant woman in a headdress. Her father's address was on it in royal-blue ink. She picked the letter up. It was heavier than she'd expected.

'Cameroon?' said Elyas, reading the name of the word printed on the stamp as he leaned over her shoulder. 'Your father had business dealings in Cameroon?'

Jia stood up and walked to the window seat, holding the envelope up to the light. She hesitated before opening it, not sure yet if she wanted to share its contents with her husband.

Elyas sensed this but he didn't seem to mind. 'I'm going to get some chai. Would you like some?'

Jia nodded, settled herself on to the seat and leaned back against the wall. For a long minute she stared at her father's garden, taking in all the things he'd planted over the years since he'd bought the house, now mature. He'd been a clever gardener, choosing plants carefully so that there was always something blossoming, blooming or bearing fruit throughout the seasons. It was the perfect testament to his ingenuity and foresight, and Jia hoped that she would always be able to do justice to the memory of Akbar Khan.

She opened the envelope and took out its contents. There were several envelopes inside, with one postmarked '1996'.

Jia thought she would begin with that one, opening it carefully and taking out the letter. Its penmanship was strikingly similar to her father's. She looked at the signature: it was from a woman named Mary.

As she started to read, Jia's long-held views of her father began to blur, like a camera moving in and out of focus.

Dear Akbar, our little one is starting law school. She'll be in London this summer, and she'd like to meet her father, the letter began.

'Who are they from?' said Elyas, returning to the room with two cups of tea and a bowl of panjeeri. 'I thought you might be hungry,' he added, placing the bowl of sweet, butter-cooked semolina and nuts in front of her.

'Just one of Baba's old friends,' she said.

'May I look?'

She folded the letter and put it back in its envelope.

'Maybe later,' she told her husband.

Jia Khan took a spoonful of panjeeri and put it in her mouth.

The crushed pistachios and almonds of the fat- and sugar-rich food filled her senses, invisible to everyone except the cook, and anyone who was able to handle the truth of what went into it.

ACKNOWLEDGEMENTS

The last year has been a strange one, but as Jia Khan's Jirga has grown, so has mine. I've been propped up and held together by so many kindnesses. If it wasn't for the support of some amazing friends, family, and colleagues, this book would not be in your hands today.

I have to start by thanking the woman who weaves magic and makes dreams come true. Jenny Parrott, you are the cleverest, kindest editor an author could wish for. Thank you for your advice, and insight, and for helping me raise my game.

Abi Fellows, I have so much admiration for you and an equal measure of love. Thank you for being my agent, and for replying to my messages whenever I've lost faith in the process.

Dear Margot Weale, I'm so grateful for your handling of emails, and for the handholding at festivals. I'd be lost without you. You are my people.

Poppy Mardall and Chris 'Corleone' Pensa, you are the best of the new faces to have joined my tribe. Thank you for scooping up my family, for taking me on winding walks, comedy tales filled with vulnerability, and of course the childcare. You are my safe harbour.

Raj Khaira, thank you for reminding me of who I am, and showing me who you are – an angel in disguise as a Punjabi powerhouse.

To Fiona Goh and The SI Leeds Literary Prize team, the best colleagues a woman could ask for, thank you for your understanding and kindness over the last year.

Thank you to Sifu Carl Jackson, for sowing the seeds that turned into fight scenes, and to my Asian Excellence crew, Rita Jackson and Kokyee Ng, for the sparring and the caffeinating – both of which saved me countless times.

Mary Utley, what would I do without you? You inspire me every day, and you are never far from my thoughts. Thank you for being a beacon on dark days.

Thank you to my family who come whenever I call. It's been a helluva ride, hasn't it? Thank you, Khola, for travelling across the country to hold the rascals and make me endless cups of chai, to Javaria for stepping in without hesitation when the world was collapsing, and to Fozia, for bringing the funny to any situation. To Khizer and Zafar for sorting trains and driving Ami and Abu across the country, without being asked. What I wouldn't give to be thirteen again in Haslingden Drive eating pizza and watching Indiana Jones with you all!

And finally, thank you to my husband, who thinks he's in the book, but is the least likely person to be in a story about gangsters. You'll do. For now.